Battlegro

CW00551369

The American E
Forces in the Great War

Montfaucon

Battleground Series

Battleground

The American Expeditionary Forces in the Great War

Montfaucon

Maarten Otte

Series Editor
Nigel Cave

Pen & Sword
MILITARY

Dedication
Dedicated to Christina Holstein.
So rich in knowledge, so generous in sharing it.

First published in Great Britain in 2018 by
Pen & Sword Military
an imprint of
Pen & Sword Books Ltd, 47 Church Street
Barnsley, South Yorkshire, S70 2AS

Copyright © Maarten Otte, 2018
Maps copyright © B. Metselaar

ISBN 978 152673 491 4

Typeset in Times New Roman by Chic Graphics

Printed and bound in England by
CPI Group (UK) Ltd., Croydon, CR0 4YY

Pen & Sword Books Ltd incorporates the imprints of
Pen & Sword Archaeology, Atlas, Aviation, Battleground, Discovery,
Family History, History, Maritime, Military, Naval, Politics,
Railways, Select, Social History, Transport, True Crime,
Claymore Press, Frontline Books, Leo Cooper, Praetorian Press,
Remember When, Seaforth Publishing and Wharncliffe.

For a complete list of Pen & Sword titles please contact
PEN & SWORD BOOKS LIMITED
47 Church Street, Barnsley, South Yorkshire, S70 2AS, England
E-mail: enquiries@pen-and-sword.co.uk
Website: www.pen-and-sword.co.uk

Contents

Series Editor's Introduction

The Meuse-Argonne Offensive (or 'drive', as the Americans called it) was the bloodiest battle in American military history (over 120,000 wounded or killed, according to one source) and is largely forgotten, not least in the United States itself. It was a huge offensive operation, conducted by an inexperienced army at all levels; and in many ways this showed through quite clearly during the battle, which lasted over six weeks and ended with the Armistice.

This book covers the ground of the 79th Division over the first couple of days of the Offensive. The failure to capture its key objectives on the first day has proved to be the action on the battlefield that attracted (and still does) the most controversy. Its primary objective, the dominating heights of Montfaucon, is where Pershing determined that the memorial for the entire offensive would be erected.

Because of the successful American attack in the St Mihiel Salient, which ended ten days before the offensive on the left bank of the Meuse opened, and the enormous expansion of the AEF in France over the previous few months, several of the divisions that opened the battle were untested in combat: it was simply impractical to shift the bulk of experienced divisions from St Mihiel and redeploy them in the time available. This meant that untried formations had to be used; not only were they inexperienced, their training was inadequate and none more so than that of the 79th, which was a National Army division, manned by men who had enlisted or been drafted; and the one to which, arguably, the most demanding task was given.

By the opening of the battle the division had only managed six weeks of the three months' training period that was laid down by Pershing for newly arrived formations in France. It formed up in September 1917 in the USA; but at first it lacked much of everything in terms of equipment; and then was plundered for reinforcements – no less than 15,000 drafted men arrived in May 1918 to fill the ranks of the 28,000 strong division, only two months or so before it sailed for France. Not even the British Kitchener's Army divisions had been so ill-prepared for battle and what lay ahead of the 79th on the Meuse.

Anyone who visits the battlefield today can see for themselves, certainly if they get out and walk through some of the woods and forests and encounter the deep ravines and the marshy ground near the numerous streams, that the 'country' would be difficult for military operations;

especially given that it had been well and skilfully provided with defensive works. What they might not appreciate is the infrastructure problem, above all the utterly inadequate road system. What is now an area well provided with good roads (albeit many of which are narrow), in effect then had only one north-south supply road for every two or three divisions. To give some idea, an American division, with its full complement of men and artillery, required some thirty to forty miles of road. The roads in the area in 1914 were far from the well designed and constructed ones of today – then often considerably narrower, certainly no more than, at the best, tracks reinforced with hard core and designed for very limited volumes of light vehicles.

'Chow time'; alas, not a common sight in the first days of the offensive. The failure in the supply system to get food and water forward to the men fighting the battle was a major factor in slowing down the First Army's advance.

It is very easy to sit here in 2018 and criticise numerous features of the plan and execution of the battle for Montfaucon; however, such judgements risk taking small account of the situation on the ground. A tortured landscape; scared and bewildered men of all ranks, lacking the cohesion of months of being in the army together; inexperience; a formidable foe, even in limited (and generally very tired) numbers; horrendous logistics problems; the very real and justified fear of gas – during the battle up to twenty percent of shells were gas; utterly inadequate communications; a failed supply system – there was much working against the 79th and the other American troops involved in the offensive.

In fact things worked out, initially, better than might have been the case. The fact was that the German army on the Western Front was on the back foot, with notable advances being made by the allies north of Reims, especially since early August. The German defence plan depended upon the presence of significant numbers of men to enable counter-attacks in a timely manner, when the attackers were off balance as they advanced. It is almost a certainty that the AEF would have been in severe trouble if more of these Eingriff divisions had been available: but they were not. The collapse of the supply system in the opening days of the offensive could have caused the AEF's First Army catastrophic consequences: but the German manpower was not there, nor was it ever present during the course of the battle.

This is a story on the ground of a notable topographic feature (albeit not so significant as has often been argued) and a very raw, untried, American division. Several recent books have been written on the subject. This one seeks to avoid polemics and looks at what happened and relates it to the ground, very much from the American soldier's point of view. We can only sit back in awe at these men of 1918.

Maarten has made full use of his intimate knowledge of the ground and the published material; once more his good friend, Bart Metselaar, has provided excellent mapping to accompany the various tours. In following the progress of the work I have spent some time on the ground in company with the author and have been further educated in what is becoming an increasingly familiar battlefield to me. There is nothing like this experience to qualify judgements of the planning and development of an offensive. Seeking as full an appreciation as is possible of those few days in September is the best way of honouring the men who fought and died at their countries' command in the fields and woods around Montfaucon.

Nigel Cave
Ratcliffe College. Autumn 2018.

viii

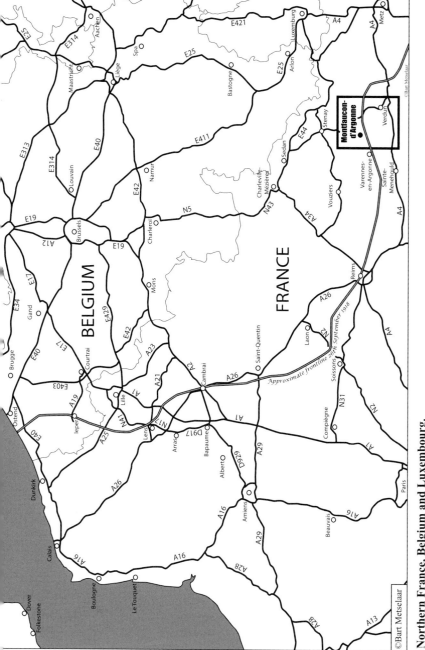

Northern France, Belgium and Luxembourg.

©Bart Metselaar

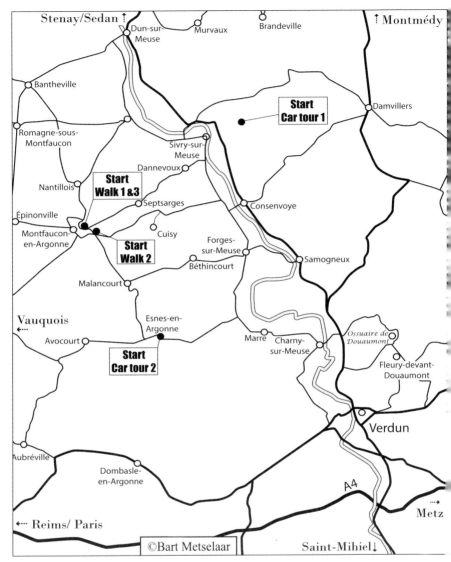

Starting points of the walks and car tours.

Introduction

Over the last decade there has been a plethora of publications on seemingly every conceivable subject relating to the Great War. Therefore, it will come as no surprise that over the last few years several books about Montfaucon have been published, of which the most recent and thorough studies are *Betrayal at Little Gibraltar* by William Walker, published in 2016, and *With their Bare Hands* by Gene Fax, published in 2017.

However, there is no comparison to be made between this book, which should not be regarded as a major study, and these large-scale works. I have written this book to give a clear picture of events that took place one hundred years ago on 'Falkenberg', as the Germans called Montfaucon, the German translation of Montfaucon: Mount of the Falcon. Both battlefield tourists and readers at home can use this book as their personal guide in order to explore the terrain. In order to provide a clear picture of events, I have divided 26 and 27 September, the two most important days, each into morning, noon and night. In the narrative, regiments are described from left to right. The axis of attack was in a roughly northerly direction.

I refer to the community on Montfaucon as the town of Montfaucon, due to the fact that in many of the original American sources and eyewitness accounts Montfaucon is referred to as a town (in fact such sources called almost any place with more than a dozen houses 'a town'). Although an important market place in this region and dating back to Roman times, it was in fact a village of around 800 inhabitants.

The word casualty is often confused with fatality, for some reason. Casualty, as well as meaning those killed, also includes the wounded, missing and those taken prisoner.

For the narrative I have made extensive use of eyewitness accounts, which, in my opinion, gives the reader a much closer, personal connection with the fighting men. I have taken the liberty of sometimes editing the original text, all in an effort to put together the facts from unit histories and journals that can, quite frankly, often be tedious and repetitive, in order – I hope – to turn them into an interesting story.

Any visitor to the site of the bloodiest battle in the history of the United States will be drawn to Montfaucon, for it is here that General Pershing, the Commander in Chief of the American Expeditionary Forces, determined that the major memorial to the AEF would be sited. Although there are many things to see at this fascinating site, most people only stop briefly at the American Monument, built after the war to commemorate all the Americans who participated in the Meuse-Argonne Offensive that started on 26 September 1918. The monument now stands at the former town centre of Montfaucon.

Many people climb the 234 steps to the top of the tower monument and take a photograph of the picturesque church ruins that lie directly behind it; but the reality is that many of these tourists really have very little idea about what happened here all those years ago. Hopefully, this book will spark further interest in the history of the AEF and the Meuse-Argonne Offensive. The book follows the 79th 'Cross of Lorraine' Division from their start line between Esnes-en-Argonne and Avocourt to the capture of Montfaucon on 27 September 1918; and for a day or

General Pershing, Commander in Chief of the AEF.

The Allied front lines on 26 September, the start of the Meuse-Argonne Offensive, and on 11 November.

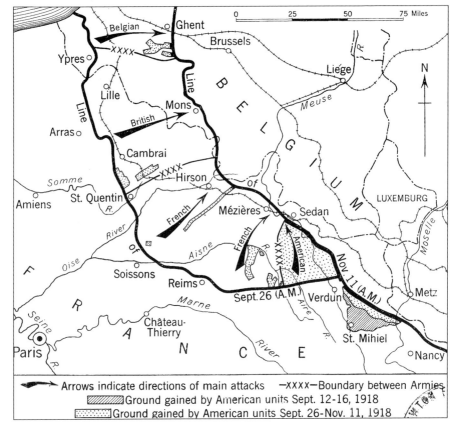

two beyond that. As usual, there are several GPS compatible walks and tours that offer a good understanding of the area and the possibility of walking in the doughboys' footsteps.

A tactical position
As one of the most dominant hills in the area and centrally located between the Argonne Forest and the River Meuse, the hill served as an important observation post for the German army, like a modern-day spy satellite. It was situated about seven to eight kilometres behind the front line, depending from where you look at it, and was not specifically built as a front line position, although it was incorporated into the third line, the Etzel Line. Therefore, Montfaucon must be regarded more as a *tactical* position than as a *strategic* position.

The value of Montfaucon to the Germans was due to the fact that this position provided them with a view of the surrounding area for miles around. From here, they relayed enemy movements to their gun batteries to the rear. Understandably, the American high command thought it was vital for the success of an overall breakthrough on the Meuse-Argonne front to eliminate Montfaucon on the first day of the offensive. The green and untried 79th Division was assigned this task; as we now know, it did not succeed in taking the town on the first day and was therefore, rightly or wrongly, branded as the division 'that held up the whole of the American Army'. The reasons for this failure have been amongst the biggest sources of controversy about the offensive and its conduct amongst military historians. Interesting though this may be, the controversy is not discussed in the main body of the text; however, in Appendix 4 I have added an affidavit on the subject written by Major H.D. Parkin, who served in the 316th Regiment.

Occupied by them since September 1914, by 1918 the Germans had transformed the hill into a honeycomb of tunnels and built an impressive number of observation and signalling posts and shelters. When the Americans fought their way into Montfacucon on the morning of 27 September, the ruins of this once prosperous little town were defended by the Germans; but this was merely an improvised last stand. Most of the garrison had already left for the intermediate line near Nantillois or the Hindenburg Line even further to the rear. Nevertheless, German snipers and other troops who were concealed in the ruins of Montfaucon made life really miserable for the doughboys, who had to spend the rest of the day in ridding the place of Germans.

The main German defence line was built across the barren fields, ridges and woods to the south of Montfaucon. Montfaucon was portrayed as an 'impregnable town', particularly in books published

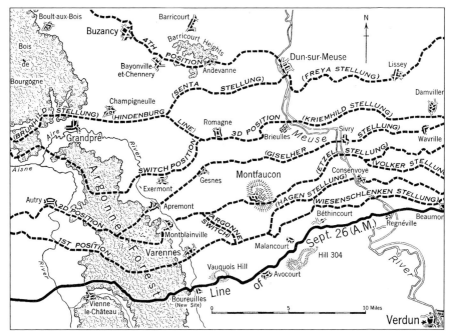

German lines of defence in the Meuse-Argonne in 1918.

soon after the war, in an effort to make its capture even more heroic. In no way do I want to belittle the achievements of the men who risked their lives or sully the memory of those who made the supreme sacrifice for the sake of democratic ideals, but the key phase of the fighting to this stage in the battle had taken place before the doughboys reached the town.

Malancourt, Haucourt, Golfe de Malancourt, Montfaucon Wood and Cuisy Wood appear in practically every battle report. In fact, one or more of these places are named in every single eyewitness account that I have found. They also usually write about the mopping up of stray soldiers and snipers in Montfaucon; but fighting in the town itself is rarely included in these accounts. All the same, heavy hand-to-hand fighting is mentioned when the Americans entered the town close to the destroyed communal cemetery.

An important aspect of the failure of the 79th Division to capture Montfaucon on the first day was the organization of the German artillery and the disorganization of their own. The Americans often advanced without sufficient artillery support, whilst on the other hand they were subjected almost non-stop to German pre-arranged artillery defensive fire.

The First World War was the first war of mechanisation and the mass production of the weapons of war between major industrial powers, all designed to annihilate; unprotected men came up against a red hot, razor-sharp iron deluge of fragmented artillery shells, withering fire from machine guns and, all too often, a blanket of gas. A lot of the doughboys died without ever seeing the enemy; seemingly out of nowhere, the German artillery simply blew many to smithereens and they just disappeared, were vaporized or blasted to small fragments.

On the evening of 26 September, the position at Montfaucon was threatened with being outflanked by the 37th Division on the left (west); whilst on the right it had already been outflanked by the 4th Division. The 79th Division had taken up positions in front of it. This meant that Montfaucon was under fire from three sides and that encirclement was only a matter of time. By noon the next day the town had been evacuated by the Germans. The withdrawal was greatly speeded up because of the continuing morning attacks of the 37th Division and the advance of the 79th Division in front of Montfaucon.

The 79th Division sailed from Hoboken, New Jersey, on Sunday, 30 June 1918, and arrived at the major French harbour of Brest between 15 and 21 July. From 19 to 29 July the division proceeded to their designated training area. This left the division with what turned out to be about eight

American troops waiting to embark for France, 1917.

Montfaucon in 1915.

weeks before the battle for training purposes, at least four weeks less than Pershing's training programme demanded. By 13 September, the second day of the St. Mihiel Offensive, the division was in the Avocourt sector in the Meuse-Argonne, relieving the French 157th Division. This left the division with even less training time: only six weeks, which made them amongst the greenest American divisions in France. The fact that just before sailing for France 15,000 men were replaced by untrained draftees did not help matters. This 'plundering' of divisions was not unusual in the AEF; completely undesirable, but a consequence of the exigencies of war.

Within days of the offensive's opening the inexperience of the AEF was laid open: there was considerable chaos on the supply routes, a failure to achieve promised results; too many inadequate senior officers; poor staff work; inexperienced junior officers and NCOs; and jealousy between divisional and corps commanders. This almost convinced the Allied *Supremo*, Marshal Foch, to withdraw the Americans from the Meuse-Argonne area; General Pershing had to work hard to convince him to decide otherwise. Although the picture was not a pretty one – and certainly a considerable contrast to the success achieved at St. Mihiel – there were many positives in the AEF's performance.

Taking everything into consideration, we should look with considerable admiration at the performance of the 79th Division during the events that took place in and around Montfaucon on those fateful days in the last week of September 1918: it was a feat of sheer determination. How was it possible that a barely trained rookie division was able to take the supposedly impregnable height of Montfaucon only thirty-six hours later than scheduled? With all the defects in command and lack of battle experience, without support on its right flank, without any artillery support worth mentioning, under almost non-stop artillery and machine-gun fire and seemingly against all odds, they achieved what they were ordered to do.

List of Maps and Diagrams

Chapter 1

The Germans and the Allies 1918

Building an American Army

On Friday, 6 April, 1917, the United States declared war on Germany. At that time the Americans had only a small standing army at their disposal – smaller, for example, than that of Belgium in 1914. There were just over 120,000 men in the regular US Army and 180,000 in the National Guard, the reserve, 'militia', troops. Participation in the war required the US army to organise itself immediately into a modern military force of a European standard; unsurprisingly, this proved to be a massive undertaking. Infantry and artillery units suitable for fighting on the Western Front, units of supply, transport, engineering and medical services, to name but a few, were needed: all had to be combined into divisions. Therefore, a radical transformation had to be implemented to meet the needs for participating in a global conflict between major industrialised nations, requiring a bewildering range of new weapons with an increasingly important mechanised capability, significant training requirements and a trans-oceanic supply system. The necessary growth and change required a complete reorganization and rethinking. This

Camp Meade, Maryland, training camp of the 79th Division in 1917.

unsatisfactory situation was, at least to a degree, thanks to President Wilson, who had refused to allow the American chiefs of staff to plan for a European involvement. To be fair to him, it is doubtful if there was the political will in the nation to take a more robust approach to preparing the country for a European war.

One of the major problems was that volunteer soldiers alone would be insufficient to satisfy the huge manpower needs of this new army. To fill the ranks, Congress passed the Selective Service Act on 18 May 1917. It called for all men between the ages of twenty-one and thirty to register for the draft, later amended to include men eighteen to forty-five years of age. All registered men received a number as part of the process. Local authorities then called registered men to service based on a national lottery. During the first draft, of 5 July 1917, roughly 2.8 million men were called up. By the end of 1918 4.7 million men had been called to arms, of whom well over two million were involved in the war in Europe. It was an outstanding success.

The need to train the newly enlisted men presented huge problems because of the size of the force, the diverse educational and cultural background of these American soldiers to be and a chronic shortage of suitable trainers. For the first time, men had to take basic intelligence tests to ensure their placement in the appropriate branch of the military. The American Government set up a national system of thirty-two training areas to manage the new soldiers. In Britain, Italy and France the AEF and its allies set up training camps to teach the Americans the latest fighting and technical skills; more than 1,000 veteran Allied soldiers served as instructors. This new army needed qualified, capable commanders at all levels, from section (or squad) commanders upwards. When war was declared there were only around 6,000 army officers (and of these something like a third had been in the army for less than a year) and so the biggest problem the Americans faced was the lack of officers; the training camp system alone commissioned 80,500 new officers. Officers were in such high demand that anyone who had a college education was regarded as possible officer material, regardless of their background. It will come as no surprise, therefore, that the lack of adequately trained, let alone experienced (in particular staff) officers, would cause tremendous problems during the Meuse-Argonne Offensive.

American divisions, for a variety of reasons, were at least twice the size of their European counterparts. This created many problems. Amongst these are the facts that large divisions move slowly, are very cumbersome and have a complex command structure. An American division on the march could easily be stretched out over fifty kilometres; it was not uncommon that the first units to arrive at a given destination

Camp Meade, inside the barracks 1918.

had to wait a full day or more for the rest of the division to arrive. The organisational problems were only solved after the Great War.

The early French and British military missions in the USA advised the military on the needs of the American Expeditionary Forces (the AEF). At the end of May 1917, Colonel Chauncey Baker of the Quartermaster Corps and an academy classmate of Pershing, was sent to Europe with a small staff to observe the French and British armies. They reported back to Washington by mid-July. While the Army considered Baker's report, the first AEF troops began to arrive and train in Europe. On 26 June 1917, the First Division (The Big Red One) was the first American division to land in France, at Brest.

Colonel Chauncey B. Baker, 1859-1933.

In eighteen months the AEF went from being a small military force to an army of millions. They trained hundreds of thousands of officers and soldiers, operated supply lines from the US across the Atlantic to France, built new port facilities, workshops, lumber mills and railway lines and used American locomotives to transport thousands of troops and material. With America's active involvement in the war, the *Materialschlacht* (the Battle of [War] Material), as the Germans called it, was finally won by the allies. The output of all sorts of material needed for the war effort by American production capability was on a vast scale. On the other hand, the AEF was almost entirely dependent on the allies for much of its equipment, such as artillery, aircraft and tanks – for example, no American built aircraft ever made it across the Atlantic before the end of the war. Again, this was largely a consequence of circumstances – the allied shipping priority was to get manpower to France as soon as possible and the British and French took on the bulk of the responsibility for providing the weaponry and support equipment.

1918: The Hundred Days' Offensive

The Spring Offensive of the German Army on the Western Front started on 21 March 1918, commencing with Operation Michael. The German High Command hoped to win the war (or at least force a favourable draw) before the Americans arrived in sufficient numbers to make the Allied manpower advantage overwhelming. By July, after a series of major attacks, the German offensives had been defeated. The Germans had managed to advance as far as the River Marne and, as in 1914, were halted about seventy kilometres from Paris; but once more they had failed to achieve a decisive breakthrough. When the Germans ended the run of offensives in July 1918 (with some, quite probably crucial, AEF assistance, it should be noted), it was the sign for the Allied *Supremo*, Ferdinand Foch, to order a counter offensive, later known as the Second Battle of the Marne. The AEF, with over 250,000 men fighting under French command, gained its first battlefield experience here. The men who fought at the Marne later successfully put to use the lessons learnt there during the Meuse-Argonne Offensive in September, October and November 1918.

The Germans, having largely spent their offensive capabilities, were forced to withdraw from the Marne and were pushed back to the north. For this first Allied victory of 1918, Foch was granted the title Marshal of France.

Marshal Ferdinand Foch, the allied Supremo in 1918.

After this success, Foch felt increasingly confident about allied capabilities and considered the time had arrived for a return to the offensive. By now the AEF was present in large, albeit inexperienced, numbers and gave new hope to the Allied commanders. The Americans were landing in France at an average rate of 300,000 men per month by July. However, Pershing was determined to use his army as an independent command, one that fitted the American commitment to the war as an associated power.

The American 27th, 30th, 37th and 91st Divisions had already reinforced the BEF, the British Expeditionary Force; the French were using several other American divisions to take over quiet sectors of the line in order to acquaint the fresh troops with trench life and to free experienced French divisions to fight elsewhere. In addition to the Americans, large numbers of British troops returned from the Sinai and Palestine Campaign, the Italian Front and reinforcements that had been held back in Britain were partly released by the Prime Minister, David Lloyd George.

David Lloyd George, British Prime Minister from late 1916 to 1922.

Several plans were considered and rejected. Finally, Foch agreed to a proposal by Field Marshal Sir Douglas Haig, Commander-in-Chief of the BEF, to strike in the Somme east of Amiens, south-west of the site of the 1916 Battle of the Somme, with the intention of forcing the Germans away from the vital Amiens-Paris railway. The Somme was chosen as a suitable site for the offensive for a number of reasons. As in 1916, it (more or less) marked the boundary between the BEF and the French Army; in the summer of 1918 the Amiens-Roye road, south of the river, now defined the boundary. Unlike Flanders, the Picardy countryside provided a reasonable surface over which tanks could manoeuvre. Finally, the German defences manned by the

Field Marshal Douglas Haig, 1861-1928.

German *Second Army*, commanded by General Georg von der Marwitz, were relatively weak: this had been illustrated by a limited but highly effective attack (involving some American troops) by the Australian Corps at Le Hamel, just south of the Somme.

During the Hundred Days' Offensive the Allies launched a series of offensives against the Germans on the Western Front from 8 August to 11 November 1918; they forced the Germans to retreat beyond the Hindenburg Line and ultimately led to the signing of the Armistice. The term the 'Hundred Days' Offensive' does not refer to a specific battle but rather the rapid series of Allied victories along much of the length of the Western Front, starting with the Battle of Amiens, and which were co-ordinated by Foch.

During the Battle of Amiens, which began on 8 August 1918, the allies advanced over eleven kilometres on the first day, one of the greatest advances of the war, with Henry Rawlinson's British Fourth Army playing the decisive role. The effects of this victory on the morale of both sides must not be underestimated; it resulted in the surrender of a huge number of German troops. On one day alone they suffered 30,000 casualties. The German losses were so heavy that Erich Ludendorff, together with Hindenburg, Chief of the General Staff, described the first day of the battle as 'a black day of the German Army'. The main concern for the Germans was not so much the length of the casualty list (bad as it was) but the fact that so many of the casualties were prisoners and this was taken as a sign of weakening morale amongst the fighting troops. From now on the German Army was forced into a defensive role; they fought a fighting and, it has to be said, often effective retreat until the Armistice came into effect on 11 November 1918. The Armistice was an agreement to end hostilities as a prelude to peace negotiations. The Treaty of Versailles, signed six months later, would act as the peace treaty between the nations; to this day, the Germans have never formally surrendered nor ratified the peace. Interestingly, the Treaty was also never ratified by the United States; they made a separate peace with Germany in 1921.

In the midst of the Battle of Amiens, the American First Army formally came into being on 10 August 1918; it was soon by far the biggest Army formation put into the field on the Western Front by any combatant power during the war. The Second American Army was formed in mid-October.

Von Hindenburg and Ludendorff in front of their headquarters in 1918.

The Allied offensives of late September
After several significant victories, a co-ordinated offensive by the French, British, Belgian and American armies, under the overall direction of Foch, started on 26 September 1918 in an all-out effort to force the German Army out of France and Belgium and to bring the war to a conclusion, with the hope that this might be achieved before the end of 1918. Foch's planning for this dated back to late August and early September, with the various national commands being informed in early September of their contribution. In France, the American Army was assigned the south-eastern part of the line, near Verdun, stretching from the Argonne Forest in the west to the River Meuse in the east, some thirty-five kilometres long, which became known as the Meuse-Argonne Sector. It also operated in other parts of the line and various AEF divisions still served with the British and the French. The French supported the AEF on its flanks.

The Meuse-Argonne Offensive.
Behind the German sector opposite the Americans was an area that included rich coal and iron deposits (Briey) as well as major railway lines (Metz, Sedan), all of which were of great importance to the German war

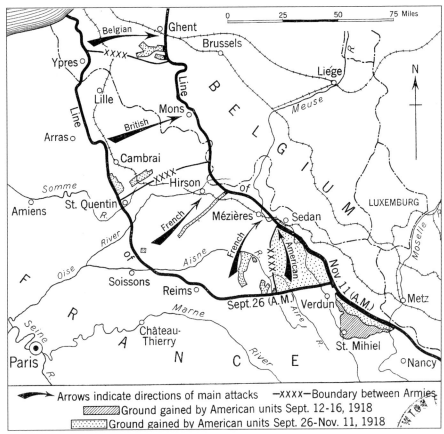

The Western Front, September 1918: the coordinated allied offensives.

effort. Due to the effective British naval blockade of Germany, it had become vital for the Germans that they maintained continued access to these deposits as they provided some seventy-five per cent of the raw materials needed for steel production. Much of the German supplies entered France at Sedan. If the Americans could achieve a breakthrough here it could prove to be decisive in deciding the final outcome of the war. By cutting off this whole sector the Germans would be forced to withdraw from large parts of north-eastern France and a very significant part of their supply system would break down. In addition, the only other line of retreat lay over the Ardennes, difficult and hilly terrain that was not easily passable in winter.

Designated the Meuse-Argonne sector, 'Black Jack' Pershing regarded the prospect with mixed emotions. The main benefit would be that the Americans would be responsible for their own troops, without coming under the authority of a foreign commander. Before the revised allied plan, the AEF had been busy preparing for a limited attack, with some French assistance, on the St Mihiel Salient, south of Verdun. After reducing the salient the Americans hoped to push on to Metz and continue into Germany, 'to bring the war within the Kaiser-reich's borders'. However, following insistence by Foch, Pershing and his staff made the decision to execute both; first the St Mihiel Salient was to be pinched out and occupied and then they would immediately switch all the AEF's energies to the Meuse-Argonne sector.

An advantage (possibly the only one!) for the Americans in this situation was that Pershing's forward headquarters were already based in Souilly, which was more or less half way between the two battlefields. Huge supply dumps, railway lines and other infrastructure were close at hand behind the line. Major problems, however, included mustering and hiding hundreds of thousands of troops within a relatively small area, with all sorts of problems close to the front line, such as poor infrastructure and the difficulty or remaining unobserved by the Germans. In a matter of little more than a couple of weeks, tons of extra supplies, guns, ammunition etc. had to be transported to the sector; not to mention the need to move huge numbers of men and resources from the St Mihiel area to the Meuse-Argonne. New warehouses, railways, roads and barracks had to be built in a fortnight. By now, an Army of unprecedented size (for any of the combatants – no other power in the war ever put together a single Army with anything close to a million men), comprising about one million, mainly inexperienced, soldiers, was under Pershing, a monumental task for just one man who also had all the responsibilities of being the commander-in-chief. Needless to say, all of these issues caused major difficulties both before and during the offensive. The AEF still had much to learn.

Fortunately, eliminating the St Mihiel Salient was a fairly easy task for the Americans. The Germans had already determined to withdraw from it, partly because they recognised that the power and quantity of modern weaponry made it all but impossible to hold the Salient and partly in order to shorten their lines; although that process was still in its very early stages when the offensive began on 12 September. The downside of this 'easy' victory was that it made many of the Americans at higher command level unduly over-confident; they seriously underestimated the strength of German resistance in the Meuse-Argonne. The troops who were waiting for them here knew that the Hindenburg Line was the last barrier between the enemy and the Fatherland, whereas at St Mihiel the Germans had merely *withdrawn* (admittedly in some considerable disorder) to the Hindenburg Line, a significant difference; the Germans were now fighting for their homes and to protect their kith and kin.

After the offensive at St Mihiel was ended on 16 September (which some historians have argued ever since was premature and a lost opportunity), the attention of Pershing's staff was focused on the preparations for the offensive in the Meuse-Argonne, some forty kilometres to the north west of St Mihiel. Immediately after the battle, the veteran 4th Division was transported to this new sector of operations. All the other divisions that moved into the Meuse-Argonne sector for the opening of the battle were fresh divisions from elsewhere. These latter divisions were transported close to their destination by train and marched off from disembarkation points to French barrack camps during the nights preceding the offensive. Soon afterwards they were moved into the forested area south of the old 1916 front line, where all sorts of hasty preparations were under way for the forthcoming offensive. The St Mihiel offensive will be considered in the next volume in this series.

John J. Pershing (1860-1948)

John Joseph Pershing was born at Laclede, Missouri, on 13 December 1860. He graduated from West Point in 1886 with an outstanding record. Assigned to the 10th Cavalry Regiment, composed of African-American soldiers under white command (and possibly the origin of his nickname 'Black Jack'), he campaigned against the Apache Indians in the southwest. From 1891 to 1895 he was a military instructor at the University of Nebraska, where he earned a law degree in 1893. In 1897, Pershing was appointed to the West Point tactical staff as an instructor. Not very popular among his students because of his strictness and rigidity, he was nicknamed 'Nigger Jack'. Later, although still not seen as a compliment, it was softened to Black Jack. This nickname would stick with Pershing for the rest of his life and into history; it was known to the public as early as 1917.

In August 1898, just a month after the American victory at the Battle of Santiago de Cuba, Pershing was commissioned a major of the United States Volunteers. A year later Pershing was fighting his next war: the Spanish-American War. On his arrival in Manila in August 1899, he was assigned to the island of Mindanao; in November 1900 Pershing was appointed Adjutant General of the Department of Mindanao and Jolo. Pershing's efforts in helping to suppress the Moro Rebellion earned him the praise of President Theodore Roosevelt (1858-1919), who wished to have Pershing promoted to colonel as a reward for his service in the Philippines. But Pershing was low down on the list of names of people who were due for promotion in the Army, which in the U.S. Army – as for most other armies – was mainly based on seniority rather than on merit.

As a kind of consolation prize, Roosevelt petitioned the United States Congress to appoint Pershing to a diplomatic posting; he was assigned as military attaché to Tokyo. While in Tokyo, Pershing served as an observer of the Russo-Japanese War (1904-1905). In the autumn of 1905 he returned to the States, where Roosevelt, using his presidential prerogative, nominated Pershing as a brigadier general; Congress approved the promotion. After the Russo-Japanese conflict ended, he returned to the Philippines until 1914, when he assumed command at the Presidio, a major base on the northern tip of the San Francisco Peninsula in California. In 1915, while he was away on special

Pancho Villa, 1878-1923, military leader of the rebel forces during the Mexican Revolution.

assignment, his wife and three daughters perished in a tragic fire, popularly referred to as the Presidio Fire; his son, Warren, then aged five, was the only member of the family to survive the fire.

Pershing's next assignment, both difficult and frustrating, made him an important public figure. In 1916 he commanded the Mexican Expedition to capture the Mexican revolutionary general and bandit, Pancho Villa. Despite his failure to capture Villa, Pershing gained considerable public approval for his dedication to duty. The expedition was withdrawn early in 1917, just prior to America's entry into the war. Pershing was now a thoroughly experienced commander of troops.

In May 1917, although he had never held an important staff position in the War Department, President Woodrow Wilson

President Woodrow Wilson, 1856-1924.

and Secretary of War Newton Baker chose Pershing to command the AEF that was to be despatched to Europe in support of the Allies. He was the

11

second choice – General Funston, who had an unusual career in many ways, was the man that they had in mind; but he died of a heart attack at the age of 51 in February 1917. Arriving in France in June 1917, Pershing immediately began planning the organization and deployment of a large American Army. He decided (albeit in line with US political thinking) to create an independent American force commanded by its own officers with its own support echelons in a distinct sector in France. In choosing this course, he challenged various allied leaders, who favoured incorporating elements of the AEF into their armies as replacements. It is worth bearing in mind that the Americans fought in Europe as an Associate Power rather than a Coalition Power – the implication being one of greater independence.

For over a year, despite the ever-growing military crises in France as the number of French and British troops reached a dangerously low level, Pershing single-mindedly pursued his objective of an independent American Army (and an equally single-minded devotion to US doctrine, which emphasised the power of the bayonet and of the élan of the infantry at the expense of machine guns and artillery). Fortunately for him, he had the support of the War Department and President Wilson (in any case, this was what he was instructed to do by them) and overcame efforts by Allied leaders to force various forms of amalgamation with their own armies. Pershing argued that national pride dictated the formation of an independent force and that the U.S. could make its most effective contribution to victory by following his course. He also believed that the outcome of the war was going to be decided on the Western Front and, more specifically, in

Headstone of General Pershing, Arlington National Cemetery, Arlington, Virginia.

France. Despite Allied protest, he finally got his way; however, perforce, American formations participated in battles under French or British command during the summer of 1918 and it proved impossible to deploy the American Army as an independent entity until late August.

After the war, Pershing returned to a hero's welcome and, in 1919, was promoted to General of the Armies, a rank especially created for him. George Washington is the only other man to hold the rank – and that was granted in 1976. In 1921 he became Chief of Staff of the United States

Army and presided over significant reforms in the War Department. He left active service in 1924 but continued to perform important duties, such as chairman of the ABMC, the American Battle Monuments Commission, that created and cared for military cemeteries and monuments in France. In 1931 he published his memoirs, *My Experiences in the World War* (which, one has to say, are not particularly inspiring), which were awarded the 1932 Pulitzer Prize for history. He died in Washington DC on 15 July 1948 and is buried in Arlington National Cemetery, Arlington, Virginia: Section 34, Site S-19.

The Germans

The night before the attack, along the Meuse-Argonne front, five German divisions, some 65,000 men, were opposite some 195,000 Americans. They were commanded by General von der Marwitz as part of the *Fifth Army*. The *117th, 32nd* and *5th Bavarian Reserve divisions* were, to a greater or lesser degree, the defenders of the Montfaucon sector; several divisions were held in reserve.

Georg von der Marwitz (1856-1929) was a highly experienced Prussian cavalry general who commanded several armies on both the Eastern and Western fronts. For some time in 1916 he was adjutant to the Kaiser; at the end of the year he left that post to command *Second Army*. In the autumn of 1918, as the BEF maintained its advances on the

General Georg von Marwitz.

Somme front, he was relieved of that command and, on 22 September 1918, transferred to command the *Fifth Army*, which consisted of nine divisions. The average strength of a German division in 1914 was roughly 17,500 men whereas, after several reorganizations during the war and due to the shortage of manpower, in 1918 a division often consisted of just 10,000 men. In reality, especially after the second half of 1918, the period when the Germans had sustained huge losses, the divisions stationed in the Argonne area were lucky if they had 6,000 to 7,000 men. But although suffering severely from battle fatigue, the German Army was still a fighting force to be reckoned with.

The activities of the Americans and French behind the front line did not pass totally unnoticed by the Germans. Although they suspected that something was brewing on the Meuse-Argonne Front, they did not expect an attack of this magnitude. However, because of the fact that between 12 and 16 September the Americans had reduced the St Mihiel Salient, the German High Command believed that the centre of gravity of the attack would be directed against Metz, which provided a plausible decoy for the American preparations in the Argonne.

For the Germans it was key to hold onto their defences on the Kriemhild Line. The importance of holding the line between the Argonne and the Meuse can be appreciated from the words of this order issued by von Marwitz, dated 15 September 1918:

> 'According to the information in our hands the enemy intends to attack the *Fifth Army* east and west of the Meuse in order to reach Longuyon. The objective of this attack is the cutting of the railroad line Longuyon-Sedan, which is the main line of communication of the Western Army. Furthermore, the enemy hopes to compel us to discontinue the exploitation of the iron mines of Briey, the possession of which is of great importance to our steel production. The *Fifth Army* once again may have to bear the brunt of the fighting of the coming weeks on which the security of the Fatherland may depend. The fate of a large portion of the Western Front, perhaps of our nation, depends on a firm holding of the Verdun front. The Fatherland believes that every commander and every soldier realises the greatness of this task and that everyone will fulfil his duty to the utmost. If this is done, the enemy's attack will be shattered.'

German storm troops posing for the camera in March 1918. Note the abundance of stick grenades, often known as potato mashers.

Chapter 2

German Military Installations on Montfaucon

It is essential to understand the basic outline of the organization of the German defences in the Meuse-Argonne area before taking a closer look at the observation posts and other German installations on Montfaucon Hill.

After the big battles of 1916 (Verdun, the Somme) had ended, Germany decided to return to the defensive on the Western Front. The Verdun Offensive had been far too costly in human lives and in materials to be able to sustain it any longer; whilst the Somme had caused considerable anxiety and a rethink of defensive doctrine in the field. The Germans also needed to review the organisation of the front line; there were many sectors that were difficult to defend and consequently sucked in too much manpower and resources. The solution was as simple as it was effective: a new defensive line was to be built close to or, as for example on the Somme, some distance behind the existing front line. Here, there was no immediate risk of an enemy attack and all the different kinds of raw building material, such as sand, gravel, cement, reinforcing bars (rebar) and timber could be more easily delivered wherever they were needed by a system of narrow-gauge railway lines, the construction of which had begun in 1915. The advantage of building in the hinterland was that the new lines could not be reached by the lighter calibre guns. The building programme, a massive undertaking in its own right, shortened the German front line in France by about fifty kilometres.

As a result of this action, thirteen divisions that could be deployed elsewhere were made available. In several sectors along the Western Front, work on this project started as early as autumn 1916 (the Somme) and continued throughout 1917. In the Argonne sector, the bulk of the work started in the second half of 1917 and included many of the structures built by the Crown Prince's *Fifth Army* in 1915 and 1916. (It should be noted that the German army changed titles of major formations as the war progressed – the Crown Prince's Army becoming, for example, Group of Armies German Crown Prince.) The additional benefit of building new lines several and more kilometres behind the front line was that the enemy was forced to advance further, generally across an utterly devastated No Man's Land, thus wearing the men down before the battle had even started. It would cause significant problems for supply trains, artillery and, of course, troops, sapping their energy before they had even reached the principal line of defence.

The Hindenburg Line

By 1918 the Germans had radically altered their defences from the basic arrangements of the winter of 1914-1915. Vast increases in the number of guns and shells available, particularly those of heavy calibre, aircraft, tanks (albeit limited in number), shock troops, light machine guns and many other inventions and new tactical insights had changed the way war was fought. For example, the composition of an artillery regiment was transformed; the total number of guns remained the same, but by 1918 about fifty per cent of the light field guns had been replaced by heavy guns and mortars, significantly increasing firepower. The Germans no longer relied on continuous defence lines (though these still existed); defence in depth meant that the defences had become more like a network of lines and groups of strongpoints. Another significant difference was the number of machine guns in a division and their organisation. The number and type had increased substantially, more than tenfold: from twenty-four in 1914 to 288 in 1918, thus multiplying the firepower of a division several times. In comparison, in 1914 there had been one machine gun for every 750 men, whereas in 1918 there was a machine gun for every fifty-six men.

Both sides were producing machine guns at an extraordinary rate, in turn enhancing the capability of small units, such as platoons. Platoons themselves became more specialist: a war which had depended to a large extent on deploying masses of manpower was replaced by the effective use of technological advances and availability of war materiel – as well as developing battlefield doctrine – to deal with the extraordinary changes in the means available to wage the war. Concepts such as the 'empty battlefield' and 'elastic defence' (effectively allowing an enemy thrust to get forward and then hitting it with counter-attack units as the advance lost much of its artillery cover and the attacking troops were off balance) were introduced as the balance between the defensive and the offensive gradually changed in favour of the latter.

Thus by 1918 machine guns and predicted artillery fire largely compensated for the lack of manpower that was such a major issue for the German Army by late summer 1918 and would prove a horrible obstacle for the Americans. Manpower was a fundamental problem for the German High Command, as a central pillar of defensive doctrine and the one which enabled the concept of elastic defence to be effective was

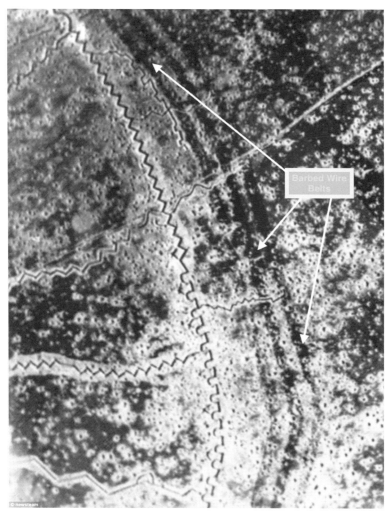

Barbed Wire
Belts

A good example of the Hindenburg Line; note the three different belts of
barbed wire on the right.

the availability of counter attack (or *Eingriff*) divisions to the local Army
or Group commander. These were sorely lacking when the Meuse-
Argonne Offensive opened – as they generally were for the whole of the
battle.

The Maxim machine gun
One of the most famous machine guns of the First World War was the
German Maxim, nicknamed 'the Grim Reaper'. Notably invented by
American inventor Hiram Stevens Maxim, it was the first to use the recoil

The German Maxim MG 08 machine gun.

force generated by each exploding cartridge to reload the gun automatically. The machine gun could theoretically fire 500 rounds per minute, but it was much more common to fire in short bursts. This prevented the gun from overheating and excessive barrel wear – not to mention acknowledged the sheer physical problem of carrying around huge quantities of cartridges. Maxim's invention revolutionized future warfare, as armies around the world were still using hand-cranked guns like the Gatling. Incidentally, he also invented the canvas belt that fed the cartridges into the machine-gun. Perhaps surprisingly, the British Army, often accused of being hide-bound and unwilling to innovate, was the only one interested in Maxim's invention. After several flawless trials, the Maxim was adopted by the British Army, thus making them the first to enter the world of mechanized, industrialized slaughter. Before the war the gun had been successfully used in several colonial campaigns, becoming 'the gun most associated with British Imperial conquest'.

Now one weapon, occupying a few square metres of space and operated by a handful of men, could do the same job as fifty trained riflemen. Quickly, although not in great numbers, the Maxim was adopted by several other European nations. By 1912, the original gun designed by Maxim had been modified by the British; fewer working parts, less weight, more reliable and adapted to the .303 cartridge (as also used by riflemen), the Vickers machine gun was in fact superior to the Maxim – the British army retained it in use until the early 1960s.

The Germans adopted the Maxim only as late as 1908. In the German army, the MG08, as the gun was officially called, was aimed and fired by a gunner but directed by the gun commander, who was usually an experienced and highly trained NCO. Using a specialised set of binoculars for direct firing missions, he observed bullet strike and called corrections to the gunner.

The Americans were forced to use the machine guns delivered by their allies as, to date, they had produced no modern guns of their own. These guns were mostly French-built 8 mm Hotchkiss and Chauchat guns. British (light) Lewis guns were also in use and were much preferred. The American-made (light) Browning 30.06 came in production too late to change the outcome of the war; only 1,200 made it to Europe before the war ended. Several guns of the first batch of Brownings were used by the 79th Division. All the same, the BAR, the Browning Automatic Rifle, was widely used by the Americans by the end of the war. Although only equipped with a twenty round magazine, it supplied the infantry with much-needed extra and, more importantly, reliable firepower.

In spite of all of the technological changes on the battlefield, none of the belligerents had been able to achieve a decisive breakthrough by the opening of 1918 and a war of movement was something that still only existed in the realms of fantasy. By 1918 the trench system was still the backbone of the defence on both sides, but with the difference that by now individual sectors had become much more organized. A more flexible and lightly held front line was adopted which meant that the first lines could be (temporarily, it was hoped) abandoned to the enemy. In between the main lines several intermediate lines were created. These were mostly makeshift defences; shallow trenches hastily dug on high ground or adapted shell holes, defended by machine guns to stall the enemy in order to buy time to salvage as much material as possible and regroup at the next line. Today in the Argonne countless shallow, knee-deep trenches can still be found in the intermediate sectors; at first glance it looks as though they were never properly finished. This is what distinguishes these trenches from trenches that were developed before 1918. Here, the main trench lines, in the Kriemhild Line, for example, were about two metres deep.

Another important feature of the defences were broad belts of barbed wire, sometimes fifty metres wide and erected in front of the trenches. Gaps were deliberately left in the wire so that enemy troops would go in the direction of concealed machine-gun emplacements or predicted artillery zones, so-called killing zones. The wire the Germans used was

German tren:hes on the Western Front in 1918.

so strong th. it was almost impossible to cut it by using a standard-issue wire cutter. Large cumbersome cutters were needed, which added to the soldier's already heavy load. To tackle the barbed wire problem, the Americans counted on their artillery. It was expected that a preliminary bombardment of seven hours would suffice to cut it to shreds. With hindsight, v e now know that this strategy usually failed miserably. Even today, a hundred years after the battle, the wire is still so strong that you need brute force to cut it. (It might be added that many of the wire cutters issued to the troops by the AEF were quite inadequate for the task.)

Many of the structures the Germans had built in the area were made from timber and earth, but over the years the Germans also built great numbers of deep concrete shelters and tunnels; very often this was the reason why many Germans escaped from the preliminary American bombardment largely unscathed. Besides shelters and tunnels, they also built concrete observation posts, machine-gun posts, signalling posts, artillery emplacements, railway stations, water points and hospitals. It needs to be kept in mind that the construction, design and use of bunkers also evolved during the war; the popular image of numerous machine guns operating from inside such structures is a considerable exaggeration.

The Germans christened the whole length of the new defence system the Siegfried Line; the allies referred to it as the Hindenburg Line, after Field Marshal Paul von Hindenburg (1847-1934), commander of the German Army. The unofficial name stuck and the main German line of defence is referred to by that name to this day. The principle lines of

German barbed wire.

defence along the front were often taken from characters in Wagner's *Ring des Nibelungen* cycle. From the front line to the rear, the German defensive positions in the Meuse-Argonne consisted of four zones; each zone was made up of several defence lines. This layer of defensive zones is the significant feature of the Hindenburg Line – that is it was not **a** line at all but a series of lines, the whole designed to be part of a complex defensive arrangement.

1. The *outpost zone.*
This was the zone closest to the enemy and basically covered No Man's Land; this sector was usually lightly held and could easily be evacuated as prescribed by the doctrine of flexible defence. Therefore, there was almost no artillery in the *outpost zone* except for a few isolated batteries; most of the guns were placed in the *battle zone* and more to the rear. However, especially as the battle developed, individual field guns were often brought forward to bolster the defence of this zone.

On the Meuse the number of German soldiers per metre was significantly less than on other fronts. There are several reasons for this: principally, since the Second Battle of Verdun had ended on 28 September 1917, the Meuse-Argonne had been a quiet front for almost a year; fewer troops were needed. After the promising but ultimately fruitless German spring offensives that were fought on other sectors in 1918, the Germans, who had been almost continually engaged by the allies since late July, were desperately in need of manpower replacements in areas such as the Somme and before Arras. This meant that there were even fewer troops deployed in this sector than normal. However, a few weeks before the Americans launched their offensive, German intelligence officers suspected that something was going to happen on the Meuse-Argonne front – though they still had major concerns about Metz, concerns reinforced by imaginative American deception operations. As a precaution, the high command decided to reinforce the Montfaucon sector; on 23 September, just three days before the American attack was launched, the *5th Bavarian Reserve Division* arrived at Dun-sur-Meuse, about fifteen kilometres north east of Montfaucon. Coincidentally, two weeks before that, the *117th Division* relieved the *37th Division*. The *37th Division* was not withdrawn to another part of the front; it stayed in the sector and was thrown into the fray on the second day of the American assault.

2. The *withdrawal zone*.
The area between the *outpost zone* and the *withdrawal zone* was the terrain the enemy was allowed to take but, in doing so, naturally making them pay the highest possible price in lives. The zone was mainly situated in an area that had been the Verdun battlefields in 1916 and all along the destroyed southern part of the seemingly impassable Argonne Forest. Any army advancing over such utterly destroyed terrain would face immense logistical problems; utterly inadequate roads (which withdrawing troops would mine as well) and nothing but wasteland for miles around.

The *withdrawal zone* itself contained, from south to north, the Wiesenschlenken, Hagen and Etzel Lines. Montfaucon was situated on the Etzel Line. Although most of the guns were in position behind the *battle zone*, there were in fact several close support field gun batteries in the direct vicinity of Montfaucon. Two batteries of four guns were positioned in Fayel Wood, four between Montfaucon and Septsarges, one in Beuge Wood and, prior to the American attack, several guns were spotted in Nantillois and on Montfaucon Hill itself, the latter firing point-blank at the advancing Americans and inflicting heavy casualties. As for machine guns, artillery pieces that had been at a premium in 1914 were plentiful by 1918; the risk of losing numbers of them was a price well worth paying for the direct support they offered.

The *withdrawal zone* here varied from four to eight kilometres in width and the Germans defending this zone were ordered to hold the enemy for a minimum of three days. If necessary, they could retreat to an intermediate line and keep the enemy engaged without the immediate

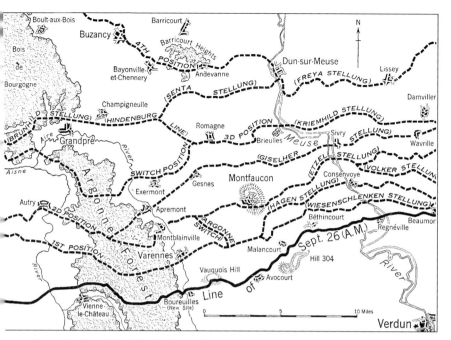

Organization of the Hindenburg Line.

danger of a hostile breakthrough. This provided the time that the Germans needed to bring reinforcements to the front, launch a counterattack and ultimately destroy the enemy or to push them back to their start lines.

However, the German plan was based on sector enemy attacks; they did not expect and certainly could not handle an all-out Allied offensive that stretched from the North Sea in Belgium to Verdun and beyond. If their whole front line was seriously engaged by the enemy, where would they find the reinforcements to plug the holes in their defence lines and the manpower for their *Eingriff* divisions, the latter essential if their defence doctrine was to be effective? By late September 1918 this was exactly what was happening on the Western Front. Still, the Germans somehow managed to find extra regiments, although in most cases these were rated as third and fourth class and often were far from full (or establishment) strength.

3. The *battle zone.*
This line is confusingly known as the Hindenburg Line but in fact consisted of two lines, the Giselher and the Kriemhild Line. The battle zone varied in width from one to one and a half kilometres. This zone was where the enemy had to be stopped and preferably pushed back all the way to the original No Man's Land and even beyond. The line was

23

looked upon as a border line; there were barely any other defences beyond the Hindenburg Line. If the enemy managed to reach this line, it was all or nothing for the Germans. With this at the back of their minds they were willing to fight for every metre. It took the Americans several weeks (instead of a few days, according to Pershing's initial plan) to reach this line. Not surprisingly, the heaviest fighting took place in the battle zone.

4. The *ultimate withdrawal zone.*
The total width of the first three zones varied from four to twelve kilometres. The *ultimate withdrawal zone*, locally the reserve or Freya Line, as the Germans called it, was built at a distance of three to twelve kilometres to the rear of the stop zone, making a total depth of twenty-four kilometres of defences in this sector.

For heavy labour, the Germans made use of Russian prisoners of war (after the peace treaty with the Russians this provided a construction manpower problem, although Italian PoWs were available in large numbers after Caporetto); most of the Freya defences were only partially completed. If the Freya line was taken, the only thing left to do for the Germans was to retreat in the direction of Sedan, cross the River Meuse, and withdraw to the River Rhine (an Antwerp Line was in preparation), where they would begin their defence of the Fatherland. However, by the time the Germans surrendered Sedan to the French the Armistice had been signed.

Although the Germans had been building and perfecting their defences for years, many of the more permanent Hindenburg Line defences in this sector, e.g. concrete shelters, were only built in 1918. In contrast, many of the intermediate lines, in Beuge Wood and Brieulles Wood for example, were hastily constructed once it became clear that the American offensive had started. The intermediate lines mainly consisted of shallow earthworks but were highly effective in slowing down the American advance. For example, the shallow trenches at the southern edge of Beuge Wood inflicted serious casualties on the troops of the 79th and 37th Divisions. Here, the Germans managed to stall the American advance for about three hours; this time was used to reinforce the garrison in Cierges, where the Americans were held up once again and failed to breach the defences. Without such German tactics to slow them down, Cierges would most probably have been wrested from the Germans on 28 September; but it remained in German hands until 4 October. At the end of that day it had taken the Americans twenty-four hours to advance a mere 1,000 metres.

The method of occupation of the lines was in conformity with new German doctrine. The lines were lightly held, with one battalion, by now (theoretically) 800 men strong, in the outpost position in echelon formation; while a second battalion took up a reserve position and a third was in rest billets well to the rear, in this case the village of Nantillois and Beuge Wood. Each company, about 200 men strong, held its position in the front line in a system of *stutzpunkte*, or strongpoints, garrisoned by a non-commissioned officer (a corporal or a sergeant) or, rarely, a lieutenant (the Germans were very reluctant to 'dilute' the 'quality' of their officer corps and so NCOs or temporary officers often performed command tasks that would be done by officers in other armies) and with eight men in each. These strongholds did not necessarily or even usually have to be concrete structures; in the Argonne area they were often set up in camouflaged shell holes or made from timber and earth. There were eight machine guns per company, four in position and four in reserve, giving them formidable firepower. As noted previously, the Germans largely compensated for the lack of manpower through the use of numerous concealed machine-gun positions with interlocking fields of fire. The wire in front of the line was at least ten metres in depth although wire obstacles could cover an area as wide as fifty metres. The nature of the Meuse-Argonne region, with its series of lateral valleys and deep ravines, was such that it made for an ideal area for defensive fighting. By the time the Americans launched their offensive, many of the heights on which the Hindenburg Line was built had been organised into powerful positions by the addition of machine guns, artillery, concrete underground shelters, trenches and wire entanglements.

An improvised German *Stutzpunkt* or strongpoint in 1918.

German military installations at Montfaucon

In 1920, the 304th Engineers, 79th Division, published an interesting military evaluation of Montfaucon.

'As a post of command and observation the position is unexcelled, and it was for that purpose that the Germans used it, taking advantage of and improving every natural feature of value. As an element in the defensive system, the position of the hill made itself almost impregnable if organized for that purpose, but it was apparently the plan of the Germans that the outer lines along the ridge of the hills south of Malancourt and through Malancourt Wood, Montfaucon Wood and Cheppy Wood were to prevent any assaulting force from getting within striking distance of Montfaucon. Once through the prepared lines of defence, however, the natural features of the place asserted themselves as shown by the difficulty in its capture. Had the town of Montfaucon and the flanking Tuillerie Wood been organized to the extent met with in other positions less favored [sic] by topography, its capture by infantry assault would have been even more difficult than it was.'

This statement clearly shows that the Germans used Montfaucon as a tactical rather than a strategic position and that its most important support to the German defences was primarily one of observation. The hill, a left over from the last ice age, is more or less situated in the centre of the Meuse-Argonne region, with the Argonne Forest to its left (west) and the River Meuse to its right (east). As one of the highest hills in the area, with its summit 336 metres above sea level, it was perfectly situated to direct artillery fire at the French lines. Naturally, Montfaucon played a pivotal role in Pershing's plans. If during the first crucial days of the offensive the Germans remained in control of the hill and refused to give it up, it would cause serious problems for the AEF. French intelligence revealed that the hill was honeycombed with observation posts and that the garrison, for obvious reasons, was very well supplied. Although the sector was expected to be lightly held, it was feared that the dominating prominence of Montfaucon would hold up the entire centre of the American advance and consequently delay all other operations along the line of the offensive.

The American High Command fully realized the difficulty of capturing Montfaucon; they planned to drive deep wedges into the German lines on each side of the hill. Then, by threatening the rear, it was hoped that the German garrison would either withdraw or surrender.

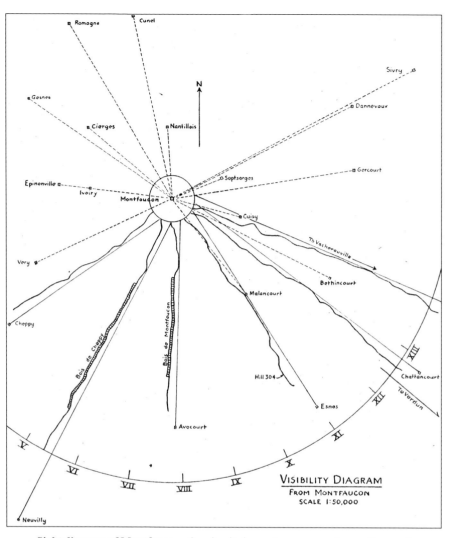

VISIBILITY DIAGRAM
FROM MONTFAUCON
SCALE 1:50,000

Sight diagram of Montfaucon, showing its importance as an observation post.

Once Montfaucon was eliminated, the advance on the German second and third positions, the Giselher Line and Kriemhild Line, could continue. But, in another scenario, the Germans could stay put and continue to relay information to their gun batteries; in theory, the garrison could hold out for weeks.

Montfaucon, dubbed the 'Little Gibraltar of the Western Front' by the French, had been used as an observation post ever since the Germans had taken it from the French in September 1914. The hill offered an

A service for the German garrison in the church in Montfaucon in 1915.

unobstructed view across the French front line and rear areas. Since early on in the war the French had tried to dislodge them from this commanding hill by means of shelling. The Germans, obviously not impressed, had no intention whatsoever of abandoning Montfaucon. As a result, by September 1918 much of the village had been reduced to little more than rubble; a few walls were still standing, most notably those of the church. Sadly, this was not the first time that Montfaucon had been destroyed by foreign invaders; this was its fate eight times, this war included; all invaders wanted to take control of the high ground.

To counter the French shelling, the Germans developed a complex system of underground shelters. They also made significant use of reinforced concrete to build signal posts, large shelters for the garrison and, above all, observation posts. Underground cellars were connected to provide subterranean passages. They also made use of the medieval tunnels that the people of Montfaucon had dug to protect themselves from foreign invaders.

Instrumental in the development of Montfaucon as a major intelligence centre was General of Artillery Max von Gallwitz. Von Gallwitz (1852-1937) grew up in a Catholic family in Breslau, Silesia (after 1945 a part of Poland). He started his military career as a loader with the artillery when he volunteered for the Prussian Army after the

Franco-Prussian War broke out. Intrigued by that war, he studied ballistics at the Prussian War Academy. On completing his education his star rose quickly; in 1906 he was promoted to lieutenant general, in 1911 to general of artillery and eventually was raised to the nobility by Kaiser Wilhelm II in 1913. He helped to develop indirect fire, close coordination between artillery and infantry units and the rolling barrage, among many other innovations of the use of artillery. Nowadays these are standard practices in the military. It should be noted that the development of modern artillery started in around 1870 and that many inventions, such as breechloading guns, rifled barrels and the smokeless cartridge, still had to be made or were under development.

General of Artillery Max von Gallwitz, 1852-1937.

Each time a new technological innovation was made it took years to find the best way to use and adapt it under battle conditions, more especially so in peace time conditions, when budgets were restricted.

During the first two years of the First World War, except for a brief time when he participated in the siege of Namur in 1914, von Gallwitz fought mainly on the Eastern Front, where he achieved several victories under Field Marshals von Mackensen and von Hindenburg. In March 1916 he was transferred to the Western Front, where he commanded *Fifth Army* during the Battle of Verdun (on the left bank) and from July to December *Second Army* during the Battle of the Somme. He was in the Meuse-Argonne from December 1916 until the Armistice on 11 November 1918, once again commander of *Fifth Army*, relieving the Crown Prince. He became well-acquainted with the area and was in fact the brains behind the defences built during this period. Besides commanding *Fifth Army*, in January 1918 he commanded the new *Army Group Gallwitz*, much of which was equipped and trained according to the latest military insights, such as shock troops, armed with sub-machine guns and automatic pistols, trained to capture their targets quickly and then move on to the next, leaving the mopping up of prisoners and the elimination of the last enemy resistance to the troops that followed.

Von Gallwitz did not believe that anyone would attack an area with such a difficult topography as the Meuse-Argonne – an opinion shared by higher command. As a consequence, the German lines were mainly occupied by veteran divisions weakened by combat or by divisions with regiments still in training. New regiments were made up of either old or young men, commanded and trained by veterans. Most regiments only had half the number of men prescribed by the establishment figures. Notwithstanding this situation, these men were well-trained and skilled in comparison to the freshly-arrived Americans and were still very capable of putting up significant resistance. On the other hand, there were also sectors where the Germans easily surrendered, hardly firing a shot; these troops often were Alsatians, men from the Franco-German border region.

As an artillery expert, it was von Gallwitz and his staff who were mainly responsible for the organization of the German guns. In fact the positioning of the guns in the Meuse-Argonne was so brilliantly executed that this became one of the most significant reasons why it took the Americans five weeks to break through the Hindenburg Line instead of a few days. It has been estimated that about sixty-five to seventy per cent of the casualties during the war, dead and wounded, were inflicted by artillery fire; to make matters worse, in 1918 as many as one out of three shells were gas shells.

Gas shells were a common feature of both sides artillery programmes at this stage of the war. For example, the AEF had arranged that approximately twenty percent of all shells for the St Mihiel Offensive would be gas. Mustard gas was favoured – and worked particularly well for the defence. Its properties ensured that the gas lingered on the ground for a considerable time after it had been deployed and it had a significant impact on the troops, causing numerous casualties (many were affected to a greater or lesser extent but few died as a direct result) and making life even more uncomfortable for the men in the battle zone. This was often mixed with shells that fired irritating gas, designed to force men to remove their gas masks.

The Crown Prince's observation post

Artillery support was a paramount consideration in the German defensive strategy of 1918. However, without proper observation, the guns were 'blind'. To tackle this problem, an elaborate network of observation posts, observation balloons and signalling stations were set up, supported by reconnaissance aircraft. Since the start of the occupation of the Argonne, the system had been constantly improved. The most important asset of this network, centrally situated on the battlefield, were the installations at Montfaucon.

At the beginning of the war Montfaucon was used as a makeshift observation post by troops of a French Colonial regiment. In early September 1914 the French were pushed off the hill by the *Fifth Army*, commanded by Crown Prince Wilhelm of Prussia (1882-1951). It has

Château Leriche (on the left): part of the Crown Prince's massive observation post is clearly visible emerging through the roof.

been said that he personally joined the final cavalry charge to secure Montfaucon. Several of the houses in the town centre were on fire when the Crown Prince mounted the hill and enjoyed the magnificent view for the first time. Many visits were to follow in the next two years when he commanded the Meuse-Argonne sector.

The opening battles of the war moved on; but after the Germans failed to take Paris and lost the Battle of the Marne (6-10 September 1914), the temporary defences several kilometres to the south of Montfaucon gradually developed into permanent lines. Montfaucon was now conveniently situated in the hinterland and offered an unprecedented view across the battlefield, from Verdun, the Meuse Heights, Mort Homme and Cote 304 to the east and Vauquois to Clermont-en-Argonne and the Argonne Forest to the west.

The start of the German occupation resulted in the removal of the local population; about 800 people were evacuated and their homes were used to house the garrison. In 1914 and 1915 most of the homes and the church were still intact, although frequently shelled by the French. Several attics were soon converted into makeshift observation posts in order to gather information about French troop movements and so on. Streets in the area were renamed and Germanized: by 1915 you could find a Haupt Strasse or Wilhelm Strasse in every occupied village. In Montfaucon the more significant buildings, such as a number of little chateaux and villas, were occupied by officers, whilst the *mairie* (town hall) served as a headquarters. Cafes and shops were taken over by the army; the garrison was a small village community of its own. Until March 1916 it stayed relatively quiet on this part of the front.

At the end of 1915, German Supreme Headquarters developed plans to strike a knock-out blow against the French, based on a major, strategic offensive (the first on the Western Front by the Germans since the opening moves of 1914, if one discounts relatively minor offensives, such as Second Ypres, April-May 1915) in the area of Verdun. To the French, Verdun was a city with mythical status. During the Franco-Prussian War of 1870 the city had refused to surrender to the Prussian army and therefore served in the collective French mind as one of the few positive events of an otherwise disastrous war. To the French, Verdun epitomized fortitude and hope.

At some time in 1915 (it has been impossible to establish the exact date) the Germans decided to improve the installations on Montfaucon by adding a new, technologically advanced, observation tower. German engineers started to search for an intact and sturdy building that was about three stories high and, preferably, possessed a large basement that could be converted into a shelter for its operators. Eventually, Château Leriche was selected, located about a hundred metres north west of the church. It was called a chateau but was in fact a modest two-story mansion with a large barn-like attic, providing unobstructed views to the south west. The Germans needed a building that was still fairly intact for camouflage and, of course, it would reduce any necessary building work. A heavily fortified concrete observation tower and shelter was built up inside the chateau. The wooden floors and ceilings of several rooms were demolished to make room for the tower. According to the American engineers, 'from a standpoint of military engineering it was a classic example of the use of reinforced concrete'. Besides the observation tower inside the church, a more favourable site for the purpose on the hill could hardly be imaginable. Realizing this, the Germans anticipated that such a point would receive considerable attention from enemy artillery. Therefore, the Germans built a tower with a characteristic Teutonic thoroughness; it could defy any ordinary bombardment. Only one direct hit was ever reported on the tower, though it was slightly brushed by shrapnel fire; it was still standing at the end of the war, though by then the mansion surrounding it had been severely damaged by shelling. Even

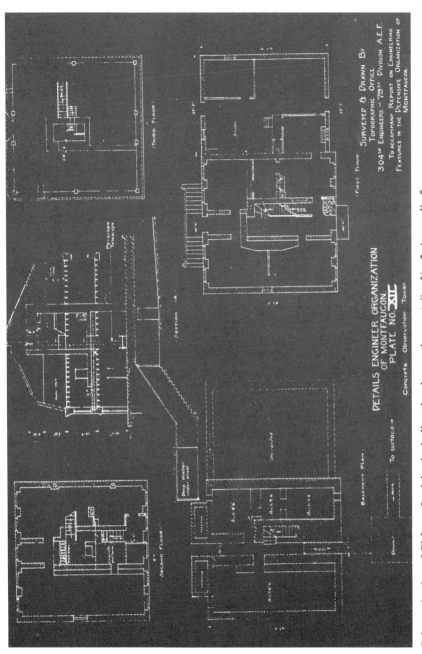

Schematic plan of Château Leriche, including the observation post. See No. 2, Appendix 5.

33

after its liberation, Montfaucon was an extremely unhealthy place; it continued to be an important target for German artillery for the remainder of the war.

Château Leriche was a building with three floors and a cellar, constructed with the massive outside and inside walls common to the architecture in this area. To adjust the building to their needs, the Germans first laid a heavy course of concrete over the first floor, making the arched cellars excellent shelters, with from two to three metres of masonry and the added seventy-five centimetres deep concrete slab as additional cover. The cellar walls were also reinforced with concrete and, in addition, a dugout was built under the road in front of the building, providing an additional five and a half metres of cover. This shelter was connected to the basement by an underground gallery and staircase. From the basement a tower was built, reaching a height of almost eleven metres from its foundations. The tower was well-protected, having for most of its height one metre of concrete and two one metre thick masonry walls (a thick outside and an inside wall within the house; the tower was positioned centrally in the building) on the side facing towards the French lines. At the point in the attic where the protection of the outer walls ended additional concrete slabs protected the upper 6.7 metres of the tower. A 1.30 metre deep slab covered the top. A small chart room at the highest point of the opening through the roof sheltered the observer and his instruments.

The Periscope
The chateau's practical function was provided by a powerful, retractable, reflecting telescopic periscope mounted on a gun carriage that was put in place on the first floor, with the tubing running through the tower and out of the roof. The instrument was so constructed that observation could be carried out either through selective eye pieces at the base of the tube on the first floor or by means of reflectors and prisms from the second and third floors. It was built by the Zeiss Optical Company, a well-known German firm that still exists today. A large and elaborate observation map was found mounted in the chart room. It was scaled in millimetres and oriented to compass points on the 360-degree radius of the periscope. For any point on the map, all that was necessary was to get its millimetre deflection from the map, turn it on the traversing scale of the telescope and bring it into focus with the eye piece. The data gathered was then relayed to a central telephone exchange in Nantillois by telephone or telegraph. In case of technical problems, a signalling station that was equipped with electric signal lights was built at the back of the hill, about fifty metres distance from the observation post.

Although the installations were unusable, the Americans used the structure itself for several weeks.

Interior of the *blinkstelle*, the German signalling post, that was connected to the Crown Prince's observation post. Note the apertures for transmitting light signals: see No. 1, Appendix 5.

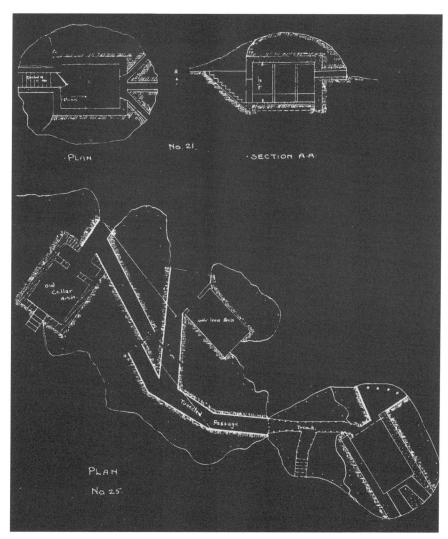

Schematic plan of the German signalling post and tunnels. See No. 1, Appendix 5.

The *History of the 304th Engineers* notes that the periscope was captured in serviceable condition but that before it could be turned around to bear down on the enemy lines some thoughtless souvenir hunter stole the eye-pieces, rendering it useless. Since the 304th Engineers' history was published in 1920, several writers have commented on this. Who was the 'thoughtless souvenir hunter' who stole the eye pieces? Private William Schellberg, of the 311th Machine Gun Regiment, was there and

36

made an interesting entry in his journal. Could one of these soldiers have been the guilty party?

Private William Schellberg, 311ᵗʰ Machine Gun Regiment.

'Friday 27 September 1918. During the day, in clearing [out] in the town, the Crown Prince's observation post was discovered. A house had been reinforced with steel girders and concrete, with a thick concrete tower running through it. It was nearly shell proof, except from a direct hit by a heavy gun, and a wonderful field of view in all directions was obtained from it. However, there was still a further price to be paid for the capture of the tower and its contents. Armstrong was carrying a big metal map case, like a stovepipe; Eugene Martenet and two other men were lugging the great telescope, and Conway was ahead with an armful of maps. Stooping over to get the protection of the embankment, they had walked about 25 feet when a great shell skimmed over their backs and the edge of the bank and exploded in the road, just ahead of Armstrong. He got most of the fragments in his back and fell dead instantly. Conway got most of the other fragments and was seriously wounded. After these two had been looked after, the rest of the party carried on with the maps, telescope and the map case. Privates Bob Armstrong and Bill Conway were both former newspaper men on the staff of the Baltimore Sun.'

On 30 September the exhausted 79ᵗʰ Division was relieved and the veteran 3ʳᵈ Division, the 'Rock of the Marne', replaced them. They found the periscope in place but useless; they decided to dismount it and sent it back to the rear on 30 October. They reported that it was in excellent condition except that some of the hoisting cables had been broken, the telescopic eye-pieces smashed (!) and one section of the elevating pole dented by shrapnel. In February 1919 the periscope was shipped from the port of St. Nazaire directly to the United States Military Academy at West Point. Subsequently it appeared that the whole contraption had disappeared; but in 1999 it resurfaced in the U.S. Army Field Artillery Museum at Fort Sill, Oklahoma, where it had been in storage for decades. Today, fully restored, the periscope, minus its eye-pieces, is now

US troops observing the Germans from underneath the roof of the Crown Prince's observation post.

exhibited in the main gallery of the museum. Thanks to the 3rd Division's quest for souvenirs, a rare piece of German Great War military engineering has survived.

Today almost nothing remains of this historic site. The whole complex was in such a state that it was blown up and demolished after the war. Besides the periscope, the only remainders of the former Château Leriche that still exist are the concrete walls of the cellars (not accessible to the public) and the wrought iron gate facing the modern-day D15a.

It has been claimed that the Crown Prince himself ordered the building of the observation post in order to follow the outcome of events in the Battle of Verdun. This idea, appealing as it may sound, is highly unlikely. Although the Crown Prince was in command of *Fifth Army*, which controlled the sector,

The German Crown Prince, William of Prussia, 1882 -1951.

38

the army was in reality 'commanded' by his Chief of Staff, Konstantin von Knobelsdorff (1860-1936). However, there is a far more practical reason why the story is implausible; the 'Crown Prince's Periscope' was more than twenty kilometres west of the main action; Château Leriche was situated on the further slope from the action east of the Meuse below the crest of Montfaucon; from this position it would be simply impossible to observe Verdun. Stories like these were already circulating amongst American soldiers in September 1918. Later, this 'fantasy' got mixed up with events that had actually happen and the story consequently became recorded in several unit histories.

All the same, the observation post *was* used during the Battle of Verdun, but for targets on the left bank of the Meuse, whereas Verdun and its defences could only be observed from the observation tower in the church. The main purpose of the Crown Prince's observation post was to survey south-southwest to guard against a French attack from that direction and to direct artillery fire. The Americans named the observation post after the Crown Prince without knowing if he had ever actually been there. On the other hand, there is ample proof that he actually visited Montfaucon on numerous occasions. There is an entry in his own diary relating to a visit to observe the front, probably from the observation post that was built inside the church walls. On 29 December 1915 he wrote:

'I was inspecting the front of the 6th Reserve Corps from the observation post of Montfaucon and from this magnificent viewpoint my eyes first sought out the eastern bank [direction Verdun] of the Meuse. Usually my first glance is focussed on the Argonne Forest.'

Interestingly, the observation post is also the site where three men were awarded the Distinguished Service Cross, the DSC, the second highest military award of the American Army (the Medal of Honor being the highest). Sergeant Thomas M Rivel, Private First Class Arthur J McCain and Private Arthur S Roberts of the Headquarters Detachment were awarded this medal for extraordinary heroism in action near Montfaucon on 28, 29 and 30 September 1918. For several days they remained constantly on duty in the ruins of the Crown Prince's Observation Post while acting as divisional observers. The chateau in which the observation post was built took several direct hits and portions of it were destroyed by high explosive shells. At one point the German shelling was so

The Distinguished Service Cross.

intense that other observers located there withdrew to a safer location. Rivel, McCain and Roberts, however, remained constantly at their post and obtained important information. From what they provided it was possible to organise counter battery fire, which put several German batteries out of action, thereby saving many American lives.

Other observation posts
Next to the famous Crown Prince's Observation Post, the Germans also spent a lot of energy, labour and material in building other observation posts on the hill. In total, seventeen heavily reinforced concrete and masonry observation towers were built at various positions in the town, of which twelve remain today. The usual manner of construction was to build up the observation post in the form of a concrete shaft inside a house, using the outer wall of the house as additional cover. Depending on the size of the building (more specifically, the size of the rooms that the engineers wanted to use), the shaft was usually 1.50 to 2.50 metres square, with a slit about 2.50 metres wide at the top for observation. These structures were certainly not built, as some say, for defensive reasons; they were solely built for observation purposes and to protect equipment and personnel. Only in a very few cases would it have been possible to mount a machine gun or even fire a rifle from such a point and, were it possible, the thickness of the wall would have prevented sufficient depression to cover the front. The observation posts were usually directly connected to some underground shelter by trench, gallery or protected passage, normally a trench that was revetted with sandbags and timber. In 1918, standing walls and rubble afforded perfect camouflage, both from the ground and from the air. As well as that and in spite of all the shelling, there were several tall trees, many of which survive today.

The observation post inside the church ruins at the highest point of the hill had the best view of all. It is highly likely that this post, built in 1915 from recycled building material from the church, and the Crown Prince's Observation Post later formed the two principal points in a triangulation system. Maps and data found by American soldiers in the afternoon of 27 September 1918 strongly point to this conclusion. By means of this system, the Germans could measure the distance to an object by sighting a distant object from two different locations and using trigonometry to calculate the distance between the locations.

Interestingly, the Germans also used countless improvised observation posts. Possibly the most bizarre of these discovered by the Americans was built in a marble burial vault in the graveyard of Montfaucon. The bodies had been removed from their graves to make room for two bunks to house the observers (see photograph, p. 193).

40

Stones of the original building seen in the concrete of Observation Post 20, Appendix 5.

The observation post amidst the bombed out ruins of Montfaucon Church: See No. 9, Appendix 5.

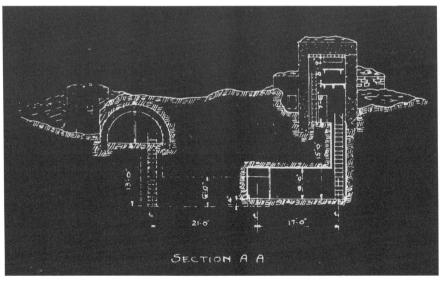

SECTION A A

Schematic plan of an observation post. See No. 8, Appendix 5.

41

Galleries, shelters and dugouts

When the Germans started their offensive on 21 February 1916, they originally intended to launch a massive attack on the relatively small but well-fortified French garrison town of Verdun on the right bank of the River Meuse. On 25 February an almost farcical series of events resulted in the capture of Fort Douaumont, a great German victory and a slap in the face for the proud French. However, Germany's fortune changed when the offensive quickly bogged down and became a slogging match between infantry, mud and seemingly endless artillery barrages – whilst the German's right flank was painfully exposed to French enfilade fire from the Left Bank. On 6 March 1916, in an attempt to break the impasse, the Germans decided to jump-start the offensive by launching another attack, this time directed at the positions beyond the left bank of the River Meuse, in particular targeting Mort Homme and Cote 304, two commanding hills, bristling with French artillery. These guns had seriously hampered the German advance on Verdun as they fired shell after shell into the German flank. However, this meant that instead of a limited though massive attack directed at one objective, the battle zone now extended over a front that was now twenty-five kilometres long. By 15 December, when the Battle of Verdun officially ended, the whole area had been laid waste. Most of the villages on or directly behind the front line were completely destroyed or at least heavily damaged by the intense shelling, Montfaucon and its sister village Nantillois included. In fact, Montfaucon had been damaged so badly that now there was an urgent need for new underground shelters and passages to protect the garrison.

One thing is absolutely clear: the Germans spared neither labour, material nor effort in providing shelters. Most of the houses in Montfaucon had arched stone wine cellars, from three to six metres wide and five to twelve metres long, with one to five metres of cover, thus making ideal shelters. Ironically, later in the war the protection provided by the shelters was further greatly improved thanks to the metres of debris from the collapsed houses that had been standing above them. Anyone hiding in these types of shelters was not safe from the heaviest artillery shells; but, due to the fact that the thick masonry of the houses acted as a bursting course, the shelters provided adequate protection against ordinary shell fire. In the majority of cases no reinforcing was required to give the protection desired, but in places arches were supported by timbers and the stone walls reinforced with concrete. The 304th Engineers recorded that very few of the cellars so used were destroyed or penetrated by the intensive shelling that the hill had undergone for three years and more.

Besides reinforced cellars, many deep dugouts had been built at a depth varying between six to ten metres below the surface, often

Entrance of a German dugout.

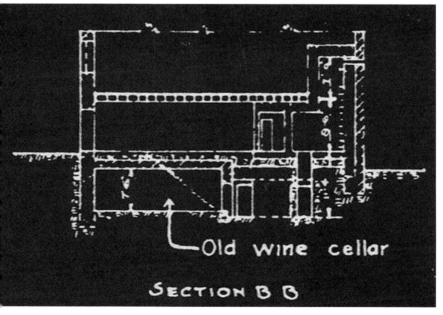

Old wine cellar

SECTION B B

Schematic plan of a reinforced wine cellar on Montfacucon.

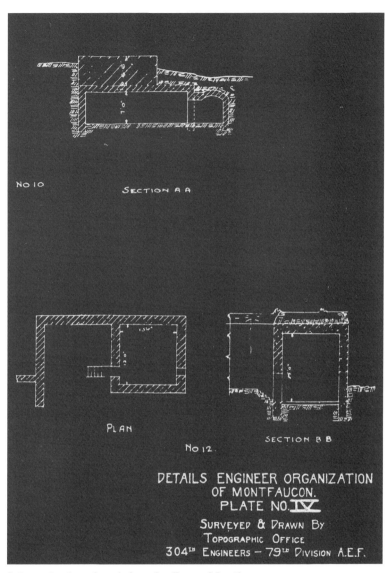

NO 10

SECTION A A

PLAN

No 12.

SECTION B B

DETAILS ENGINEER ORGANIZATION
OF MONTFAUCON.
PLATE NO. IV
SURVEYED & DRAWN BY
TOPOGRAPHIC OFFICE
304TH ENGINEERS – 79TH DIVISION A.E.F.

Schematic plan of a reinforced cellar on Montfaucon.

connected by two shafts and a gallery. After 1916, most shelters were provided with a minimum of two entrances or shafts; if one appeared to be blocked, the other could serve as an emergency exit. In some cases several shelters and cellars were connected by galleries to form continuous shelters. When the Americans took Montfaucon they discovered that in several places work was still in progress; several

Interior of a typical German dugout.

mining operations were underway to connect shelters farther back on the hill. The average shelter could accommodate thirty to forty men if necessary; but larger shelters and dormitories were also built. A huge shelter, more like a barracks, was built under the site of the present-day car park in front of the tower monument. It was discovered years ago when workers of the ABMC who maintain the Montfaucon American Monument found that during the night part of the parking space had disappeared into a huge hole; apparently, part of the roof had collapsed. The hole was filled in and the parking spaces repaired but, so far as is known, nobody took it upon themselves to survey the site at that time. Fortunately, in September 1918 Lester Muller, a reporter for the Baltimore Sun, described some of the underground installations:

'On entering Montfaucon, we learned that the Huns had lived there for several years most comfortably, the evidence of luxury being everywhere. We found a moving-picture house with many films intact, a cafe stocked with wine, luxurious dug-outs with papered walls, and one underground chamber large enough to accommodate hundreds of men. It might be said here that we found the telescope on the citadel standing as the German officers had left it. Their retreat was so sudden that when our doughboys reached the officers' quarters they found its previous occupants had left before finishing their meal, much of which was still on the tables, including cigars, cigarettes and wine.'

The generating station
In 1915 the Germans built several generating stations in the area to provide electric lighting for the billets. Naturally, one was built on Montfaucon to power the numerous signal lights about the town. In 1918 the Germans replaced the old generating station; it was too exposed and more power was needed to light the galleries etc. that had been added since it was built. The engineers decided to build a concrete structure, of 5.5 metres square, in a steep bank in a cut back from the road that leads to Nantillois. It was built as far away from the enemy as possible and offered very good protection; today there is no sign of shell damage to the structure.

A large, single cylinder, liquid gas engine that drove a generator furnished the power. A chimney was built at the far end of the shelter to evacuate the toxic fumes given off by the engine. Small trenches of fifty centimetres deep carried the power lines to various points. Practically every shelter and dugout of any size in the vicinity was powered by electricity from this station. Next to the station underground store rooms and shelters connected by galleries were built. Only the generating station bunker itself survives.

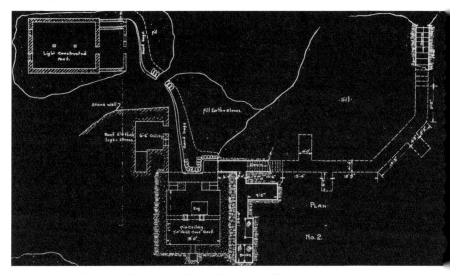

Schematic plan of the generating stations and other underground structures.

46

Entrance to the generating station, March 2018.

The same entrance, photographed on 27 September 1918.

After the Germans retreated from Montfacucon, the Americans took possession of the shelters; all the entrances were heavily protected by masses of sandbags as the hill was a daily target for the German artillery and, naturally, the entrances were all facing in the wrong direction, ie towards the Germans. Still, weeks after Montfaucon had been liberated, doughboys died or were wounded at this dangerous place that lay in full view of the batteries on the Meuse Heights and the high ground to the north of Montfaucon.

Machine-gun bunkers

It has been repeatedly claimed that there were hundreds of machine guns on Montfaucon. Were there, in fact, any concrete structures built to serve that purpose? After years of surveying the hill, I have found no remains of concrete machine-gun emplacements. This does not mean, of course, that they were not there at the time, but most likely the structures built to protect the machine guns and their crews were made from timber and earth and have disappeared with the passage of time. Another possibility is that such concrete structures were destroyed during or after the war. The Americans were well-known for dynamiting German bunkers in case the Germans retook positions by counter-attack. However, to this day, no documentary reports, photographs or anything else has surfaced to support the theory that concrete machine-gun shelters were constructed on the hill.

Anti-tank barriers

During the latter stages of the war the Germans widely used anti-tank obstacles. There were two distinct types. The first was the trap mine, a wooden ammunition box that was placed in the ground with the lid flush with the surface. The box was filled with unexploded ordnance and a detonator that was set to go off at a certain weight; the first primitive anti-tank mine was born. The second type was the anti-tank barrier. This kind of obstacle was built with the idea of delaying a tank long enough so that the artillery could destroy it. Naturally, both types of defence were largely dependent upon the element of surprise for their effectiveness. They were usually built in village streets, ruins, roads and other places where aerial observation would have difficulty spotting them. Often both were used together and were positioned in such a way so that if troops managed to avoid the first there was no avoiding the second. It also was not unusual that certain types of barrier were boobytrapped.

When the Americans entered the town on the afternoon of 27 September they found that all the main roads leading into Montfaucon were blocked with anti-tank barriers. The barriers consisted of three

An anti-tank barrier on one of the roads leading into Monfaucon. The middle one of three reinforced concrete pillars has already been removed by the 304th Engineers.

Detail of a concrete anti-tank barrier, with part of the metal reinforcement sticking out from the top.

reinforced concrete pillars, each with one metre wide sides forming a square, spread across the road. Buried one metre into the ground, the pillars were about three metres high. The construction was strong enough to halt the heaviest tank. Added to this, machine guns were trained on the barriers to prevent infantry blasting the obstacles. These structures were permanent and did not permit the use of the road by either friend or foe. To make things even more complicated for the attacker, and if the terrain permitted, the barricaded road was either in a heavy cut or fill, so that the tank could not pass around it. If this was not possible, the area on both sides for a distance of a minimum of fifty metres was mined. No mines were reported in Montfaucon.

Lieutenant Colonel DuPuy, 311th Machine Gun Regiment, was there when eleven tanks were confronted by the barriers.

49

'About nine-thirty pm small French tanks came lumbering along to help in the attack on 'Little Gibraltar', as the French had nicknamed the hill. The coming of the tanks gave the men assurance and strengthened their morale. The tanks (eleven in number) approached the town in pairs, through five of the principal streets. All went well until they reached certain points, where the Germans, with their usual cunning, had foreseen just such an attack, and had erected barricades across the streets, formed of high concrete blocks reinforced with steel rails, which later were bent backwards and planted in the ground some twenty feet. Here the tanks were useless, so we were again compelled to fall back in the face of hundreds of machine guns.'

It is worth noting that the Americans only had relatively light (French) tanks available. There had been a plan for the use of heavy British tanks at St Mihiel, but a couple of weeks before that offensive Haig had to inform Pershing that there were no spare tanks available; and none could be produced for the Meuse-Argonne.

Camp Montfaucon

The Germans, as well as the French and British, constructed numerous support camps in the area immediately behind the front line, intended for soldiers who were not on active duty at the front. Here, soldiers could recuperate from the hardships experienced at the front; amongst the luxuries at their disposal were bathing facilities, canteens and cinemas. Because of the close proximity of the front line, deep shelters were essential at these locations and many were dug at Camp Montfaucon. Nowadays, these deep dugouts are still to be found all along the old front line, but for some reason the ones at Montfaucon have all disappeared. According to old engineer reports, it is safe to say that at least one hundred dugouts were found in the immediate vicinity of the destroyed town, especially on the slopes to the north and east, close to the junction with the road to Nantillois.

Camp Montfaucon was a camp of considerable size. All along the bottom of a steep escarpment, safe from all but very high angle shell fire, the Germans constructed two groups of approximately thirty buildings, consisting of barracks, offices, officers' quarters and store rooms. The buildings were built as close to the escarpment as possible and connected by a series of very large dugouts driven straight back into the hill. When the hill was captured by the Americans, the Germans were still working on several tunnels and at least one building. According to the engineer report, the details of these dugouts were very interesting because they

A good example of a hill honeycombed with German dugouts.

Schematic plan of part of Camp Montfaucon.

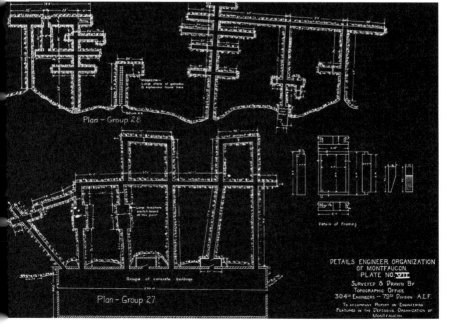

were built differently than other shelters; the entire length of the gallery was timbered solidly with the standard frames of five centimetre thick planks instead of corrugated iron. The ground into and on which the dugouts were built is very heavy and the excavation must have been difficult.

For the most part the buildings in the camp were constructed of chicken wire gabions, filled with earth and stone and plastered inside and out with a sort of cement, giving the appearance of concrete and making a very strong, substantial and comfortable shelter. Today, only a few concrete pillars and knee-high walls remain. Not one of the dugouts has remained. NOTE: Camp Montfaucon is built on private property and is not accessible to the public.

Artillery protection and Fayel Wood

Besides artillery support from the gun batteries in Epinonville, Cierges, Nantillois and Brieulles Wood, Montfaucon was also protected by at least two gun batteries that were situated in Tuillerie Wood, present-day Fayel Wood. During the war, Fayel Wood was much larger and continued all the way up to Montfaucon. Now only roughly a third of the forest remains. The guns in the wood were mounted in well-protected earth emplacements sunk in several small gullies and were hidden away within the wood. The usual shelters for ammunition and deep dugouts for personnel were built at each emplacement. Ammunition supply was accomplished by means of a forty centimetre gauge tramway, connected

A German gun emplacement in Fayel Wood.

up to a sixty centimetre narrow gauge line at the eastern edge of the wood. This line ran to an ammunitions dump located between Septsarges and Nantillois, which in turn was supplied by the railroad that ran from Brieulles to Nantillois.

Although not organized for defence, some resistance by machine gunners was encountered at Fayel Wood. The greatest defensive preparation in the immediate vicinity of Montfaucon was to the south-west of the hill, where numerous hedges and orchards offered concealment for a considerable number of artillery pieces. From the piles of empty shells found here and along the ridge to the south, it was apparent that a large number of batteries, in addition to the heavy concentration of machine guns, had been in action in this section the previous day. Fortunately, when the Americans reached this area on the morning of 27 September it had been largely evacuated; the guns were already being withdrawn in the direction of Nantillois, some two kilometres to the north.

Conclusion

Colonel J. Frank Barber, CO of the 304th Engineers and author of its history, reached the following conclusions:

1. The Germans were turning Montfaucon into a highly protected position for observation and for the garrisoning of a considerable number of troops in comparative safety against hostile fire; they were not counting on it as a significant element of defence in the general defensive scheme of the sector.
2. Reinforced concrete, used inside masonry buildings that had walls with an average thickness of between forty and sixty centimetres, provided additional protection and proved very effective against the violent and heavy artillery fire. The outer masonry walls proved good bursting courses.
3. The concrete work here, as well as in other parts of the sector, seemed to be of recent construction and had only been partially completed. [This suggests that most of the observation posts and other concrete structures were constructed in 1918.]
4. It would appear that the Germans were not counting on offensive warfare in this sector but were building for an indefinite defence.

Chapter 3

23–25 September: Preparing for the attack

'While cleaning our gun I saw Frank Miller. Glad to see each other. He had had nothing to eat for a couple of days so I took him to our kitchen and got him something. Every chance we got we saw one another. Did not know if we would participate in this drive or not. [...] Walked around and saw some of the big cannons. Every place you went you saw them.'

Private William Schellberg, 311th Machine Gun Regiment.

First Army's plan to take Montfaucon.
To support the infantry attack along the entire First Army front, roughly thirty-five kilometres wide, about 2,700 guns, 189 Renault FT17 tanks and 821 aircraft were assembled. There was an average of one gun for every eight metres of front. At certain points in the line where stiff opposition was expected, the average interval was even less; opposite the Malancourt-Montfaucon sector the artillery was almost sufficient to be literally hub to hub if extended in a single line.

For the first phase of the Meuse-Argonne Offensive, the First Army deployed nine divisions, some 193,000 men in the immediate battle zone. The front was roughly divided into three major sectors; an army corps, which in this case contained three divisions plus reserve troops, was assigned to each sector. From left to right, these were I Corps, V Corps and III Corps. To put everything into context, this approximated to what the British made available on the first day of the Somme in 1916, but with crucial differences, the most notable of which was the huge increase in artillery capability.

The 79th Division, assigned to V Corps, was to launch a frontal attack on Montfaucon, thereby pinning down the German garrison. In the meantime, the 37th, also in V Corps, was to advance on the left to drive the Germans out of Montfaucon Wood and to outflank the town. The 4th Division, on the right, assigned to III Corps, was expected to do the same, but with the difference that, after they passed the hill, they were to wheel left in an encircling manoeuvre. The encirclement of the hill and an attack from the rear would hopefully be sufficient to force the Germans into

54

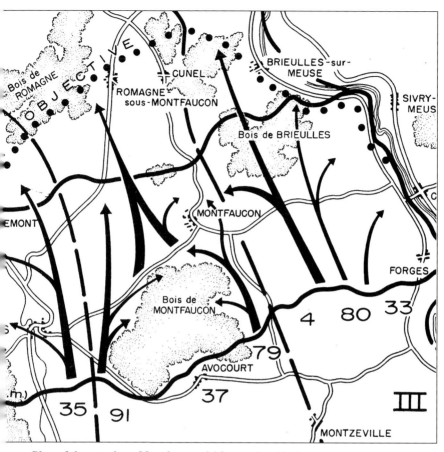

Plan of the attack on Montfaucon, 26 September 1918.

surrender. In theory a textbook exercise – a weak division keeps the enemy engaged in the centre, while a strong division outflanks the enemy and attacks from the rear and another threatens the other flank.

And this is where the controversy started: according to V Corps' plan, the 4th Division was tasked with attacking Montfaucon from the rear. However, in III Corps', which included the 4th Division, the encircling manoeuvre was not mentioned; on the contrary, the 4th was ordered to advance as far into German territory as possible. These contradictory orders lie at the root of the question of why the 79th failed to take Montfaucon on the first day.

The 79th Division's plan of action

The 79th Division was commanded by Major General Joseph H. Kuhn and comprised:

> 157 Infantry Brigade: the 313th and 314th Regiments, under the command of Brigadier General Nicholson, who were to lead the attack.
> 158 Infantry Brigade: the 315th and 316th Regiments, under the command of Brigadier General Noble, were to act as support: the 315th to follow the 314th and the 316th to follow the 313th. The support regiments were to clear areas of German resistance that the assault regiments had passed. They would also take care of any prisoners who were sent to the rear.

Major General Joseph H. Kuhn, GOC 79th Division.

The plan of action, as outlined in 158 Brigade's Orders, provided that the 315th and the 316th would support the attack of the 314th and the 313th at a distance of 1,000 metres, advancing in line with two battalions, about 2,200 men, and one battalion, about 1,100 men, in support, the latter to serve as a brigade reserve. Supporting the infantry regiments were the 311th and the 312th Machine-Gun Battalions and the 304th Engineers. In total, roughly 11,000 men would advance on Montfaucon.

The final objectives for the first day lay at an unprecedentedly distant twenty kilometres away from the start lines. They were expected to:

The 'Cross of Lorraine' insignia of the 79th Division. Worn on the left shoulder of the tunic, this particular one is made of silver bullion and was used during the victory parades o 1919.

1. Cross No Man's Land and capture Haucourt and Malancourt.
2. Frontally attack and capture Montfaucon.
3. Attack and capture Beuge Wood and Nantillois.
4. Ultimately, push on to the Kriemhild Line in Romagne and Cunel.

In short, they were expected to assault and capture four major German defence lines all in one day; this was an unrealistic assignment, even for highly experienced troops. Territorial gains of this magnitude had never been

56

achieved before on the Western Front. Naturally, the ordinary soldier was left totally in the dark about the goals. They only knew that they had to go forward and follow their officers, no matter where they would lead them.

Preparations

On Monday *23 September,* a rainy day, it had been decided that the attack was to be launched on 26 September; the 79th Division would form part of the attacking line as a shock division. NCOs and soldiers had not yet been informed. Every night thousands of soldiers were moved to the front. A letter from First Lieutenant FT Edwards to his father graphically describes the situation behind the front at this period:

'AMERICAN EXPEDITIONARY FORCES, FRANCE
September 21, 1918

DEAR DAD,

This has been a gala day, seven letters from you, one from Virginia, and one from Uncle Ben. Your letters are full of the things I like to hear about, the new cistern, the building, what you know of the war; little home things, all of them. We have been moving so much that it is a wonder that we ever get mail at all. You don't know what real discomfort is back there at home. For two weeks now we have been steadily on the move; as soon as it gets dark we pull out on the road. We march nearly all night; with one or two exceptions, in the rain; a cold, chilling autumn rain. Towards daylight we pull into some deserted town; sometimes we just curl up on the seat and try to

**First Lieutenant
Frederick Trevenen
Edwards, 3rd
Division.**

sleep; or again we crawl into some haymow or into some barn. More often we sleep on the ground. But the rainy season has begun and we have it nearly every night. Everything we own gets wet; there's no nice place to get to eventually, where you have a bath and a warm room and a bed; you just keep on. I have my office to set up and run during the day and between times snatch an hour of sleep. The nights are getting cold; I shall soon have to put on my winter stuff and keep it on. Would you believe it, if I told you that I had not washed my face in three days; I haven't had my underclothes off in four weeks; my breeches have not come off in over two and my coat has been on for a week. I did manage to change my socks the other day. When I looked at my feet the air currents waved as they do on a hot day. Tonight I have a palace, if we don't move. I am in a wooden building with a roof

57

over it. Yes sir, a Real Roof, so let 'er rain! There is a bunk made out of four boards, which some Poilu [nickname for French soldiers] owned once. I shook the straw out of it, as being suspicious, and spread my blankets out. So, I am really luxurious. All my love, TRAVENEN'

On *24 September*, a sunny day for a change, the front line sector that had been occupied by the French was taken over by the 316th Regiment in the evening. The following evening the 314th Regiment passed through the French 129th Regiment from the rear and took over their front line positions. During the preceding forty-eight hours the French had positioned outposts along two entire divisional fronts so that during expected trench raids the Germans would not discover that the French were quietly trading places with the Americans. Thousands of doughboys were secretly massing in the rear areas and were preparing for the forthcoming attack. For Lieutenant Colonel DuPuy, 311th Machine Gun Battalion, it had been a busy night:

Lieutenant Colonel DuPuy, 311th Machine Gun Battalion.

'At 3.30 am on 24 September, I was awoken by one of General Nicholson's orderlies with an order to report at his dugout at once. Upon my arrival there, I found Colonel Oury, Colonel Sweezey, General Nicholson and his Adjutant, Major Pleasanton. They were sitting in the small dugout that the general was occupying, with a box as an improvised table, on which stood a small candle to light the room. In this sombre light their faces seemed to have a drawn expression, for the general had just received word that we were to attack the following day at five-thirty in the morning. He gave us only the important details and stated that the attack order would be in our hands later in the day. It was sufficient to be told that General Liggett, V Corps Commander, had decided to make our brigade shock troops. The map was minutely gone over, and the sector which we were to attack carefully marked on the map with the axis of liaison clearly shown. After leaving the general, I immediately sent for my four captains together with Captain May to give them instructions. I was in a dilemma to know just which companies to throw into the fight first. I had great confidence in two of my captains, and less confidence in the other two. Should I sacrifice the two worst ones first and hold back the two best for the final onslaught, or should the best be thrown in at the start, with the hope that they would be spared until the final attack?'

American troops on their way to the front.

Advertisement for
marching boots,
autumn 1918.

Obviously, down in the lower ranks information was much less detailed,
as Private William Schellberg of the 311th Machine Gun Regiment wrote
in his diary: 'Received orders that we would figure in this drive but did
not know where. Got orders not to leave; be ready to leave at any time.'

Trench raids
Trench raids were carried out by small teams of experienced (so far as
practicable) men; under the cover of darkness, they left the relative safety
of their own trenches and crossed the barbed wire in No Man's Land to
infiltrate enemy trench systems. The distance between friendly and enemy

front lines varied but was generally a few hundred metres. Any attempt to raid a trench during daylight hours would have been pointless because it would have been quickly spotted; enemy machine gunners and snipers had a clear view of No Man's Land and could easily eliminate anyone who was foolish enough to show their head above the trench parapet.

Standard practice was to creep up slowly on the sentries guarding a small sector of an enemy front line trench or a sap (an extension from the trench), then kill or incapacitate and take prisoner the occupants as quietly as possible and establish identification. This was not as easy as it sounds; flares were fired at regular intervals, lighting up the better part of No Man's Land. Going over the destroyed terrain was far from easy; it was a land filled with shell holes, rusted strands of barbed wire, putrefying corpses from earlier attacks and other obstacles. Very often it was necessary to cut the barbed wire just a short distance from the enemy in order to reach their trench. As a makeshift alarm, often empty ration cans were hung on the wire. A major hazard was that the enemy might also be operating in No Man's Land, either on the same mission or keeping fighting patrols out with the objective of intercepting enemy patrols. It is quite obvious that trench raids were amongst the most dangerous undertakings of front line duty.

American trench raider clipping enemy wire. Note the M1917 trench knife and the very rarely seen grenade vest.

Trench raiders with sandbags filled with hand grenades slung around their necks.

Having secured the part of trench that they had entered, the raiders would complete their mission objectives as quickly as possible; the longer they stayed in the trench, the greater the likelihood of discovery and consequently enemy reinforcements arriving. Hand grenades would be thrown into dugouts where enemy troops were sleeping before the raiders left the enemy lines to return to their own; sometimes large charges were used, with the intention of destroying the dugouts. The main reasons for undertaking such highly dangerous missions were, in no particular order:

1. Intelligence. To secure documents, note the conditions in the trenches attacked, state of the wire and so forth, secure identification of the troops holding the line (often by cutting off any identifying insignia on a uniform) and – probably best of all – to take an enemy prisoner back for interrogation, the more senior the rank the better.
2. Destruction of valuable enemy equipment like machine guns.
3. Keeping the pressure on the enemy, through intimidation; letting them know that even in their own beds they were not safe, thereby reducing their morale and efficiency.
4. To kill enemy troops.

Unfortunately, there also were many friendly fire incidents. Returning raiders could mistakenly be fired on by their own troops, especially when these were inexperienced. In the chaos and confusion, men who had started out from one section of trench often ended up crawling back to another. Therefore, it was standard procedure to notify sentries along the line whenever raiding parties were sent out and to use some kind of password so that returning raiders could identify themselves when challenged in the dark. Of course, it sometimes happened that sentries were not informed about a raid or were given the wrong or an outdated password; it was by no means a fool proof system. Returning with a prisoner was another discipline; often the only means of taking an enemy soldier back was by knocking him unconscious. Once the alarm went up there was the further problem of the enemy's artillery fire reacting: guns were set on SOS lines at night time and, given the appropriate signal, would open up in the affected area: by this stage in the war and in an ideal world, fighting patrols like this involved a complex inter-arms arrangement and extensive rehearsals.

Trench raiding was very similar to primitive warfare insofar as it was fought face-to-face, often with crude weaponry. Trench raiders were lightly equipped for stealthy, unimpeded movement. Typically, raiding parties were armed with homemade trench raiding clubs, bayonets, sharpened entrenching tools, trench knives, hatchets, pickaxe handles and brass knuckles, 'knuckle dusters'. Firearms were not used, at least initially, because of the nature of the operation, although pistols were extremely useful when it came to close quarter fighting, only used if their activities were discovered by the enemy. The reality was that many trench raids had to be aborted because the raiders were prematurely discovered or had to be abandoned early because of the alarm being raised and the effectiveness of the enemy's response.

One trench raid, executed on 22 September by the Germans, was particularly successful and nearly gave the American game away. After a heavy German artillery barrage that started very early that morning, a strong German raiding party attacked a French outpost: among the French were about twenty Americans, of whom one was killed and one captured. It remains unknown what happened to the captured soldier and if the Germans were able to extract information from him. Luckily for Pershing, despite this incident the Germans were still not aware of the fact that every night thousands of Americans were pouring into the sector. But they were expecting something; shifting so many men and necessary equipment causes a lot of noise, especially during the night, when sounds are amplified. The sheer scale of the movement, combined with the utter inadequacy of the transport infrastructure, meant that it would be hard not to be aware of changing circumstances. The question for, in this case the German, high command was always one of making an assessment on the basis of intelligence and most likely enemy options. By the opening of the Meuse-Argonne Offensive, they had identified some divisions on the move from the St Mihiel area and also of the quality of the ones that were being shifted.

A testimony to this move to the front is provided by a letter from First Lieutenant FT Edwards (18th Field Artillery, 3rd Division) to his father.

'HEADQUARTERS 18TH FIELD ARTILLERY,
FRANCE, September 24, 1918.

Dear Dad,

A bright fall morning, crisp and clear; the sky seems miles high and full of white clouds. I can hear American aeroplanes circling over; I know they are American, because one soon learns to differentiate the sound of the motors, the Boche drone and the heavy purr of the big Liberty machines. I am in a little town; on the face, it seems asleep; there is no traffic going by the door, the wide streets are deserted. In reality it is a beehive. With the dawn I could hear the last of the trucks and guns going by. All night long they banged and clattered along; a road more jammed than ever Fifth Avenue was. At daylight they all disappeared. I have just had breakfast, shaved, cleaned up my leather equipment, and I am sitting on one feed box with the machine on another, in the door of an ancient stable. Behind me the clerks are unpacking their trunks and boxes; in an hour the place will be Regimental Headquarters, with

The headstone in the American Cemetery in Romagne of Trevenen Edwards, killed on 6 October at Montfaucon by a German shell. Plot D.11.3.

every stall a department. Thank Heaven, at last we have a clear sunshiny day. For the last month it has rained almost continually; heavy driving rains that go right through you.

All my love, Trevenen'

At nightfall on *25 September*, the second day, the weather had cleared; in the Avocourt-Malancourt sector the preparations in and behind the 79th Division lines were becoming more intense. In the darkness, the roads, so deserted by day, suddenly became filled with panting horses, rumbling guns and caissons, trucks and long columns of infantry. In the rear areas, from Dombasle to Rampont, came convoy after convoy, bearing

Observation balloon hovering over Montfaucon, 29 September 1918.

ammunition to the reserve dump in Deffoy Wood and the forward dumps near Camp de Civils, and rations and engineer supplies for Esnes Wood. A narrow gauge train ran non-stop between the Camp de Civils and Avocourt, delivering engineering material, ammunition and rations, in that order of priority, until German shells put the Avocourt end of the line out of operation. Engineers would then arrive to patch up the line, only to see it destroyed again within an hour or so; the skilled German gunners knew exactly what to aim for. The motorized heavy batteries emerged from concealment in the woods and forged towards the front, heading for pre-arranged battery positions. Much effort was put into camouflaging the guns; unlike at St Mihiel, German planes dominated the skies and made full use of their many observation balloons.

One of the observation balloons that would cause a lot of trouble for the attackers on Montfaucon was one to the north of Beuge Wood, a kilometre to the west of Nantillois. A strong winch deployed a 2,000 metres long steel cable attached to the balloon; from the balloon a telephone wire led to a large concrete shelter, about twenty-five metres long, built in the north-eastern corner of Beuge Wood. Close to this shelter, a howitzer battery was in position, the guns trained on Cote (Hill) 304. This battery was also connected by telephone. Another telephone line, in fact several in case one line was cut, was connected to the German telephone exchange in Nantillois, a three-chambered shelter built in the bank of the road to provide maximum protection against incoming fire. From here coordinates were passed on to the appropriate batteries, which would then try to destroy, or at least severely disrupt, the enemy before it could reach Montfaucon. Needless to say, the Nantillois telephone exchange was connected to the telephone exchange at Montfaucon. Nantillois also relayed much of the information from the Montfaucon observation posts as appropriate and was therefore an important link in the German defences.

Preparing for the big push, in front of the jump-off lines and ahead of the outposts, American reconnaissance patrols were sent out to establish sixteen points where the German barbed wire entanglements were to be cut; a group of officers from the 313th and the 314th Regiments measured and fixed a white tape line to create lanes for the infantry. The tape line was very important, as it guided the infantry in the right direction when the attack was launched. The soldiers were operating in a country where they had never been before. Notwithstanding this, they were expected to launch an attack on a foggy morning, still in darkness, from the middle of nowhere across unknown terrain and against an experienced enemy; they had had inadequate training (at all levels of command); and this was to be their first offensive engagement.

Cutting wire was a serious and dangerous business that had to be done under the cover of darkness and carried out under the nose of the enemy. With flares lighting up the sky it was even more dangerous. To prevent detection, wire cutters were wrapped in cloth to muffle the sound of clipping. Wire was only to be cut prior to the attack; if cut any earlier it was very likely that the gaps would be detected by the enemy, thereby losing the element of surprise. The wire cutters had to be alert to enemy patrols, tasked with intercepting such activity; whilst the barbed wire would be covered by machine guns, set on fixed lines, and so stealth and silence were essential. Lieutenant Colonel DuPuy recalled:

'The captains were ordered to make their reconnaissance at once so that there would be no confusion in entering the jumping off trenches that night. Our own wire was to be cut that night before twelve o'clock with lanes from ten to twelve feet [3.5 metres] wide and about two yards [1.8 metres] apart, cut, removed and taped so that the men in the early morning mist could find their way through the entanglement. Major Harry Parkin, of Pittsburgh, handled this job admirably.'

Throughout the night of 25 September the American post of command (this use of rather strangulated English rather than the simpler 'Command Post' was likely because the Americans made a literal translation from the French, *poste de commande*, as most of the AEF operated in what was or had been the French sector) was as busy as a bee-hive, crowded with battalion and company commanders who assembled to receive copies of the field orders and to get maps, which had just been distributed, marked with sector lines for the advance. It was only at that time that many officers learned that Montfaucon was immediately in the sector of the 79th Division. From the front line trenches, Montfaucon lay distant over eight kilometres beyond the wild tangle of No Man's Land, German wire entanglements and trenches and a series of defended ridges and woods. First Lieutenant Arthur H Joel was informed about his mission in front of Colonel Oury's dugout and noted:

> 'At the last officers' call in Hesse Wood came the first news of the coming Argonne drive. The regiment's mission was to take over the front line at Dead Man's Hill [Mort Homme], and in the big drive to capture Avocourt, Malancourt, Cuisy, Septsarges, Montfaucon and Nantillois beyond. The colonel talked like a strict father to the semicircle of lieutenants, captains and majors collected in front of his dugout in the woods. It was the last meeting of 314th officers before going over the top, and they knew that a few at least would be missing before the next summons to Regimental Headquarters.'

Along the way to Montfaucon were several significant obstacles; the Forges Creek at Haucourt, the strongly fortified village of Malancourt and, beyond that, the defences leading up to Montfaucon, the dominating presence towering over the whole region. Rising 336 metres above sea level, it was higher than any other hill between the Meuse and the Argonne on either the allied or German side of the front line. The sloping terrain in front of the hill was covered with trenches, barbed wire and anti-tank barriers. According to the latest intelligence, only a couple of thousand German troops were believed to be in the area in front of the hill, which was in fact true. To protect their positions, the Germans had erected broad belts of barbed wire in front of the trenches. The Americans expected that the preliminary artillery barrage would suffice to cut it.

The heavy artillery started its preliminary bombardment at 11.00 pm and was to continue for the next six and a half hours. Later on, the lighter calibre guns were to join in; trench mortar crews were to wait until dawn to contribute their part in the destruction of the German front. The sky was ablaze with fire and, while officers worked in their dugouts, busy with maps and orders, the noise outside was absolutely ear-shattering. At about that time thousands of soldiers were now being informed about the attack. Private William Schellberg (311th Machine Gun Regiment) recalled:

'Received orders that we would start the drive off in our sector Argonne Meuse Sector [sic]. This drive is on a forty kilometre front. Biggest drive in history leaves for front at 6.00 pm. The Allies started bombarding at 11.00 pm. The heavy artillery kept this up for six hours, then the light artillery started. The Germans bombarded us, killing some of our men.'

One American officer, sitting on a rickety chair in a lice-infested French dugout, was trying to have a shave. Every time the heavy gun battery close to his dugout fired a salvo the water in his canteen rippled noticeably. Earth and small pieces of chalk fell through the cracks of the

Shell exploding on the German front line.

American HQ in Hesse Wood, September 1918.

ceiling and, although he was about eight metres underground, after an hour or so the air was heavy with thick dust. Some of the men with him were playing a game or were smoking cigarettes, adding to the fetid atmosphere; some were just sitting on the floor with grim looks on their faces, one was reading the Bible. Everybody, in his own way, was preparing himself for the inevitable: in a few hours they were going to go over the top; nobody knew if they would be still alive tomorrow. First Lieutenant Arthur H. Joel, F Co, 314th Regiment:

'On the evening of 25 September, an officer and four scouts from each company were sent to the front lines to locate platoon positions among the battered trenches, shell craters, and masses of rusted wire on desolate Dead Man's Hill [Mort Homme – in fact almost certainly he meant Cote 304]. The pitch black night and the necessity for silence made this a very difficult and spooky mission. Towards midnight these same guides met their platoons at the regimental dug-out and guided them in single file to their respective areas of holes, ditches, barbed wire and mud, there to await the approach of their first zero hour. The troops were fully prepared for battle; more or less a matter of increasing their supply of ammunition and lessening the amount of clothing, bedding and other such luxuries of the march. Each soldier carried his rifle, at least two hundred rounds of rifle ammunition, bombs, emergency rations, raincoat and overcoat, a canteen of water, and any extra firearms he might be using. With these he was ready to go over the top from Dead Man's Hill and trust to God for food, water and luck for an uncertain length of time.'

On the right, on the left and from far behind the line, the 'heavies' belched out a steady and seemingly endless number of shells that smashed whatever remnants of Malancourt and No Man's Land might still have remained. Observers in Hesse Wood watched shell after shell hitting the ruins and the battered trees on Montfaucon and wondered if anyone could survive such a barrage. In their hearts, the officers hoped for the total destruction of the German trenches and wire obstacles so that their men could advance reasonably unscathed. It was anticipated that most of the wire would be cut and the German lines blown to smithereens by the time the doughboys made their advance. However, most of the American barrage fell in the area that had already been destroyed during the fighting in the Battle of Verdun in 1916. Beyond this, the lines were fairly intact.

More and more batteries joined in; during the night the deafening roar of the big 155s and 210s, which could be heard from twenty

American gunners operating a 155mm Schneider gun of French make.

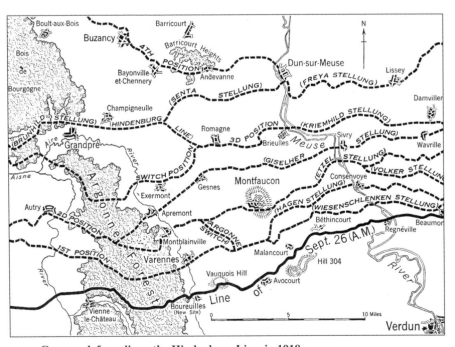

German defence lines, the Hindenburg Line, in 1918.

kilometres behind the front line, concentrated their terrific bombardment upon the Wiesenschlenken, Hagen and Etzel Lines. Many of the doughboys when they moved up to the line had passed alongside the positions of the heavies. It was the first time the men of the 79th Division had been so close to such large calibre weapons in action, and the roars which splintered the darkness, the weird red glare accompanying them and the pungent battle smoke filtering under the trees made, as one soldier recalled, 'many a stout heart tremble'. For the draftees, many of whom had been working on farms only a few months ago, it was an impression that they would not forget for the rest of their lives.

Preparations were made to march to the jump off area. The troops had to get rid of all the excess weight in their packs. Hand grenades, rations for two days and specialist equipment was issued; every fourth man carried an extra shovel, pick axe or some other heavy tool. However, in many cases supplies did not arrive on time or in sufficient numbers. Lieutenant Colonel DuPuy, 311th Machine Gun Battalion, wrote in his diary:

'All paraphernalia, which could not be carried by the men, was piled up by companies and cached. This included everything of company and personal property with the exception of the pistol-belt, water bottle, condiment can, meat can, knife, fork and spoon, overcoat, slicker, ammunition and guns. After this work had been completed, at about 2.30 am, I received a message to report to General Nicholson and was told that owing to the fact that supplies had not come up, the attack had been postponed until the following morning. […] We again loaded the material which we had discarded, pup tents were pitched in the woods and the routine of camp life temporarily resumed.'

A few hours later, the leading battalions of the 313th and 314th Regiments began to enter the support trenches, platoons feeling their way along in the darkness, past the quiet lines of the forward battalions of the 315th and 316th Regiments, leaving every soldier with his own thoughts. The muzzle flash of the guns showed them the way for the first couple of hundred metres, but once out of the light it became pitch-dark and the men had to hold on to the webbing of the man in front of him. Several men lost their way, became entangled in the masses of wire or slipped into flooded shell holes; although it was a dry night, there had been a lot of rain during the previous days. Occasionally, a German shell exploded in the vicinity, which made these battlefield novices hug the ground.

Utter devastation: No Man's Land 1918.

After a chaotic night most of the AEF troops, well-equipped or not, had made it to the start lines. In the densely packed trenches German shells caused the first casualties of the day. For many doughboys this was their first confrontation with the horror of war. Most men had never seen a dead man before and were shocked by the conditions in No Man's Land.

The orders were to attack at H hour on D day, which was in this case 5.30 am. The terminology of H hour and D day were first used during the St Mihiel offensive (or 'drive' as the Americans generally called it); in the Second World War, 'D-Day' added a whole new meaning to the expression. Facing north, the leading regiments of the 79th Division were the 313th on the left and the 314th on the right; the 316th was in support of the 313th and the 315th in support of the 314th. The support regiments were to follow the leading regiments at an interval of 1,000 metres. Cold and hungry, the men waited for the signal to go over the top.

Chapter 4

26 September, Over the Top

'Early in the morning I made every effort to secure reserve rations, but without success. For some reason the quartermaster did not arrive and I was downhearted to see, finally, that my men had to enter the fight absolutely without food, and with no apparent place to draw it during the attack, because by studying the map it could easily be seen that it would be days before a road could be completed across the devastated country over which we were to pass; I knew that artillery and ammunition must give way to either supplies or wounded.'

Lieutenant Colonel DuPuy, 311th Machine Gun Regiment.

In front of the American lines lay the *117th Division*, which consisted of three regiments, *the 11th, the 157th* and *the 450th*, in total some 6,650 men. Initially, about 3,500 German soldiers manned the Wiesenschlenken and Hagen Lines, aiming to force the 11,000 men of the 79th Division to a halt. The Germans had prepared two death traps for the Americans: the Golfe de Malancourt and Demon Redoubt. The 313th and the 316th Regiments, the left wing, were up against the Golfe de Malancourt, the 314th and 315th Regiments, the right wing, against Demon Redoubt.

The *Golfe de Malancourt* was partly developed as a defensive work in 1916 to protect Montfaucon against the French. From the edge of Malancourt Wood, on the south side of the clearing, the ground gradually sloped up to the edge of Cuisy Wood, thus affording the *117th Division* a very advantageous defensive position. The positions were well constructed and were still largely intact. Up in Cuisy Wood, numerous machine-gun nests were perfectly concealed and ideally situated to support those in the trenches below them with overhead fire. This position held up the 313th for nearly five hours and effectively obstructed the capture of Montfaucon, an objective on the first day. The German positions resisted several frontal attacks. It was simply impossible for the doughboys to break through the devastating wall of machine-gun fire directed at them. The slaughter there was indescribable.

Demon Redoubt. Malancourt is built in a wide valley that tapers in a north-western direction and ends on a ridge that runs roughly parallel

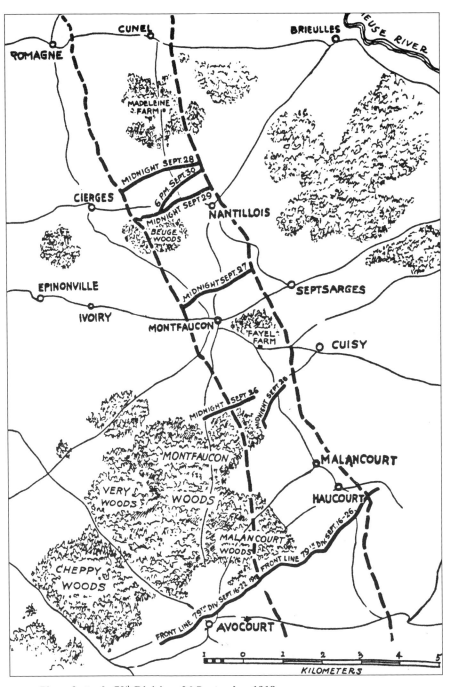

Plan of attack, 79ᵗʰ Division, 26 September 1918.

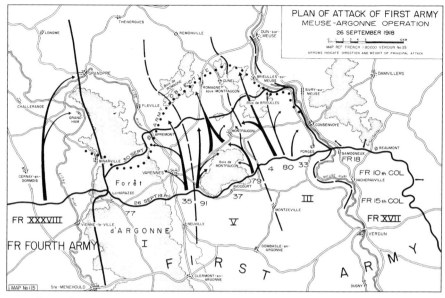

Plan of attack, First Army, 26 September 1918.

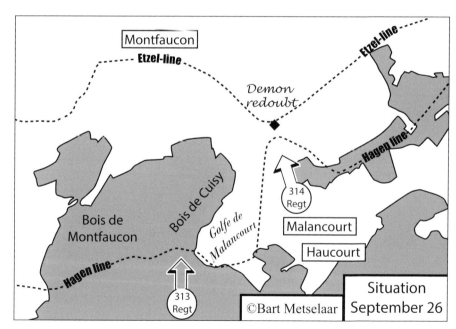

Golfe de Malancourt and Demon Redoubt.

with Montfaucon Hill. The main road, the present-day D18, runs across the valley from Malancourt to Montfaucon and is the only way of reaching the ridge leading to Montfaucon. On top of the ridge, to the right of the road, the Germans built a concrete bunker that the French christened *L'ouvrage du Demon*, Demon Redoubt, as well as a powerful defence line, the Hagen Line, that ran in the direction of Cuisy. To the left of the road, the defences continued in the direction of the Golfe de Malancourt, where they connected with the Wiesenschlenken Line. The fighting in the valley leading up to Demon Redoubt was terrible and, despite the efforts of the doughboys, it was not overcome on day one.

At 2.30 am on 26 September the intensity of the bombardment increased. This was the moment that all the different types of heavy guns opened up, firing at a high rate. Flares flew up into the sky and the noise of the guns became ear-splittingly loud. Smoke and dust filled the air. Ahead of the front line, the ground became silhouetted intermittently by the deluge of shells over or upon the German positions. To add to the mayhem, the Germans shelled the American front line in return but, according to American reports, with little effect. Colonel DuPuy was close to the batteries when,

'...at 2.30 am, bedlam broke loose. The guns belched and thundered for miles around us. The earth actually trembled, and the air was full of screeching, ripping, whistling express-car noises. The night was a beautiful starlit one, and it was a marvellous sight to see those flashes on all sides go up, as the guns spoke from their hidden, camouflaged positions. I stood just back of six batteries of 75s, and they shot by salvoes from a whistle signal, each time throwing three hundred and twenty pounds of steel at every salvo. The flash of the guns was so intense that one could have read a paper any place within the area of my post of command. Apparently the Boche was taken by surprise and was thrown into a state of frenzy. Flare after flare went up, vainly calling for a barrage from their own guns, and after the first fearful outburst from our side their return shells started to come in, which resulted in some casualties in our thickly packed trenches. At 5.30 am, all the guns ceased for a moment, while the barrage was raised. Daylight was just coming on, and over went the men, bayonets fixed.'

In the division the first casualties started to fall. The Second Battalion of the 315th, making its way through the communication trenches toward the jumping-off position, was hit by a bursting shell in the midst of a

A 155mm battery close to Esnes.

A trench mortar crew at work. These French mortars were called 'crapouillot', or little toad, could fire various weights of bombs weighing between 18 and 35 kilos with ranges between some 500 and 1500 metres.

platoon, killing one and wounding six others. Meanwhile, the company commanders were working non-stop; directing their men to the jump-off lines, moving men into the line, who were then standing shoulder to shoulder in the trenches. Bayonets were fixed, hand grenades handed out. Shortly before 5.00 am most of the division was ready for the attack.

Morning, 26 September, left wing: jump-off.
The 313[h] Regiment was leading the attack
The 316th Regiment was in support

A few minutes prior to H hour, the trench mortars of Company D, First Gas Regiment, added a protective screen of smoke and flame to the heavy fog that was already shrouding No Man's Land. These, of course, were the perfect circumstances needed in order to obscure troop movements from enemy observation; but there was also the real danger that the doughboys would lose their way. Indeed, the fog was so thick that the officers had to rely on their compasses to find their direction. However, promptly at 5.30 am the first waves of infantry went over the top and swept forward. The American First Army, with nine divisions on a thirty kilometres' long front, was finally on the move: the Meuse-Argonne Offensive had begun.

The preliminary barrage lifted and then the rolling barrage started; every few minutes the field of fire moved forward towards the enemy, for example, by one hundred metres, with the attacking infantry as close as possible to the exploding shells, the artillery protecting their own troops with a wall of steel and forcing the enemy to take cover.

The battalions were attacking in companies, one on the left and one on the right, each company maintaining an interval of ten to fifteen metres between them, covering a width of 800 metres in total. The German guns, which up to this moment had largely remained ominously silent, now started shelling the American lines. The experienced German gunners knew that the moment the barrage lifted the American trenches would be packed with men, ready to start the attack: an easy target. Private William Schellberg (311th Machine Gun Regiment) was one of the thousands of doughboys who had been waiting for the signal to go over the top:

> 'We had nothing but light packs and two days' rations and at 5.30 am we went over the top. It sounded like all hell had broken loose. We only went a few yards when three big shells burst only a few yards from us, knocking dirt in our faces. It was still a little dark and cloudy. Barbed wire was all around; some of us getting hooked in it. We had four extra men carrying ammunition for us. The men from Gas and Flame put up a cloud of smoke in front of us to keep the Germans from seeing us. During this we lost the four extra men and two other men. This leaving [sic] us five men and a corporal in our squad. Having lots of trouble with machine guns killing a lot of our men. Captured lots of Germans. We were with the fourth line to go over the top.'

Scarcely had the leading units of the 313th and the 314th Regiments cleared their own wire than they were plunged into the dense smoke barrage. This smoke, combined with the fog that lay over No Man's Land, made it extremely difficult for companies and platoons to keep in touch with each other. The going was difficult on ground that had served as a No Man's Land for nearly all of four long years of war – ground that had been blown to bits, was covered with shell holes and clogged up with rusted, twisted and shot up barbed wire that had to be cut in order to make a passage through. Fortunately, detachments of the 304th Engineers, equipped with heavy wire cutters, preceded the infantry to cut the German wire. First Lieutenant Arthur H Joel recalled:

'From 6.00 to 6.30 am scouts crawled out with wire cutters and opened passage ways in the belts of barbed wire. During the same half hour a dense smoke screen was placed ahead by a gas regiment in the rear, in order to conceal our movements. The outfit was ready to go over the top of trenches and shell holes at the command of its officers at exactly 6.30 am.'

The air was alive with whining, whistling, and screaming missiles. Through all of this mayhem the assault companies made their way, crossing shell holes, craters and trenches that had been blown apart. The first waves of the 313th and 314th Regiments soon passed the thinly held German front line trenches.

The Americans met little resistance at first, though men were falling because of the German shelling. At 6.25 am the barrage began to move forward, a hundred metres every four minutes, with the units of the 313th and the 314th following on behind as closely as possible. The 315th and 316th Regiments, in support, were keeping their eyes on the advancing lines, waiting for the 313th and 314th to have gained the desired 1,000 metres. Around 7.00 am the support regiments also went over the top and started to mop up any German soldiers or machine guns that had not been cleared by the leading regiments.

The Regimental History of the 316th Regiment vividly describes the advance:

'Trench six winds through Malancourt Wood, and part of the regiment struggled forward over its rocky bottom as the 313th, now well out in front, moved on. At a turn in the trench, as the head of the column approached, there lay a group of grotesquely huddled figures in American olive drab. Dead. It was the 316th's first sight of grim horror. War had all at once taken on a new

Over the top!

A heavy shell exploding in No Man's Land.

meaning. In No-Man's-Land for some distance the regiment moved on without loss, undisturbed save by artillery shelling. As the German part of Malancourt Wood was neared, there was a queer bzz-zz-zz overhead, an instant's puzzle as to what the **** that might be, and then that much taught lesson in the little red book on the importance of 'keeping down' was being graphically illustrated.'

The 313th, advancing well into Malancourt Wood, was met by the withering fire of hidden machine-gun positions and snipers. The thick woods made it difficult to keep the line intact. In spite of this, the battalions kept pressing forward. Enemy machine gunners and individual riflemen were taking their toll, but a number of them were soon captured and sent to the rear – or otherwise dealt with. The fire was still intense; however, the attack had to proceed and the line could not halt to deal with all the snipers and machine-gun nests. Meanwhile, the 316th Regiment started to mop up the first German machine-gun crews:

'The assaulting regiment, moving steadily ahead, had unsuspectingly passed by a number of concealed machine-gun nests, and the German gunners were now demonstrating their skills to the 316th. Followed a speedy issuing of orders to platoon commanders, cautious flank movements followed, and the regiment was sending back its first prisoners, casting a hasty glimpse at its first war trophies, and leaving behind its first dead and wounded. It was this character of fighting which marked the entire Meuse-Argonne action. Concealed machine gunners, allowing the first waves to pass on, opened up on the second, and

Golfe de Malancourt from the German viewpoint; the Americans came from the forest and walked into plain view of the German machine guns.

either bravely fought to an inevitable finish or shouted "Kamerad" in time to save their lives.'

At the same time the 313th ran into a serious problem; they lost contact with the rolling barrage. They had to cross the shattered remains of Malancourt Wood, an area covered by an unusual quantity of old wire, cratered and shell-holed to an extraordinary degree, the product of heavy calibre shells during nearly four years of war. The infantry's progress was reduced to a snail's pace while trying to cross this wasteland. As a result, the barrage gradually drew away from the struggling infantry, leaving them to meet the heaviest opposition without artillery protection. At first the troops did not meet any significant opposition aside from an isolated pillbox or machine gun, allowing them to concentrate on the terrible conditions underfoot. Gradually, however, German opposition stiffened and their artillery started a counter-barrage. All the same, the worst was yet to come.

At about 09.00 am, at a point some three kilometres beyond the first German defences, the 79th Division's fortunes changed rapidly. Here, Malancourt Wood suddenly opened out into a clearing, the Golfe de Malancourt. Directly opposite and to the left lay Cuisy Wood and behind that the slopes leading up to Montfaucon. On the other side of the clearing the Germans had built the Wiesenschlenken Line; the 313th marched into the first death trap.

Morning, 26 September, right wing, jump-off:
314th Regiment was leading the attack
315th Regiment was in support

The leading 314th Regiment had not yet encountered a lot of resistance; for the first hour or so they slowly moved forward across the difficult terrain. Fortunately, the German front line on this part of the battlefield was only thinly manned. First Lieutenant Arthur H. Joel (F Co, 314th Regiment):

'The division's mission this first time over the top was to capture the territory thus far held by the Germans against all attacks. Montfaucon, the city [!] on the high point across the broad desolate valley, was the main objective. The Germans called it Little Gibraltar and boasted that it was impregnable. It had been the Crown Prince's headquarters in the Battle of Verdun. Sometime after midnight, shortly after the moonlight had broken through the screen of dense, black clouds, cannon of all sizes began belching a steady stream of high explosives and gas shells [one out of three or four], the deadly messengers of destruction flying over the heads of the waiting troops and falling somewhere on the enemy position. Tons and tons of steel shrieked and whistled, each type of missile sounding its weird warning of destruction and death. Accompanying the roars and shrieks were intermittent flashes of the guns lighting the horizon as far as the eye could see. At the same time, over toward Montfaucon, one could see the flashes of exploding shells doing their deadly work of destroying barbed-wire entanglements, trenches and dug-outs, as well as the town of Montfaucon. Now and then a shell from an enemy counter battery exploded somewhere on Dead Man's Hill, adding to the clamor and thrill of the weird night.'

At about 8.00 am the rattle of the German machine guns could be heard in the fog ahead, as the 314th came into contact with the defences in and around Malancourt. The first rush, overwhelming the German first line, had occurred with surprisingly little resistance from the Germans, due to their retreat from the front line to the Wiesenschlenken and Hagen Lines. Now the Americans ran into the first line of organized defences. During the advance of the 314th Regiment, the 315th had been following behind at 1,000 metres distance. Snipers became a real pest and were hiding in the most unexpected places, opening fire when the troops had already passed. The first battle casualty of the 315th was First Lieutenant

Raymond T. Turn. He was killed when a sniper bullet detonated a hand grenade in his pocket. Pressing forward, the supporting battalions mopped up what the other battalions had overlooked in the way of snipers (it seems that all individual riflemen had become known as 'snipers') and machine-gun positions.

Meanwhile, the 304th Engineers, commanded by Colonel James F Barber, were faced with the monumental task of rebuilding the road leading from Avocourt and Malancourt to Montfaucon. About a kilometre north of Avocourt the road had more or less completely disappeared (Avocourt itself had become a hopelessly snarled up bottle neck) and the whole area was a maze of shell craters – while, to make matters worse, some of the roads along the advance of the First Army had been mined, leaving deep craters. Therefore, the progress of troops or transportation of any significant size was all but impossible, even though it was of the utmost importance during the first crucial hours of the day. To keep the momentum of the offensive going, a constant supply of ammunition was needed.

To get an idea of the quantity of materials that were being used at the height of the fighting in the battle zone, the AEF was getting through 70,000 hand grenades daily. Another example is provided by tobacco. Back in those days, smoking or chewing tobacco was one of the few pleasures combat soldiers could look forward to; the British troops on

A well-known photograph of a traffic jam in Esnes-en-Argonne, 26 September 1918.

Infantry advancing to the front line with Bangalore torpedoes; this was a pre-war (1912) British invention to blow up barbed wire obstacles; a broadly similar, if much modified, weapon is still in use today.

the Western Front were supplied with 1,000 cubic metres of tobacco each day. For building material, many thousands of tons of sand, rock, gravel and timber were needed but were scarce in supply. As all of the roads in the area were congested, the engineers were forced to use what was available on site. The road was virtually non existent for at least two kilometres and had to be rebuilt, effectively, from scratch and therefore huge quantities of material were needed. There was a great shortage of everything, especially of sandbags. The 304th Engineers, some 800 men, started work on the road at about 9.00 am.

One of the first men awarded the DSC on the 26th was Albert C Rubel, a captain in the 304th Engineers. Rubel's actions are proof that engineers were doing much more than building roads and bridges. While trying to locate a section of the Avocourt-Malancourt road, he was held up by an enemy machine gun on the parapet of a trench running parallel to the road that the support battalions had obviously failed to mop up. Challenged by the Germans, he proceeded ahead with two men of his platoon and personally killed the two gunners. He received his medal in 1919.

Meanwhile, the forward battalions of the 314th were fighting in the area between Haucourt and Malancourt – two destroyed neighbouring villages that now existed in name only. There were many snipers and seemingly countless machine guns to take care of before they could cross the boggy terrain around Forges Creek. Fog and uncut wire also seriously hampered the attack.

'The path of the drive led over desolate country completely cut up with shell holes, mine craters and trench systems. Early in the advance it was necessary to go through a swamp, waist deep, near the outskirts of Malancourt, the first objective. [This was, in fact, the destroyed hamlet of Haucourt.] Pop! Pop! Pop! Tzing! Tzing! The singing, cracking and whining of machine-gun bullets was good evidence that at least a few Prussians had survived the intense hurricane of high explosive and gas shells of the previous night's barrage. But for several hours very little strong resistance was encountered, Fritz having retreated to new lines of resistance.'

The pathetic remains of Haucourt on 26 September 1918; note the helmet and scull on the bottom right.

Once past the creek the men made good progress, but it took another hour to reach the destroyed villages of Haucourt and Malancourt, a distance of barely a kilometre. In between the villages they ran into a concrete pillbox. After the doughboys had killed the crew, they continued through the valley to Malancourt, a village that was built on the side of a ridge. Here they ran into heavy machine-gun fire coming from the three sides of the valley in which the village was located. Several fights broke out when the posts were attacked. Hand grenades exploded a d slowly the

85

Ruins of Malancourt, 27 September 1918.

Americans moved forward. One by one, snipers and machine-gun crews were taken out of action. German machine gunners were being given no quarter when captured; the Americans had seen scores of their buddies killed by machine-gun bullets. First Lieutenant Arthur H Joel, F Co. (314th Regiment), was present when two German machine gunners were captured.

'As the fog began to clear, the advance of several groups was held up by a machine gun on the opposite side of a shallow valley. But after a little resistance the gun crew surrendered the first prisoners. These men were middle-aged, dirty, miserably dressed and apparently glad to be alive no matter what the cost. A little later a score or more of the enemy were captured and sent to the rear under guard. An incident happened at the time which goes to show that the 'Kamerad' act didn't always save the Hun. A lieutenant ordered a private to conduct two husky prisoners to certain officers in the rear. Within an incredibly short time the little Italian reported back. 'What did you do with the prisoners?' demanded the lieutenant. 'I tended to them, Sir', he answered. His sheepish glance told better than words what had happened. Such occurrences were not uncommon. On either side.'

Morning, 26 September, left wing, Golfe de Malancourt:
313[h] Regiment was leading the attack
316th Regiment was in support

In the meantime, the slaughter at the Golfe de Malancourt had started. As the infantry left the protection of Malancourt Wood and emerged into the clearing known as the Golfe de Malancourt, trouble started immediately. A German map, found after the battle, showed the location, or at least the planned location, of the machine guns used in this sector. No less than 113 fixed positions were counted. In addition to this, it has been estimated that there were at least fifty-five portable guns. All these guns were in a sector that was about 600 metres wide; this provided, effectively, a wall of bullets. At some places, when the Germans saw the orderly rows of Americans marching out of the woods, they could not believe their eyes. This was a reversion to the tactics of 1914. The Americans, on the ground at least, started to realize that it was a better idea if they abandoned the AEF's doctrine of fighting and winning by virtue of superior morale, manoeuvre and the rifle and the bayonet and improvised tactics more useful to them. It was just as the French Prime Minister, Clemenceau (although other sources suggest that it was Foch), had predicted: if the Americans did not want to learn from the French and the British, the Germans would teach them.

In addition to machine-gun fire, German snipers started to pick off American officers one by one. From an examination of the number of

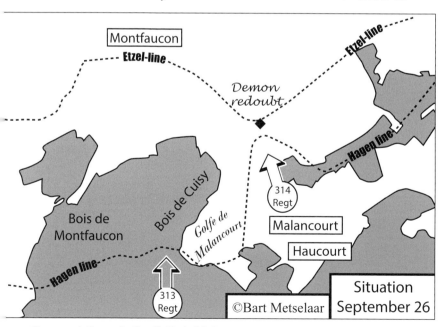

German defences in the Golfe de Malancourt.

casualties among officers on the first day, it is clear that the Germans were very successful in this. Major Benjamin F Pepper of the Second Battalion, 313th Regiment, was shot through the head by a sniper and mortally wounded; his adjutant, First Lieutenant Francis S Petterson, was killed instantly; and Major Jesse R. Langley of the Third Battalion was shot through both legs. Captain Harry Ingersoll of H Company, who was wounded several times in an attack that had been organized to eliminate

Headstone of Major B. H. Pepper, 313th Infantry, killed on 26 September.

Headstone of Captain H. Ingersoll, 313th Infantry, killed on 26 September.

Field graves of Pepper and Ingersoll. They were reburied in the American Cemetery in Romagne in plots E.20.38 and E.20.39. Captain Ingersoll (inset).

some snipers, was taken to the rear; he died of his wounds the next day. It was later confirmed that approximately twelve machines guns held up the advance along a fifty metre stretch of front. Colonel DuPuy (311th Machine Gun Regiment) recalled:

> 'Forward they had pressed on that memorable day until at dusk their lines had stopped at the north edge of the Bois de Montfaucon. But at what a cost. That gallant officer, Major Pepper (B. Franklin Pepper of Philadelphia), had been among the first to fall, shot through the head as he led his men at the machine-guns in the Golfe de Malancourt; Major Langley, whose keenness and dash had so inspired his battalion, went down with machine-gun bullets in both legs; Captain Ingersoll had been killed taking his men forward in the attack. As the giant Skip Weimard was carried to the rear with a shattered leg he good-naturedly cursed the luck that had put him and so many of his brother officers out of the scrap so early. Battalions were now led by captains; companies by lieutenants; platoons by sergeants – all after but one day of fighting.'

Captain Harry Ingersoll was posthumously awarded the DSC for extraordinary heroism in action. He showed absolute disregard for his personal safety in leading his company in an attack against an enemy position, strongly entrenched and protected by barbed wire entanglements. Although he was mortally wounded by machine-gun fire, he inspired his men by his courage, who carried on the attack and took the enemy position that had been holding up the advance. He was temporarily buried on the battlefield next to Major Pepper. After the war, both were reinterred in the Meuse-Argonne American Cemetery at Romagne-sous-Montfaucon.

There were so many wounded and dead lying in the clearing that stretcher bearers could hardly cope with the situation. If there was no other option, wounded were treated where they had fallen in order to prevent them from bleeding to death. Captain Horatio N. Jackson of the Medical Corps and attached to 313th Regiment was constantly working in the face of heavy machine-gun and shell fire. He was most devoted in his attention to the wounded, always present in the line of advance, directing the administering of first aid and guiding the work of stretcher bearers. He remained on duty until severely wounded by high explosive shells. After the war, he learnt that he had been awarded the DSC for his actions in the Golfe.

Morning, 26 September, right wing, Malancourt:
314th Regiment was leading the attack
315th Regiment was in support

The 314th experienced its own troubles, having lost contact with the artillery barrage and facing the fortified positions of Haucourt and Malancourt. They were met with heavy machine-gun fire. Fortunately, the first rush had engulfed Haucourt, the ruined hamlet in front of Malancourt, and by 10.00 am the leading companies had pushed on toward Malancourt itself, reaching the southern end of the shattered town as the fog lifted. Immediately the German machine guns opened fire on the Americans from almost every direction.

As the doughboys battled through the ruins of Malancourt they became embroiled in bitter fighting with nest after nest of machine gunners; they had been located in such a way that the fire of those at the rear protected the more exposed positions. Colonel Oury (CO, 314th Regiment), endeavoured throughout to make use of his own machine guns. At first the 312th Machine Gun Regiment, armed with heavy Brownings, managed to keep well up with the support line, but several companies had encountered rough going from the moment they left their jumping-off trenches. Just an hour after leaving the German front line trenches, the men, despairing of making fast enough time, discarded their carts and manhandled their heavy Brownings forward.

Colonel Oury, 314th Regiment.

Sergeant John E Spasio of the 312th, pushing forward with a squad of men, captured a German non-commissioned officer and, at gun point, forced him to disclose the position of a number of trench mortars. Thanks to this information, the doughboys were able to put those trench mortars out of action. Spasio later added to his tally of prisoners by capturing ten more Germans. The heavy Brownings finally reached a forward position at 10.30 am, arriving at the time when Major Gwynn of the 3rd Battalion was seeking some way of silencing three persistent machine guns on his flank. C Company as well as F Company mounted their guns and set to work, the start of yet another terrible fight.

'Sergeant Cabla of Company F, 314th Regiment, successfully manoeuvred his patrol so that he could flank the enemy machine-gun nests. He advanced to within five feet of one gunner and opened fire. At the moment he fired six other machine gunners

90

turned their fire on him. Sergeant Cabla then ordered his men to fall back and in doing so received a bullet in his breast, stopped only by the whistle he was carrying. He successfully withdrew his platoon to a better position and proceeded to use rifle grenades to great advantage. While discharging a grenade, a sniper bullet hit him in the foot. Although the wounds gave him tremendous pain, he refused to leave until the machine-gun nests had been wiped out.'

Private William Schellberg (311th Machine Gun Regiment) did not advance that fast; his company was in support and arrived somewhat later on the battlefield.

'Going along fine until 11.30 am; ran into lots of machine guns and snipers and Corporal Warfield and Private Heil were shot through arm, Heil having a broken arm and Warfield only a slight wound. I took charge of the 7th squad. Someone told me that Eberlein was shot. When I saw him he was white and cold. I got the first aid man up to him and he told me he was dead. I felt like beating Germany myself.'

A post-war reunion button belonging to Private First Class S. Vasey, 311th Machine Gun Battalion.

There was no shortage of self-sacrifice that morning: five more DSCs were awarded in due course for brave actions carried out during the terrible fighting in the area between Haucourt and Malancourt. The first was awarded to Captain Henry M Smith (314th Regiment), who was seriously wounded while leading a platoon of his company against strong machine-gun nests. Smith continued the advance until all the machine guns in his immediate front had been silenced and the crews killed or taken prisoner. He refused to seek medical attention until called to the rear by his regimental commander.

Sergeant Harry L Greenwood (Company K, 315th Regiment), personally led a patrol of four men against a machine gun that was holding up the advance. He inspired his men to greater effort; under heavy machine-gun fire and by his excellent example they managed to capture the gun and nine prisoners. He was killed while reorganizing his platoon after a counterattack.

However, the actions of Private First Class Clifford M Seiders (312th Machine Gun Battalion), dwarfed those of other DSC recipients as regards the total of guns taken and prisoners captured. Advancing ahead of his platoon in the face of heavy machine-gun fire, Seiders entered a cellar of a ruined building in Malancourt alone and discovered thirteen of the enemy. He shot one who resisted and took the remaining twelve prisoner, bringing in with them three light machine guns. As if this were not enough, later the same day he captured ten more Germans and five machine guns. It was men like this who made the difference. They forgot all about the inadequate textbook regulations they had been taught and started to improvise to reach their goals; some learnt faster than others.

Meanwhile a new problem had presented itself. General Kuhn had been waiting in vain all morning for news from his regimental commanders. Frustrated, he moved his headquarters to Cote 304, a few kilometres south of Malancourt. This did not help matters much as by now all communications had broken down; by the time he was informed of the situation by AEF Headquarters at about 3.00 pm, he still had not had any contact with his officers.

Noon, left wing, 26 September, Golfe de Malancourt:
313th Regiment was leading the attack
316th Regiment was in support

Around noon, after fruitless hours of trying to penetrate the lines in the Golfe de Malancourt, a halt was called and a more organized attack was started against the machine guns that were blocking the way. A temporary command post was set up at the northern edge of Malancourt Wood. To add to the chaos, troops of the 316th now appeared on the scene; they were not aware of the fact that the 313th's attack had bogged down; the troops of both regiments began to get mixed up, complicating command functions. Meanwhile, the Germans were continually spraying the woods with machine-gun bullets, the death toll and the number of wounded growing all the time. Colonel Sweezey, who had moved forward quickly, was bending over a map with Lieutenant Schauffler when a sniper's bullet hit the latter in the hip. This did not prevent them from coming up with a new plan of action; obviously, the frontal attacks on the German line were nothing less than suicide missions. With the help of a few newly arrived French tanks, the Americans would now try to outflank the enemy position, eliminating one machine-gun post at a time. Heavy machine guns started a powerful barrage on the enemy line and at around 2.00 pm the 313th started an attack on Cuisy Wood. The Doughboys had been very lucky that the Brownings had arrived at all, as it was extremely difficult to manhandle heavy guns and ammunition to the front. Lieutenant Colonel DuPuy (311th Machine Gun Regiment) described some of the difficulties experienced by the machine gunners:

No Man's Land between Esnes and Malancourt.

'We moved forward, taking everything ahead of us for three hours with little resistance. We crossed three miles of No Man's Land, the most God-forsaken, desolate, torn-up-place the world ever saw. Over an area of approximately four miles this land had remained a No Man's Land, changing hands, of course, from time to time, but continually being shelled so that at the start [there were difficulties], even with the careful preparation which I thought I had made by building platforms which were intended to be thrown across the trenches and craters over which to lead mules and gun carts. However, it was found impossible to take the mules and carts forward, so that everything had to be unslung and manhandled. So deep were the shell holes and mine craters that the ammunition carriers were even unable to carry two small boxes of ammunition, so that the belts were removed and wrapped around the men's necks and waists, and they crawled up and down these steep slippery banks using their finger nails and toes. At times the guns and tripods had to be thrown from the bottom of the crater up to the top to a man waiting to receive it; the man followed by hand and foot. The tactics that we had learned proved to be of little value. We had always been taught to attack and take a machine gun by the flanks, but in trying to do so we simply ran into frontal fire from a machine gun on one side or the other of the one we were trying to take, so that it was necessary a great many times to simply charge a gun from the front and both flanks, and take it regardless of our losses, which, per gun captured, averaged ten to twenty men.'

While the 313th were still trying to breach the defences in the Golfe, the 314th were fighting their own bitter struggle, forcing their way through Malancourt and beyond. Early in the afternoon the 37th Division, to the left of the 313th, had passed well beyond the German second position by pushing the attack toward its frontal objective, leaving behind the men of the 313th. The 314th, on the right, had also passed the second position. However, the Germans started to realize that their position was threatened and resistance weakened due to their belief in the greater advantage to be gained by concentrating their forces around Montfaucon. In addition, the knowledge of the rapid American advance in other sectors all along the rest of the offensive line, particularly that of the 4th Division to the right of the 79th and almost in line with Montfaucon, convinced them that their position in front of Cuisy Wood was untenable. It was then that the Germans evacuated the Golfe de Malancourt in a fighting retreat, having successfully held their positions for nearly five hours. They reorganized at the Etzel Line on the forward slopes before the hill of Montfaucon. The 314th had not been so lucky; they received no help from the 4th Division and were forced to wait for assistance.

Noon, 26 September, right wing, Demon Redoubt:
314th Regiment was leading the attack
315th Regiment was in support

The struggle to force the German defenders out of Malancourt took much longer than anticipated and wrecked the 314th Regiment's schedule. The

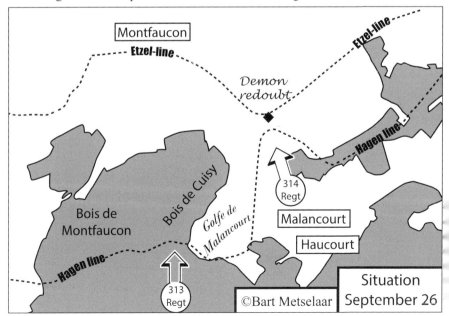

German defences at the Demon Redoubt.

315th, who were supposed to stay a kilometre behind the 314th, had now also reached the front line, adding to the chaos. Regiments mixed, units got lost; sometimes a platoon was reduced to a few men, the rest straggling somewhere in the sector. The roads leading to the front had become so congested that the artillery had trouble reaching the troops in time to support them in the attack. Finally, at around noon, the Germans withdrew from their positions; they moved back to the Hagen Line, which had been constructed about two kilometres to the north-west of Malancourt. First Lieutenant Arthur H Joel (314th Regiment) described what he saw when he first set eyes on the village:

'By midday the fog had all cleared. As the battle increased in intensity, glances to right and left over the rolling farm country gave the observer an appreciation of the bigness of a modern battle. The general plan of infantry attack was to advance in thin lines following each other at varying intervals. A distant view showed the series of human waves going forward in the tide of attack, gaining in one place and held up in another, according to the fortunes of battle. Ordinarily there were numerous high-explosive shells bursting in the lines and shrapnel overhead, but thus far Fritz's artillery was not in an effective position after its hasty retreat.'

Some of the units that still had some cohesion moved into what remained of the village and started to pursue the withdrawing enemy. However, after about 500 metres the attack bogged down in the face of withering machine-gun fire coming from Demon Redoubt and several other hidden nests. Sergeant Joseph T Labrum (314th Regiment) was leading his platoon out of Malancourt when, after about 400 metres, they suddenly came under heavy fire from Fosse Wood. Here, a stronghold was built on a steep wooded ridge that was fifty metres higher than the track on which they were walking.

'Heavy machine-gun fire from a wood directly in front kept the two platoons in a trench most of the day and part of the afternoon. The position was such an untenable one that it was well nigh impossible even to attempt to clear the obstacle, for the cover was poor and the Huns had a direct fire on the position held by the platoons. E Company off to the left managed to clear out the obstacle by flanking the guns.'

Demon Redoubt Bunker

The valley leading up to the Demon Redoubt, situated on the ridge in the distance.

A German howitzer battery, Malancourt.

The Americans were pinned down in this position for about four hours. Several attacks were made and, according to First Lieutenant Arthur H Joel, men of F Company of the 314th Regiment men fell thick and fast. In spite of all their efforts, it proved impossible to reach the German positions.

'In the early afternoon the real battle began. Thus far there had been a great deal of excitement, plenty of prisoners, but few casualties. Surely reports had exaggerated real conditions at the front, one naturally concluded – until the troops suddenly met the stonewall resistance of the concealed German machine gun defence. The Huns had fallen back of necessity but had organized a new line through and in front of Montfaucon, the lookout city which they called Little Gibraltar. Contact was made by a combat patrol. A lieutenant, Sergeant McCawley and four men, had advanced through a network of barbed wire defences to the crest of a low hill. They were just clearing the knoll in skirmish formation when fired upon by an automatic rifle in a clump of bushes ahead. Sergeant McCawley and his gunner Jones, over on the right flank, immediately returned the fire. Champa, and Calabretta on the left quickly followed suit. Then, as if by prearranged signal, enemy machine-guns, automatics and snipers located in trees, gullies, and bushes ahead and on the flanks opened with a hot fusillade that filled the air with snaps, cracks and whines of flying lead. Cut weeds, flying gravel and the harsh cracks of the bullets were proof enough that the patrol had located the resistance and were in a bad trap. The mission of the patrol had been accomplished; that of locating and testing the strength of the enemy even if it was necessary to sacrifice themselves. It was the moment of every man for himself as best he could. Whether or not McCawley and Jones heard the repeated orders to take cover in a low bushy spot to their right will never be known. McCawley was shot through the head while operating his gun and died with a smile. Jones and Champa were hit in the legs and Calabretta was mortally wounded in the stomach.

. . . .

An officer had only his revolver and two bombs as weapons; useless luggage in this situation. By crawling and wriggling with his nose in the ground, he finally managed to roll into a shell hole, wondering in a dazed way why the "lights hadn't gone out". When the helmet rings with the cracks of 'close ones' and bits of flying gravel, one just naturally feels weak in the stomach and expects everything to suddenly turn black. For hours, German snipers, machine gunners and automatic riflemen, organized strongly in depth and well-concealed, swept the area with a steady sheet of fire. Heinie saw to it that the Yanks continued to hug the ground most of the afternoon. At least five lieutenants and captains of the battalion were shot down in an hour's time, the losses being heavier that first afternoon than any other time in the drive. Not a few miracles and almost unbelievable, narrow calls happened that day. First Sergeant Joe Cable, the big Texan, forced out of one shell hole by dangerous fire, made a run for another. A bullet hit the whistle in the breast pocket over his heart, and then spoiled a little French book underneath. The whistle was flattened and the book shredded, but the sergeant was barely bruised. Another bullet took off the heel of his shoe, and a third cut him across the toes, after which he secured protection in a deep shell hole and nursed his foot. The battalion gas officer was made a casualty by the

August Schuler, 314th Regiment, died on 27 September of wounds received on 26 September.

very thing he had trained himself to combat. McCawley, Gilbert, Jones, Schuler, Shade and Weber 'went west' like real men, either this day or the following, and at least fifteen others were wounded.'

The last DSC awarded to the 314th Regiment for actions above and beyond the call of duty that day went to Sergeant Peter Strucel of Company L. During one of the last frontal attacks on the ridge leading up to the Etzel Line, he and his men ran into heavy machine-gun fire. With utter disregard for his own safety, Sergeant Strucel showed exceptional courage and devotion to duty by constantly walking up and down the line, cheering and encouraging his men to attack the nest. In the performance of this task he was killed. Once again

The headstone of Private Schuler.

an attack had been repelled and the doughboys were looking for cover. It was simply impossible to reach the enemy. This hopeless situation greatly affected morale; there were signs of panic and it had been reported that several soldiers had retreated without orders. Fortunately, the doughboys had been able to take Fosse Wood, situated on a steep ridge about 500 metres north of Malancourt. In doing so they freed themselves from enfilading fire on the right flank. This would make a future American attack on Demon Redoubt much more likely to be successful. At around 4.00 pm the order was given to stop the advance. Contact with brigade headquarters had been lost and no one in the immediate fighting area knew what to do anymore. Artillery and tanks were needed to drive the Germans off the ridge; the frontal attack had proved far too costly in human life.

Noon, 26 September, left wing, Cuisy Wood:
313th Regiment was leading the attack
316th Regiment was in support

At last the regiments of the 79th Division could move on. After the Americans took over the positions in the Golfe de Malancourt that had been occupied by the *117th Division*, they fought their way through to the southern edge of Cuisy Wood. Once the southern edge had been won, the Germans began to withdraw but, nevertheless, continued to put up stubborn resistance in rear-guard actions, with the result that there was much hand-to-hand fighting, resulting in heavy losses to both sides. Private William Schellberg remembered that when they entered the wood the Germans started to fire with everything they had, including the feared flamethrowers. This, however, failed to put a stop to the American advance; whilst on both sides many heroic deeds were performed. After the war, Private Harold P Rumberger (Company B, 316th Regiment), learnt that he had been awarded the DSC for his actions during the fighting in the wood. On his own initiative he attacked a machine-gun post with his rifle; the German crew was not impressed by his efforts and continued operating the gun. Enraged by his failure, he ran back to the American lines in order to find a more effective weapon. Eventually, he returned with a Browning Automatic Rifle, attacked the nest a second time and killed the crew.

For a brief time the fighting paused and the Germans slowly started to withdraw from Cuisy Wood; by now the 79th Division had been held up at the Golfe de Malancourt for five hours. The Germans in Cuisy Wood were being outflanked and their positions were in serious danger of being cut off and the men left there surrounded. They retreated to the Etzel Line on the slopes leading up to Montfaucon.

There was some positive news at the end of the day; the 304th Engineers had somehow managed to find a way to make the Avocourt-Malancourt Road passable again. Faced with huge problems in finding sufficient material to fill in the craters, they had started to fill in the holes with rubble from the shattered buildings in Malancourt. This speeded up the work greatly, but the makeshift road could still only be used by animal-drawn vehicles.

At 6.00 pm the final attack of the day was made by the exhausted men

Engineers using rubble from ruined buildings in Haucourt to repair the road.

One of the many French Renault FT17 tanks that supported the American attack.

of the 313th Regiment. The assault was accompanied by several French tanks that had, surprisingly, managed to reach the front. As the Regimental History explains, the success of this attack would make a huge difference to the position of the neighbouring 37th Division:

'The right battalion especially was confronted with a serious problem. The 79th Division, operating on its right flank, had, through effective resistance on the part of the enemy, been forced to delay its advance, so that when the 145th Regiment reached the edge of Montfaucon Wood its right flank was entirely exposed, due to the 79th Division being still several kilometres to the rear. Near the edge of the wood were the bodies of several Germans. One body was that of a comparatively elderly man. He lay with his head cushioned upon his arm, with wide open eyes staring glassily toward the road. Another one lay in a pool of blood with the top of his head completely blown off. The arrival of the 79th had to be awaited before an attempt could be made to attack Montfaucon. Dusk was falling when the first detachments of the 79th Division finally arrived abreast the line held by the regiment. Simultaneously with the arrival of the 79th, orders were received, calling for another attempt to force a crossing of the German defensive positions. The 79th made gallant attempts to destroy the machine-gun nests in its path, but after advancing a short distance was met with such a shower of shells, bullets and grenades that the attack had to be abandoned. The two tanks had hardly left the shelter of the woods when well directed shots fired at point-blank range by a battery of 77s reduced them to a pile of junk. The shells, striking the tanks squarely in front, smashed the steel armour and converted the interiors into a shambles of machinery, control apparatus and human flesh.'

The light had faded by the time that the advancing lines cleared Montfaucon and Cuisy Wood. Montfaucon Hill itself loomed gigantic and indistinct two kilometres ahead. Between the wood and the height lay an open field that rolled and twisted into deep folds. It was probably the most difficult place on the entire front to take by direct assault in daylight, so Colonel Sweezey ordered an attack as soon as the sun was down. Just as Montfaucon itself was sinking from view in the deepening shadows, the First Battalion was forming for the attack. Without artillery assistance or a protecting machine-gun barrage, the doughboys of the 313th Regiment silently went forward into the night, into what was supposed to be surprise attack on the fortified slope. The attack quickly became a failure. Advancing over unfamiliar terrain in the darkness, it proved very difficult to maintain contact. As a precaution, the Germans had laid a protective barrage in front of their defences. The screams of the wounded and the rattle of tanks ensured that the attack was no longer a surprise and the Germans used all the firepower at their disposal to stop it.

The headstone of Private Gilbert, 314th Regiment.

Private Weber, 314th Regiment, fatally wounded on 26 September 1918.

Proving their effectiveness, again the German heavies were aimed at pre-arranged zones, causing mayhem amongst the attackers. Under a constant hail of artillery and machine-gun fire, men and officers were falling like flies. In the darkness, the tanks lost their way and rumbled back to Cuisy Wood. Colonel Sweezey reluctantly ordered a halt to the attack and the troops drew back into Cuisy Wood to await the dawn. As far as possible, the infantry retired slowly and in reasonably good order. The 311th Machine Gun Battalion accompanied and supported Colonel Sweezey's men throughout the assault and now the machine gunners, who had carried their guns and tripods forward, silently manned their posts. The expected German counterattack, under the cover of the fog, rain and darkness, kept them a few hundred metres ahead of the infantry in Cuisy Wood. They crouched in shell holes, seeking shelter from the elements under tarpaulins and for hours, with nerves on edge, they peered into the darkness. Fortunately, the much feared counterattack did not come.

One of the medics who was tirelessly working that night to evacuate the wounded from the battlefield was Captain Frank R Wheelock of the Medical Corps, attached to the 313th Regiment. Working in areas that were continually being swept by rifle, shell and machine-gun fire, Wheelock worked voluntarily and unceasingly, giving aid, food, and water to the wounded. Throughout the entire operation he showed 'utter disregard for his personal safety', being knocked down many times by shell explosions. For two nights, he worked as a stretcher bearer, carrying patients to places of safety, after giving the wounded medical attention during the day. Men like Wheelock saved many lives with their outstanding work, especially during the first two days of the offensive, when everything, doctors included, was in short supply. For his actions, he was awarded the DSC.

Thus ended the first day. The attack had failed and Colonel Sweezey, in the face of an utterly hopeless situation, ordered the 313th Regiment back to the edge of Cuisy Wood and the shattered remains of the Hagen Line. Incredibly, some men of the 314th had reached the outskirts of Montfaucon, albeit but briefly; it had been the furthest point of advance until they were forced to pull back. The men were to spend the night on the southern edge of Cuisy Wood, staying out in the open; soldiers started to dig scrapes or sought refuge in shell holes. Private William Schellberg had a very clear recollection of the miserable night spent in Cuisy Wood:

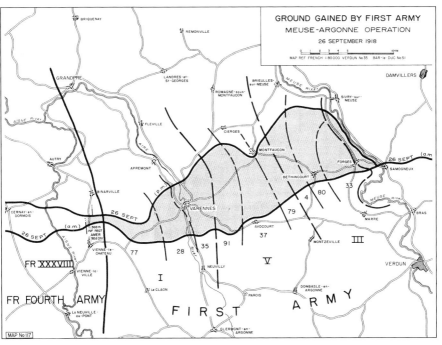

Positions of First Army on the night of 26 September 1918.

'By this time it was dark and we had taken up defensive positions for the night. The artillery was bombarding all night and we had all kinds of gas alarms. There were no blankets, so we slept on the ground along side of our guns and slept the best we could. It started to rain and got real cold. All we had to protect us with was our overcoats and slicker.'

103

Outposts were established and preparations were made to repel counterattacks. The night was cold and for a change light showers began to fall, chilling the men to the bone. All the canteens were empty; water and rations had run out. The supplies that were so badly needed did not reach the troops as the roads were in such a terrible state that they were permanently clogged by the weight of the traffic. The supply trains that transported provisions for three divisions had to use the Malancourt-Montfaucon Road, which by that time was in such a deplorable state that it was almost non-existent. The 304th Engineers were still frantically working to rebuild the road.

Entrenchment tool of a member of the 313th Regiment.

In spite of their efforts and hardship, the 79th Division had failed to take Montfaucon on the first day. Consequently, its neighbour, the 37th Division was unable to exploit their success and the 4th Division, that had advanced well beyond the town, was forced to retreat to Septsarges Wood to prevent the Germans attacking their flanks. Because of contradictory orders, the left flank of the 4th Division had failed to wheel to the left and attack Montfaucon from the rear. Now Montfaucon and its surrounding defences became, albeit very briefly, a small but dangerous salient in the centre of the whole of the attack line. On the very first day of the Meuse-Argonne Offensive the schedule of the First Army, and particularly that of V Corps, had been thrown into disarray.

Night, 26 September:
Due to the fact that the telephone lines had been put out of action, General Kuhn did not receive news of the final positions of his units until nightfall. [It should be noted that, unlike the British army, for example, the American practice was not to distinguish the level of the parts of the army by the use of 'formation' – for those of a brigade or larger – or 'unit', for those of a battalion or less: everything is described as a 'unit'.] With telephone contact broken, the chief means used that day to acquire accurate information was by the use of runners. Thanks to the terrible conditions underfoot, this system was slow as well as being extremely dangerous for the men carrying the messages – and it was inevitable that many of these never got through, the runner a casualty or hopelessly lost. Matters were not helped when various headquarters moved position or the relevant decision maker had decided, often in desperation, to go forward and try and see what was happening for himself.

Just before midnight the division's staff received an instruction from AEF Headquarters stating that the 'Commander-in-Chief expects 79th Division to advance tonight to a position abreast of 4th Division in the vicinity of Nantillois'. This order clearly showed the lack of understanding in Pershing's headquarters of the reality of the situation on the ground. To the officers who were actually in the middle of things, it was clear that artillery support was both badly needed, indeed indispensable, to convince the Germans to evacuate their positions in front of Montfaucon. However, at that moment, even if it had been possible, there was no way to motivate the disorganised troops to resume the fighting.

Brigadier General Noble, 158 Brigade.

A further difficulty was that establishing contact with Brigadier General Nicholson, commanding 157 Brigade, was not possible at this time. Fortunately, General Kuhn had been able to contact Brigadier General Noble of 158 Brigade and work out a new plan for the advance. The 315th, which had been in reserve all day, was to move forward at once. Communication with General Nicholson was not established until several hours later when the following message was sent to him at 4.53 am on the morning of 27 September:

Brigadier General Nicholson, 157 Brigade.

'Imperative orders from Commander in Chief require that the 79th Division advance at once to come in line with neighbouring divisions. Owing to your having broken liaison it was necessary to place General Noble in charge of the 315th and 314th Regiments to make an immediate advance. You are directed to take command of the 313th and 316th Regiments and to push on with all possible speed to the First Army first phase objective. Location of these regiments not definitely known.'

However, the chaos in the American command structure was such that eventually the night attack was called off. During the night the regiments were reorganized as possible, whilst plans were changed again and again. Finally, in spite of all the chaos and disorganization, the next attack on

Montfaucon was arranged for first light. The opportunity for a possible breakthrough, if in reality there ever was one, that first night of the 'drive' had been lost.

The Germans

At the end of September 1918, the Germans were fighting at numerous places along the Western Front. Apparently, for the German High Command the Meuse-Argonne was just one engagement of many. Here are some German impressions of the first day of the American assault: General Ludendorff, in his memoirs:

> 'On 26 September, a large battle was started in the Champagne and on the west bank of the River Meuse. Here, the French and Americans started an attack on a wide front. To the west of the Argonne we were masters of the situation and executed splendid defensive actions. However, between the Argonne Forest and the River Meuse the powerful American Army had managed to break through our lines; more and more, they started to become an important player on the battlefield.'

Crown Prince Wilhelm was slightly more impressed with the attack and wrote:

> 'After a preliminary bombardment of eleven hours the attack started. East from the Argonne masses of Americans smashed into the left wing of my *3rd Army* and *5th Army Group Gallwitz*. On the whole front, we were forced to withdraw two to three kilometres. Later on, unfortunately, our adversaries managed to break our lines.'

Bavarian soldiers who were so close to the front that they could actually see and hear the shells exploding, experienced the attack from a very different perspective; they were going to be the ones soon to put their lives on the line in order to try to stem the tide. A Bavarian war diary reported that:

> '[On] 26 September large scale enemy attacks were made in the Champagne and the Argonne. The left bank of the River Meuse is overwhelmed by a gigantic American Army that smashed into the right wing of the *5th Army* between Forges and Avocourt. Also the left wing of the *3rd Army* west of Avocourt is under attack.'

Bavarian shock troops on their way to the front.

During the night of 25 to 26 September, the *37th Division* and the *5th Bavarian Reserve Division* were moved into the sector. The preliminary bombardment had been an unmistakable sign that an attack was underway. The Bavarians were held in reserve in Brieulles, about eight kilometres north-east of Montfaucon. As the scale of the American attack became apparent, the Bavarians were moved to the front to support the *117th Division* in the Montfaucon sector. As the American 4th Division had already passed Septsarges, about two kilometres east of Montfaucon, Nantillois and the Nantillois-Brieulles Road were now seriously in danger. The latter was one of the main arteries that served Montfaucon; all supplies came through Nantillois. It was here that the Bavarian troops were deployed. Several units of Bavarian Field Artillery took up positions there and started to fire at the Americans. Another field artillery unit under Hauptmann (Captain) Hollidt took control of four batteries of field howitzers that they found abandoned on Hill 295, a little north of Montfaucon and Septsarges. Around noon, other parts of the *5th Bavarian Reserve Division* arrived in Nantillois. They launched a counterattack that forced the 4th Division back to Brieulles and Septsarges Woods. These actions successfully protected the right flank of Montfaucon, at least for the moment.

The Operations Section of *Group of Armies Gallwitz* reported:

Following a quiet day, at 11.30 pm, September 25, very heavy enemy artillery fire opened suddenly on almost the entire front of the *Group of Armies*. It continued throughout the night with little variation. The morning of September 26, strong attacks were launched against the front of the *Fifth Army* west of the [Meuse], conjointly with similar attacks against the left of the *Third Army*. After [considerable] fighting, during which the advantage often fluctuated, the enemy succeeded in penetrating the main line of resistance at several points and even gained ground beyond it. The line Ivoiry-Montfaucon-north of Dannevoux, as well as nests of resistance in front thereof, are still being held. Counter-attacks are in progress along the line Nantillois-Vilosnes; on the east bank of the Meuse the flank has been refused. ...'

The Americans had lost many men on the first day; but Germans losses were just as severe. To get an idea of the intensity of the fighting that took place on 26 September, the German *117th Division* alone reported about 1,500 casualties in their sector, a front approximately two kilometres wide: that is one casualty for every 1.3 metres of the front line that it held.

Chapter 5

27 September – the Capture of Montfaucon

Then the light came, the rolling plain rose to view, Montfaucon itself loomed ahead. Leaders were astir and the men were aroused. Enemy machine guns still played on the fringes of the wood and enemy artillery maintained a desultory fire, as the men munched their meagre breakfast of corned beef and hardtack. Some found a spring and filled their canteens, some drank from shell holes, some went without water.

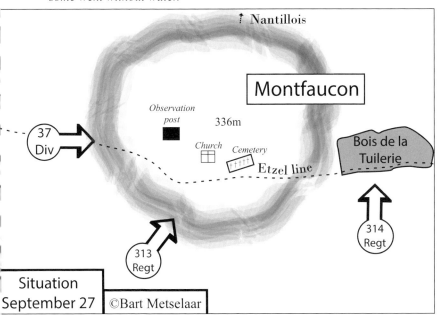

Morning, 27 September, left wing, the Etzel Line:
313th Regiment was leading the attack
316th Regiment was in support

At 6.00 am, despite huge traffic jams on every road, two batteries (eight guns) from the 147th Field Artillery had somehow, almost miraculously,

Although taken a few days after the liberation of Montfaucon, this photo clearly shows the open ground in the 313th and 314th regiments' sectors. Note the barbed wire obstacles.

A German dugout in Cuisy Wood.

arrived behind the 313th Regiment just in time to open fire on the southern slope of Montfaucon. While the officers were busy making arrangements for the forthcoming attack, the soldiers' biggest concern was breakfast. Captain Earl E. Glock (316th Regiment) recalled:

'By dawn of the 27th the men had explored the German trenches and found a number of dugouts with peeled potatoes in kettles on the stoves, ready for boiling, pots of acorn coffee, already brewed, cheese and small bags [German bread bags or *brot beutel*] of musty, tasteless biscuit. There were many valuables left behind by men who had fled in a hurry, but the men knew the weight of a pack, and had not yet acquired the souvenir habit. For water the men had to collect the rain in their mess kits. At 6.45 am the advance was resumed, the regiment still in support of the 313th.'

At 7.00 am the rolling barrage started, the signal to leave Cuisy Wood. Not everybody had been as lucky as Captain Glock's men; the 313th, hungry, wet and after a miserable night, emerged from the wood and marched down the gentle slope toward the bottom of the valley and then up the steeper slope towards the German defences of the Etzel Line. Here, Corporal George L Brown of Company K, 313th Regiment, crawled ahead of his platoon and located and killed a sniper who had wounded him and several others. Although seriously wounded, he remained in command of his platoon until he was ordered to the rear. He insisted on going back without assistance, though he was so weak he could hardly walk. For this action he was awarded the DSC, as was Chaplain John C Moore, who was attached to the 313th Regiment. Though wounded the day before, Moore remained with the attacking lines of the regiment, ministering to the dying and aiding the wounded. After entering an enemy trench with a group of men, a grenade was thrown into their midst and Moore, with utter disregard for his own personal safety, grabbed the grenade and threw it back out of the trench. It exploded just as it was leaving his hand, seriously wounding him in several places. After securing the trench line, the attack continued. However, from this point on they came under continual sweeping fire from the heavy German artillery. The whole approach was an open plain inclining upward, and it only offered a place to shelter in the valleys. While crossing the heights, they would have to advance in full view of the Germans. Fortunately, they were supported by a few 75mm field guns and several tanks. An anonymous eyewitness vividly described the events:

'8.00 am. A shrill whistle sounded off to the right; then whistles seemed to ring through the woods. [Cuisy Wood] Out of the fringe of woods came an irregular row of men. The scouts were moving slowly and seemingly aimlessly many metres apart; but they were trained to scour the ground for the enemy and keen to detect the slightest hostile movement. The tanks awkwardly followed. In the wake of the tanks came the attacking waves, marching in combat groups until resistance should make deployment necessary. Over the shell-pitted field moved the battalion, and behind the infantry

111

came two machine-gun companies. The ground to be taken would be hard won and precious, and the Brownings must be there to hold it. Here and there in the steadily advancing troops a man dropped, for the Boche artillery was increasing the volume of its fire and the light of day furnished the observation to make it effective. The attacking waves deployed on a machine-gun nest to the front, but the attack was not halted; the guns were smothered and the first prisoners of the day started to dribble back through the command post on their way to the stockades. A boche machine-gunner who had been hit the night before had lain in the field through the pouring rain until he was roused by the advancing doughboys. It was a poor semblance of a face that he carried, smashed in as it was by rifle butt and cut by bayonet. Captain Barber dressed the wounds and laid the man aside to wait for stretcher bearers. The poor chap shook as if with ague for an hour and then quietly passed away.'

Captain Barber died a fortnight after performing his heroic deeds. He is buried in the American Cemetery in Romagne, F.32.4.

The 313th attacked with the Second Battalion on the left and the First Battalion to the right, the Third Battalion acting as support. As explained earlier, the 146th Regiment of the 37th Division on the extreme left had already started the attack on Montfaucon but withdrew once they had eliminated the machine guns that had been holding up the attack in the area in front of Cierges and Hémont Wood. In the meantime, six French tanks had rolled forward ahead of the 313th. After advancing 300 metres they ran into terrible machine-gun fire, though not as heavy as on the previous day. Despite strong resistance, the 313th pushed forward and surged ahead to the last roll of ground in front of Montfaucon; all of this was accomplished with an unexpectedly low number of casualties. An anonymous soldier noted:

'The advancing waves appeared on the crest of the next fold of ground, still intact though fewer in number. The tanks had suffered too, for only half as many mounted this roll as had set out from the woods. Some had been struck by artillery fire; some had been ditched in shell holes or trenches, for the French FT17 tanks cannot surmount the obstacles that are taken so easily by their

German barbed wire obstacles.

grown brothers; some were stranded with killed or wounded crews and no one to drive them. Frequently the forward moving lines deployed to reduce machine-gun nests. The 77s had almost ceased to fall; evidently the Germans were moving the field pieces back to safer positions to prevent their capture.'

Montfaucon had been surrounded on three sides and, combined with the recent breakthrough of the 37th Division, the Germans' main worry was that they would be encircled. During the night they had already partially evacuated the site and it was now just a matter of time before they gave up their positions altogether. That moment came when the heavy artillery located on the Meuse Heights slackened fire noticeably. To add to the Germans' woes the Americans had managed to destroy many of the machine guns that had been located at the base of the hill and which now left the Etzel Line practically undefended. As a result, part of the German garrison evacuated Montfaucon and moved to the intermediate line at Beuge Wood and Nantillois. But they left a surprise for the Americans. Dozens of snipers and so-called suicide squads were left amongst the ruins in order to keep the enemy engaged as long as possible, thus enabling the garrison to make a safe retreat and with time to prepare new defences. Two German observers remained on the hill, passing on details of troop movements to the heavy artillery. The lull in the enemy barrage was immediately used by the Americans to advance to the foot of the hill.

Morning, 27 September, right wing, Demon Redoubt:
314th Regiment was leading the attack
315th Regiment was in support

At 4.00 am, several patrols left Fosses Wood and moved forward through the darkness and heavy fog. They had been tasked with reconnoitring the area and ascertaining the locations of the machine guns. Corporal William J Walsh, Company H, 314th Regiment, was leading a scouting patrol 300 metres in advance of his company when he was fired upon from enemy machine-gun positions. Several of his patrol were wounded but, after carrying one man to shelter and assisting the others, he continued on under heavy fire. He was

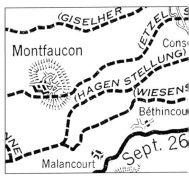

The Wiesenschlenken and Hagen Lines in the 314th and 315th Regiments' sector.

able to locate six machine-gun posts and managed to kill the entire crew of one of them. For this action he was awarded the DSC. Personal initiatives like these often saved the day; they made the difference.

First Lieutenant Samuel J Marks, Medical Corps, 314th Regiment, was also awarded the DSC. Marks advanced with the first wave of attack of his battalion, dressing and evacuating the wounded under heavy machine-

An American first aid container found on the battlefield in 2017.

gun fire for a period of twelve hours. He had already been working tirelessly for days when his aid station was shelled. Several patients and attendants were killed and wounded; although he was wounded himself, he remained at his post, caring for patients who had received fresh wounds and assisted in their evacuation.

From the moment the 314th Regiment emerged from the old German trenches the resistance began, stiffening as the men pressed forward. Moving up along the right side of the Malancourt-Montfaucon Road, they were welcomed by a heavy machine-gun barrage from the front and enfilading fire from both flanks. However, they pressed on and just as daylight appeared all opposition directly in front of them was eliminated. It had taken them the better part of two hours to clear the scattered German points of resistance, and now the regiment was reorganizing for another push forward to the Hagen Line and Demon Redoubt on the higher ground ahead. The first hurdle had been successfully overcome. Sergeant Joseph T Labrum, 314th Regiment wrote:

'Long before daylight the battalion started forward again and continued their advance for about two and a half kilometres before they met resistance along the main road [the present-day D15] that runs through Montfaucon. Cover was quickly taken and because of the darkness no effort was made to overcome the obstacle. The company on the left flank cleaned out two nests of guns and, supported in the rear, the second and fourth platoons cleared their resistance.'

The 304th Engineers tearing down the walls of ruined buildings to use the resulting rubble as hard core for road repairs.

Men of the Signal Corps working on telephone lines.

Meanwhile, the supply routes were still congested and were continually being repaired and rebuilt. The men of the 304th Engineers worked frantically to keep the Avocourt-Malancourt road open. To add to the already massive supply problems, the 79th Division had to share the only road available in the sector with the 37th and 91st Divisions for a distance of some 800 metres. Naturally, the result was a horrendous traffic jam; the bad situation was made worse by the fact that everybody thought they had right of way. Miraculously, a few gun batteries managed to get through and were in time to support the 314th, while repairs and rebuilding continued around the clock. First Lieutenant Arthur H Joel (F Co, 314th Regiment):

'The 314th regiment lined up in battle formation on the reverse slope of a big hill [Hill (Cote) 308, roughly near the junction of the present-day D15 and the road that forks off in the direction of Cuisy] to the right of Montfaucon, to take part in the big flanking movement, while the 313th Regiment made a direct attack on the city itself. Scores of French tanks took positions near the crest of the hill, while in modern battle array followed twelve companies of infantry, a machine-gun company, trench mortar and one-pounder platoons. Beyond the crest of the hill big things immediately began to happen. The storm of high explosive increased in intensity, gas clouds became a great deal more concentrated and the whining and snapping machine-gun and sniper bullets added to the toll of casualties. Gas masks had to be donned several times. Sneezing, choking and lachrymal varieties made one cough, shed tears and sneeze at the same time. These gas concentrations might not be very dangerous, but it was at least exasperating to try and keep on a mask under such conditions. [Note: Thousands of soldiers who survived the war died only a few years later because they had been exposed to gas.]'

The attack successfully drove the Germans out of the Demon Redoubt defences and off the ridge but at a heavy cost; it had taken practically

German prisoners moving off to the rear, carrying a wounded American soldier.

twenty-four hours to dislodge the Germans from the Hagen Line and there were hundreds of casualties on both sides, the ridge was littered with dead and wounded. Infuriated American soldiers decided that it was payback time. Officers tried all they could to calm their men down but during the first few chaotic minutes of 'celebrating' their victory several of the German machine gunners were killed on the spot. Eventually, the prisoners were sent to the rear, some of them, it was claimed, mere boys, fourteen or fifteen years old. Finally, Demon Redoubt was taken and the advance continued.

The 37th Division's sector, 27 September:
The 37th Division found themselves in an awkward position. Their mission had been to outflank Montfaucon and to leave the attack on the town itself to the 79th Division. However, the Germans were constantly harassing them with machine guns hidden at several spots on the hill. Even worse were the 77mm field guns that fired almost point blank into their ranks. At 7.00 am it was decided to send two strong patrols toward Montfaucon in order to solve the problem. After heavy hand-to-hand fighting, the Americans succeeded in silencing several machine-gun positions on the west flank of the hill. A few soldiers even made it into the outskirts of the town; they were in fact the first Americans to set foot in Montfaucon itself. After eliminating the opposition on the west side of Montfaucon, the 37th Division returned to its own sector. Later, the Montfaucon-Ivoiry Road was secured, but not for long. Heavy shelling from the Meuse Heights forced them to withdraw to a point south of this road. No further attempts to advance were made that day and the attack on Cierges was called off. It must be noted that the actions of the 37th Division contributed greatly to the final success of the 79th that day; by putting the German defences on the left flank out of action, they paved the way for the 79th Division's own left flank.

Morning, 27 September, left wing, Montfaucon:
313th Regiment was leading the attack
316th Regiment was in support

The attack still pressed on. As the forward battalion passed over the second wave of ground and was disappearing from view, the support battalion emerged from Cuisy Wood and started across the field. Now the machine gun companies with the attacking battalion took up positions on that second rise of ground, from where there were great possibilities for overhead and indirect firing on Montfaucon and the flanks of the height. The position they had taken up allowed them to beat off any stiff resistance and to hold on until the two remaining companies could leapfrog them and take up positions on the slopes nearer the town.

As the support battalions of the 316th and 315th moved across the plain, the attacking waves climbed up on the last stretch of open ground facing Montfaucon. Here they seemed to hesitate, waver a moment, then fell to the ground; it appeared that they had walked into their own barrage and, frustratingly, they would have to wait until the barrage lifted. The support battalions also halted and took cover, however slight the cover in that bare open field may have been. The machine guns, ready for action, pressed on until the forward slope of the last rise offered a wide field of fire. Hugging the ground, everyone was tense and waiting for the shock; awaiting the lifting of the barrage and the final attack on the town itself. Lieutenant Colonel DuPuy, 311th Machine Gun Regiment:

'Our 155s and 240s were playing on the heights and Montfaucon could not be stormed until the barrage was lifted. The rat-tat-tat of the Brownings sped the doughboys onward as they rose and, making tortuous ways through the mazes of barbed wire and trenches, approached the town. Many fell as they pressed forward, for the Maxims were playing upon the advancing waves. Through the wire, around shell holes, up the steep hill in front of the town and finally into the town itself they charged.'

Artillery observers at work.

Cleaning the barrel of a 155mm Schneider gun.

When the barrage finally lifted, the 313th Regiment's Second Battalion entered the outskirts of the town on the western side, the First through the centre, and the Third in support. The doughboys had been expecting considerable problems while carrying out the task of getting rid of the snipers lurking among the ruins. DuPuy again:

'About nine-thirty a.m. small French tanks came lumbering along to help in the attack on 'Little Gibraltar' as the French had nicknamed the hill. The coming of the tanks gave the men assurance and strengthened their morale. The tanks (eleven in number) approached the town in pairs, through five of the principal streets. All went well until they reached certain points, where the Germans, with their usual cunning, had foreseen just such an attack, and had erected barricades across the streets, formed of high concrete blocks reinforced with steel rails, which later were bent backwards and planted in the ground some twenty feet. Here the tanks were useless, so we were compelled again to fall back in face of hundreds of machine guns. [...] This was really the heaviest hand-to-hand work encountered, for here our men used the bayonet and rifle butt, the pistol and the trench knife, and it was told to me by one of my lieutenants that one of my sergeants accounted for seven men in less than an hour, three with the pistol and four with the trench knife. The hardest fight of all seemed to be centered in a graveyard to the right [east] of the town.'

As the attack entered the town, rifle shots mingled with the sound of the Brownings. Hand grenades were thrown into every dugout and cellar to blast the enemy out. The doughboys were slowly and laboriously making their way through the ruins. All the while the machine guns fired at the flanks of the town. The stiffest resistance was encountered near the ruins of the church; here, determined machine-gun crews were putting up a considerable fight, often until the last bullet. When all seemed to be lost, several of the surviving Germans managed to scurry away through the tunnel system. Snipers were a real plague, as experienced by Major Effingham B Morris Jr., 313th Regiment. While leading his battalion in attack, Major Morris, then Captain Morris, was shot in the leg, but continued in command during the four days of action that followed. He was awarded the DSC and, according to the citation, 'By his persistence in remaining, despite his severe wound, he set an example which contributed largely to the success of the operations'.

A good example of a deep German dugout.

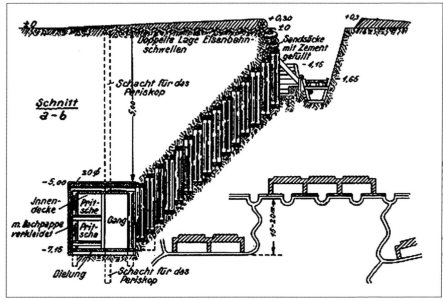

A schematic plan of one of the many German dugout designs.

On the outskirts of the town a nosey army chaplain almost got himself killed. He had advanced with the first wave and while some machine-gun nests were being put out of action he went underground to investigate a dugout. Unknown to him, the attack moved forward and the next wave overran his position. An ambitious corporal in the mopping up detail, who had been having a frustrating morning because there had been so little left to mop up, saw possibilities in the dugout. The corporal threw one of his F1 hand grenades down the steep staircase, where it exploded with a loud bang; after a few seconds the chaplain emerged from the dugout with all due haste, uttering some astonishing words, the likes of which are not usually heard coming out of the mouths of holy men. Fortunately, the chaplain was only slightly wounded in the arm whilst the explosion in the confined space caused a terrible ringing in his ears.

While the attacking waves cleared the top of Montfaucon Hill, other troops were already preparing for the advance into the valley leading to Beuge Wood, situated on a ridge two kilometres to the north. The edge of the wood was well equipped with machine guns and trench mortars and meanwhile heavy German artillery opened up in the valley between Montfaucon and Nantillois to protect the retreating Germans. Shells also started falling on Montfaucon, as Colonel DuPuy recalled:

'More explosions followed, however, as the mopping parties sought the hidden depths of the hill. Severe hand-to-hand struggles took place in the deepest and darkest tunnels. Finally, the town was quite cleared. The Colonel [Sweezey] moved to the south of the height with his headquarters; Major Jackson set up his first-aid station in a little hollow below the main road; once it must have been a spot of idyllic beauty, but now it was undermined with trenches and overgrown with brambles.'

Later, a message came from the attacking battalion that the front line had advanced 500 metres north of Montfaucon. A company of machine guns was sent around the right side of the hill, another company around the left, to protect the infantry advancing on the Beuge Wood-Nantillois defences. At around the same time Colonel Sweezey ordered the men from the Signal Corps to establish an improvised headquarters, connecting the new front line with the rear area. At 10.00 am, he phoned back to Brigade HQ that, 'I have established regimental headquarters in Montfaucon. Sweezey, Colonel.'

By approximately 11.45 am most of the resistance had been mopped up and the 313th's post of command had been established on the eastern slope of the hill, near the cemetery. It was hoped that the telephone lines would remain in working order; higher command was still largely in the dark about the 79th Division's current positions. At the end of the day, two hundred Germans, thirty machine guns and eleven field guns were reported to have been captured on Montfaucon alone.

Morning, 27 September, right wing, Tuilerie/Fayel Wood:
314th Regiment was leading the attack
315th Regiment was in support

Leaving Demon Redoubt behind, the 314th was now on its way to Tuilerie Wood, now known as Fayel Wood. After the regiment passed the small wood at the fork of the Montfaucon-Malancourt-Cuisy Road, they came under very heavy German artillery fire. The artillery that should have been supporting the 314th could not get through the traffic jam on the Esnes-Malancourt Road, so once again they had to advance without artillery support. Fortunately, the 314th had a few one pounders, which proved effective. [This was a French 37mm quick firing gun, reasonably easy to manhandle in the advance and designed, in the infantry role, to deal with machine gun nests; the British never used this calibre of weapon, although they had one of the same type of their own, preferring to leave this task to mortars. The gun was moderately successful.]

However, during the advance across the open ground between the Hagen Line and Fayel Wood shell fire proved more deadly than machine-gun bullets. The men jumped into abandoned Germans trenches that were to the left and right of the road; but even the relative protection of the trenches could not prevent the death of a number of Americans. After a while, one battalion continued on to Fayel Wood, but as they entered it they were met by heavy artillery fire. Sergeant Joseph T Labrum, 314th Regiment:

> 'The impeded advance was once more renewed and continued for a short distance when they were fired on from all sides. The two platoons had been marching up the road in platoon columns when fired upon. They immediately dropped to the shell holes and narrow trenches on the right side of the road. It was late in the morning before this obstacle was overcome, and then it was necessary to do mopping-up work, half of Lieutenant Hollinger's platoon going through part of a wood [Fayel Wood] and bombing dugouts. When they returned, the platoons once more reformed and started forward. The resistance was finally overcome and the company started forward toward the woods to the right of the city of Montfaucon [i.e. Fayel Wood. Before the war the wood continued all the way up the right (east) slope of Montfaucon Hill.]. Here we expected to find hard fighting, for the wood was powerfully fortified with trenches and dugouts, formidable enough to hold us off for a long time. But, fortunately, the wood was not as infested with machine guns and snipers as was anticipated, though there was a sprinkling of the latter who made considerable trouble for us. The companies had hardly reached the [northern] outer edge of the woods before they were met by a terrific barrage of overhead shrapnel which made things unbearable in that vicinity for some time, with the result that the entire battalion was forced to withdraw and take up a position in the field just before the town.'

German 77mm guns lobbed shell after shell on the American lines. At around 11.00 am the leading elements of the regiment attacked between Fayel Farm and Fayel Wood, only to discover that it had been largely evacuated. With the Americans now swarming over Montfaucon, General von Gallwitz thought it wiser to withdraw his troops in the direction of Nantillois rather than sacrifice them to a lost cause.

German prisoners under guard in Haucourt, 27 September 1918. Note the Maxim machine guns in the foreground.

Noon, 27 September, left wing, Beuge Wood:
313th Regiment was leading the attack
316th Regiment was in support

At 12.15 pm Colonel Sweezey sent a message to the divisional P.C. by carrier pigeon with the good news that Montfaucon had finally been taken. However, the message did not arrive until about 1.30 pm. Meanwhile, another message, asking for artillery support at Beuge Wood, revealed that Montfaucon had been captured:

> 'Took town of Montfaucon 11h55, after considerable fighting in town. Many snipers left behind. Town shelled to slight extent after our occupation. Am moving to corps objective and hope to reach it by 16 H. request artillery fire on Beuge Wood beginning 2.30 pm. and lifted at 4.00 pm.'

At 12.50 pm Colonel Sweezey, commanding the 313th, dispatched a message asking for a battalion of the 316th to protect his regiment while they were reorganizing. At 1.00 pm, the battalions of the 316th were in Montfaucon, while the 313th had already moved forward to a plateau to the north of the town.

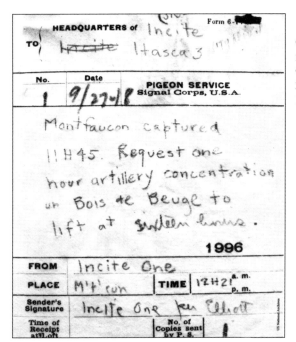

One of the
messages sent by
Colonel Sweezey,
27 September
1918.

The afternoon attack on the left of the 79th Division line did not begin until 3.30 pm, preceded, as requested, by an artillery barrage from 2.30 pm to 3.30 pm on Beuge Wood. This was a woodland stronghold lying in the direct path of the 313th Regiment, its southern edge two kilometres north of Montfaucon and west south west of Nantillois. During the preparations for the advance the 313th had been reorganized; the First Battalion of the 316th prepared a defensive position in shell holes along the base of the northern slope of the town, with the 313th in the open ground in front of it. While the 313th got underway, the remaining two battalions of the 316th moved up until both were on the northern side of Montfaucon. Two platoons from C and F Companies of the 316th went forward with the 313th in the assault. DuPuy recalled:

'After the town had fallen into our hands and been completely and thoroughly mopped up with the bayonet and grenade, the advance was continued north towards the third objective, Nantillois, and from that point on we began to realize what artillery really meant. Up to that time it had been severe for a few moments, but for the most part desultory; but here we ran into a real barrage coming from two sides and getting us by enfilade. We had now broken through the Hun's line, and were just at the edge of the so-called

Hindenburg Line. So intense was the fire from the Austrian 88s and German 77s and the long-barrelled 210s, that it was necessary to dig in temporarily to rest the men. Field dressing stations were established, only to be shelled repeatedly by the Germans. Frantic orders were sent back to the rear for artillery support, but without avail. The Boche planes seemed to have entire air supremacy and flew low over our lines, raking us with machine-gun fire. The Allied planes which did come up were soon in flames and dashed to the ground by the superior numbers of the enemy. All of our captive balloons had been destroyed the afternoon before, with the exception of one.'

The advance of the 313th and the two battalions of the 316th was halted in the open fields north of Montfaucon, the Germans pouring in withering fire from machine guns and mortars concealed in Beuge Wood and with enfilading artillery fire from the east, from the German guns situated on the Meuse Heights that overlooked most of the battlefield.

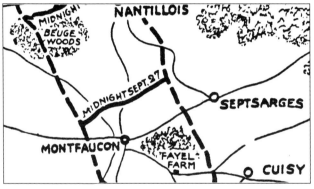

Beuge Wood, an objective of the 313th and 316th Regiments on the afternoon of 17 September 1918.

Shortly after that the front line of the regiment came under fire from their own artillery. A call was made for a volunteer to carry back a message, asking that the fire be stopped before any serious damage was done. First Lieutenant Thomas G Bradlee responded and returned through the artillery fire with the necessary orders. During the attack Colonel Sweezey had moved his regimental P.C. forward to a shell hole at the top of Montfaucon Hill, overlooking the entire country to the north. When the German artillery proceeded to rain high explosives all around it, however, it was considered prudent to withdraw from such an exposed position to the former P.C. near the cemetery on the other side of the hill.

127

The light French tanks, several of which had been the victims of direct hits, failed to keep up with the infantry. During this attack, First Lieutenant Hank Welling, 316th Regiment, was severely wounded in the side. Welling refused to be evacuated but continued to lead his platoon in the attack. Throughout the afternoon and evening he remained with his men, 'inspiring them by his courage and fortitude in spite of intense pain'. The enemy fire grew so severe that Colonel Sweezey, the supporting tanks gone and the men exhausted, ordered a halt and ordered the men to dig in for the night. By now it had become necessary to carry Welling to the rear. After the war he was awarded the DSC.

The doughboys now held a line that ran through the bottom of the valley between Montfaucon and Beuge Wood. The bank of the Nantillois-Cierges railroad offered reasonable cover against fire coming from the edge of the wood. The final position of the 313th Regiment during the night of 27 to 28 September was about a kilometre north of Montfaucon. The 316th Regiment remained to the rear of the 313th, spread out along the roads to Cierges and Nantillois.

Noon, 27 September, right wing, Nantillois:
314th Regiment was leading the attack
315th Regiment was in support

After the capture of Faycl (Tuilerie) Wood and the advance to the Montfaucon-Septsarges Road, the regiments needed time to reorganize. The 314th had been so badly mauled that it had to be bolstered by troops from the 315th. This operation took considerable time; headquarters had to be set up, telephone lines laid, runners sent out to gather information about other regiments' positions and so on. After a few hours' rest, it became apparent that strong resistance was developing north of Montfaucon in the direction of Nantillois. Therefore, after the troops who were still in Fayel Wood had been reorganized, the 314th was placed under the command of Lieutenant Colonel McKenny, who was given orders to support the attack of the 313th on Beuge Wood with an attack on Nantillois on the right flank. The First Battalion of the 315th was called up from the reserves, taking over the line in the 314th left sector. The attack started at 3.30 pm but was short-lived as, according to the 79th Division's History,

'[...]the moment the advance began it was apparent that it was going to meet terrific resistance, particularly from the Boche heavy artillery, which swept the entire area with a decimating fire. Added to this, the men of the 314th and 315th Infantry were in a state bordering on exhaustion. They had received no supplies of

A dugout in Fayel Wood, September 1918.

The HQ of Major General Kuhn from 27 to 30 September, along the Cuisy Montfaucon Road. Pictured is Lieutenant Colonel S Gillis, Divisional Signal Officer.

any sort since the advance had begun on the morning of 26 September and had secured only a few hours' rest since the memorable H hour. They strove frequently to press forward towards the objective, but high explosives, shrapnel and machine-gun bullets were too much for them, unsupported as they were.'

It proved impossible to continue the advance without artillery support. The Americans once again experienced the might of the German artillery; the wall of steel made it impossible to reach the German troops in Nantillois and they were forced to retreat. No further attempts were made that day and the men started to dig in.

In the meantime, General Kuhn had moved his division headquarters from Haucourt to Demon Redoubt, the German trench system near the fork in the Montfaucon-Cuisy Road.

Night 27/28 September:
When evening came it was clear that the advance had been so minimal that there was no prospect of any further attack by the division until the men could secure rest and rations. Therefore, Colonel Oury called a halt to the 314th Regiment's attack and ordered the men to dig in. First Lieutenant Arthur H Joel (F Co, 314th Regiment):

'The advance stopped about dusk, on a hill ahead, the men digging in like excited nugget hunters. Each doughboy carried a trench tool – either a small pick or shovel – for just such emergencies. Lying on the ground the soldier dug a hole big enough for his body and built a rampart around the depression with the dirt. 'Dig in!' was a familiar order in a shell attack.'

The 314th Regiment's bivouac was about 500 metres north of the line Montfaucon-Fayel Wood and the 315th were in a field close to the T-junction leading to Nantillois, the present D15. Fortunately, some rations reached the exhausted men but the wounded especially were suffering from lack of water. By nightfall the troops of the division were in a truly deplorable condition. Most of the men of the 316th were too tired even to be bothered to get up to go and get their rations; they fell asleep where they were, in the middle of the valley between Montfaucon and Nantillois.

During the night the artillery was called upon to fire on Beuge Wood, but once again the 79th Division had been left with practically no artillery support. The guns' advance had been painfully slow and still the guns could not keep up with the pace because of the shell-torn roads and terrain they were picking their way across.

Seemingly endless traffic-jams between Esnes and Malancourt.

Between 10.00 pm and midnight the Germans brought down a heavy barrage on the small plateau north west of Septsarges. This fell in the area occupied by half of the front line of the 315th Regiment and caused them to withdraw to a system of old German trenches, just north of the Septsarges-Montfaucon Road, called Artisan Trench.

In the meantime, while the rain was bucketing down, the 304th Engineers were still trying to keep the road open; anything that could be found was used to fill the holes in the road. It had been partially widened, a job that had to be carried out along the whole stretch of the route. The road, which had originally been a mere farm track, built to take limited numbers of horse-drawn (largely farm) vehicles, was not able to support the traffic of almost half an entire Army. To add to the congestion, every few minutes a vehicle broke down and blocked the way, so they had to be pushed off the road to one side as quickly as possible so that traffic could continue to flow. Such vehicles sometimes ended their days ignominiously as building material for the road. The estimate was that it would take at least another week until the road was finally completed. Even after that it was still in constant need of repairs because of German shelling and heavy use. Lieutenant Colonel DuPuy (311th Machine Gun Regiment) saw that literally everything to hand was used to keep the road serviceable:

'Meanwhile the engineers were frantically working on the road across No Man's Land, where great shell craters were being filled up with any material available; dead horses, motor trucks, automobiles, stones, logs, anything that would make a bed. The only road available became immediately jammed, because when we went into the fight we went in short of horses, and those we had were so completely exhausted that they fell in their tracks. Literally, the country in that section was filled with thousands of carcasses of dead horses.'

The Americans had broken through the original front line, the Hagen/Wiesenschlenken Line and the Etzel Line. Finally, Montfaucon was taken; but the amount of ground gained that day was a meagre two kilometres – impressive in the trench deadlocked years of 1915-1917, not so much in 1918, a year of mobile warfare. The number of men in the division killed and wounded during the first two days of the attack was estimated at about 2,000. The 79th Division was lagging behind once more. First Army's job was to break through the Giselher Line, the last German defences before the infamous Kriemhild Line – reaching the latter, it will be recalled, was the first day objective of the Offensive. To reach the Giselher Line, Nantillois and Beuge Wood needed to be taken first.

The Germans.
Of the third day of the offensive, Ludendorff wrote in his memoir: 'On 27 September, we were reasonably successful, and on the 28th, besides our planned retreat, we kept our lines.'

The Bavarian 5th Reserve Division War Diary noted:

'The previous day, because of sheer determination from our side, the worst was avoided and the enemy partially paralyzed. On the morning of 27 September, however, Reserve Regiment 10, without any support whatsoever, was almost overrun and had to be withdrawn to the Nantillois-Brieulles Road. On the whole front, the enemy resumed the attack. Around noon we lost Montfaucon. *Reserve Regiment 7* was thrown into the fray and came to the aid of the *5th Bavarian Reserve Field Artillery Regiment*; together, they managed to save Nantillois. *Bavarian Reserve Regiment 12* and *Infantry Regiment 147* of the *37th Division* managed to hold the line Nantillois-Moulin de l'Etanche-Brieulles [opposite, from left to right, the American 4th, 80th and 33rd Divisions]. At nightfall, several positions in front of Cierges and Apremont, west of Nantillois, were lost [the American sector in which the 28th, 35th, 91st, 37th and 79th Divisions were positioned].'

The Intelligence Officer of Supreme Headquarters reported on the situation up to 6 pm on the 27th:

'General: As far as can be determined to date, the possibility of an imminent, large scale, Franco-American attack in Lorraine has not been decreased by the Franco-American offensives which opened yesterday in eastern Champagne and between the Argonne and the Meuse; however, it is worth noting that three of the French reserve divisions recently identified as being on that front … are now in the Champagne …

All other indications pointing to the imminence of a full-scale attack in Lorraine remain valid. Intercepted radio communications indicate that strong American reserves are being moved up. The front between Verdun and Lunéville is still occupied by large numbers of fresh, trained, troops.'

In other words, the AEF's deception plan was doing its job in keeping German attention in the St Mihiel – Moselle area and further to the south.

Group of Armies Gallwitz reported:

'During the night and morning the enemy forced the troops of our *Fifth Army*, west of the Maas [Meuse], back to the line: Hill north of Ivoiry – northern edge of Nantillois – Wald von Brieulles [Brieulles Wood] – hill south of Brieulles. South of Vilosnes the bridgehead is being held. Nantillois was recaptured later in the day and held throughout the afternoon against heavy attacks, supported by tanks. [In fact, Nantillois was not captured until the next day...] At noon and during the afternoon hostile attacks against Montfaucon and against the Beuge-Holz [Beuge Wood] were likewise beaten off with heavy enemy losses.'

The Operations Section reported to Group HQ:

'Estimate of the Situation. By his attacks, from morning September 26 to noon, September 27, the enemy has succeeded in pushing back our front between the Argonne and the Meuse for a distance of ten kilometres. A continuation of the exploitation of this success should not be taken for granted. However, should such an attack occur it is not improbable that it will be extended to the east side of the Meuse.

Although the enemy attack between the Meuse and the Argonne was conducted with strong forces (four American divisions confirmed in front of this army to date), as well as conjointly with the attack in the Champagne, this does not necessarily mean, especially in view of the information available, that the enemy is striving for a breakthrough, with a distant strategic objective in this area.

Various indications, [such as] increase in railway traffic and density of billeting, as well as statements of prisoners, seem to point much more to the possibility of an impending major attack east of the Meuse, against the front of *Composite Army C* [ie St Mihiel/Moselle area] and the left wing of the *Fifth Army* [ie Group of Armies German Crown Prince].'

Chapter 6

28 to 30 September: the Aftermath

'We remained in position until almost daylight, when we withdrew and returned to the trenches to the right of the woods at Montfaucon, where we rested for some time that morning until Major Caldwell came up and told us that there was something to eat for us about half a kilometre back. That meant a short respite and that the battalion was placed in support for the morning. The half kilometre vanished toot sweet [tout de suite, immediately], for we had had nothing but hard tack and corn bill for two days, and that had been exhausted the first day out. To say that the meal was appreciated would be putting it mildly, though the quantity was anything but sufficient to satisfy our appetites. That was one time the mess sergeants were given a good word, for they had braved the heavy shelling of the back area to get up and feed us.'

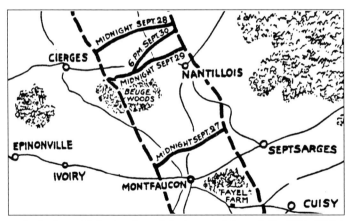

Area of attack on 28 September; this day would mark the 79th Division's furthest line of advance; over the next two days they were forced back by withering, accurate artillery fire.

As the sun rose on 28 September, the American lines ran across the open ground between Montfaucon, Beuge Wood and along the Montfaucon-Septsarges Road. The 313th Regiment's outposts had moved up to the embankment of a railroad that skirted the woods to the south. The 316th Regiment were right behind the 313th, which was positioned at the northern base of Montfaucon, along the road to Cierges, the present-day D104 and the road to Nantillois, the D15. The 314th Regiment had been relieved by the 315th and spent the previous night in an abandoned German trench system, the Artisane Trench, a little north of the modern-day Montfaucon-Septsarges Road. Today, the 315th was to spearhead the attack on Nantillois, with the 314th in support. The *450th Regiment, 117th Division*, held the line Beuge Wood-Nantillois; it was considered a good fighting division. The division had fought at the Lys in April-May 1918 and got roughly handled on the Somme at the opening of Haig's Hundred Days Offensive. The 450th Regiment was transferred to the Division in late August to replace a disbanded regiment in the division, itself coming from a division that had been disbanded after heavy losses. Despite all of this, the division was rated as second class and generally performed quite well in the early, trying days of the Offensive. The *5th Bavarian Reserve Division* was defending Nantillois itself. It also was rated as second class and had enjoyed a relatively quiet 1918. It was moved from Douai, a town in the north of France, east of Arras, on 22 September and detrained at Dun-sur-Meuse on the 23rd.

The 79th Division should have reached Nantillois and Beuge Wood on the first day of the offensive. Now, on the morning of 28 September, they were still two kilometres short of their objective. The determined resistance of the Germans on the second day of the drive showed how vital it was to have clear lines of transport so that food and ammunition could be brought up from the rear to the men at the front, as everything was in short supply. The weather grew worse by the hour; it was raining heavily. The men were wet and miserable, and the roads were still in an almost impassable condition. The ordeal of the artillery in keeping pace with the infantry during those two days almost equalled that of the men in the front line. The terrific fighting and stubborn resistance of the Germans clearly demonstrated that an error had been made in determining the fighting power of the enemy; relatively easy success at St Mihiel, just a fortnight earlier, had proved to be a deceptive indicator of German capability.

Morning, 28 September, the left flank, Beuge Wood:
The 316th was leading the attack
The 313th was in support

Beuge Wood, sited on a hill and crowned with trees, was organized with a defence of machine guns, trench mortars and field guns; 88 mm guns,

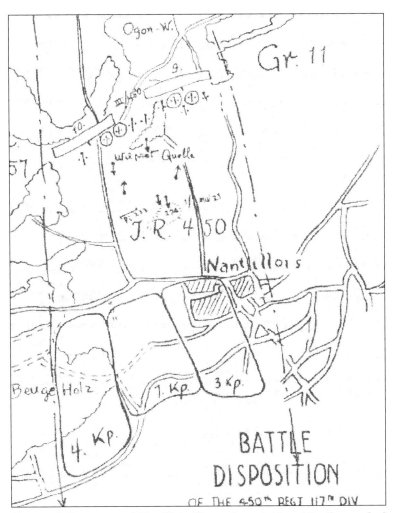

German defences around Nantillois. The centre point lay at the line marked Gr. 11, 11th Grenadiers. This is the Giselher Line, the southern branch of the Kriemhild Line, the German stop line. The 79th Division could not break through it.

positioned on the Meuse Heights, supported the German defenders. The interior of Beuge Wood was defended by using the latest military tactics; numerous short and shallow trenches, some twenty to thirty metres long, supported by machine-gun posts. These thinly manned trenches were spaced about fifty metres apart, running left and right, but also to the rear, thus creating a flexible line of defence. If one trench was under threat of being taken by the enemy, the men could fall back on another. There were

View of Beuge Wood; note the open country to be covered by the Americans. The forested area in the background held the Giselher/Kriemhild positions.

Artillery observers in the ruins of Montfaucon.

three to four of these lines in the wood. The task of the German troops was to stall the American attack as long as possible in order to give the rest of the garrison time to retreat to the Kriemhild Line. Once again, these tactics proved very successful, as it kept the Americans engaged for two hours, buying the Germans time to evacuate as much material as possible.

The 316th Regiment launched their attack in the pouring rain at 7.00 am. They immediately came under heavy artillery fire, for they had to cross an open valley before reaching Beuge Wood. As soon as the advancing lines came within range of the machine guns along the edge of the Wood, a torrent of bullets hit them. The Doughboys immediately went to ground and the attack lines now crept forward. In spite of the terrific fire, some groups of men rushed forward, dropped to the ground and crawled along on their bellies, leaving many dead and wounded behind. By 8.00 am the 145th Regiment of the 37th Division had entered the woods to the left of the 316th. Captain Earl E Glock wrote in his diary:

'At 7.00 am the attack was launched, the troops immediately falling under heavy artillery fire. As soon as the advancing lines came within range of machine-gun fire from the edge of Beuge Wood, a terrific rain of bullets descended on them. The lines dropped. 'First aid, this way, first aid, this way!' German artillery, some of it from beyond the Meuse, dropped a hail of shrapnel and high explosives; machine guns spewed over the ground with a deadly shower. At 8.51 am Major Atwood sent the following message: 'Our troops now entering southern edge of Beuge Wood.' Nine minutes later he was killed. The advance into the woods had cost the 316th Regiment heavily. It had stripped many companies almost completely of their officers and in the ranks had taken a ghastly toll.' [It should be noted that it had taken the doughboys two hours to advance about 200 metres uphill.]

Headstone of Major Atwood, American Cemetery, Romagne, E.21.25.

At 8.30 am regimental headquarters received a message that the American artillery had laid down a barrage on their own troops. Communication with the artillery had broken down, the telephone lines had gone dead; in the meantime, casualties were mounting. At the edge of Beuge Wood, Corporal George D Livelsberger of C Company took command of a platoon that had suffered severe losses, led it around to the flank of an enemy trench and charged the machine gunners nestled inside. These particular guns had been holding up the advance of the entire battalion, by this stage maybe 800 men. The corporal and his men took the position after a brief struggle and cleared the path so that the attack could continue.

With the death of Major Atwood, the command of the 316th Regiment devolved upon Captain Somers, who pressed on with the attack. (It needs to be remembered that an AEF regiment equated in infantry manpower to a then British brigade – ie three battalions, commanded by a brigadier general; that such a junior officer should have command of a regiment is, therefore, a good indicator of the problems that the AEF had in officering their units.) The advance into these woods had cost the 316th Regiment heavily. In the inevitable confusion, many small units had almost become isolated. At 11.00 am Major General Kuhn sent a message that tanks needed to come forward to assist in the attack. However, by the time that message reached the 316th, Beuge Wood had already been captured and the advancing companies were moving out in the open towards their next objective, Hill (Cote) 268. This was easier said than done; as soon as they appeared at top of the ridge where Hill 268 was situated, the Germans opened fire and laid down such a barrage that the doughboys were forced to fall back to Beuge Wood.

28 September, The 37th Division's front:
With the 79th having captured Montfaucon the previous day, the 37th Division could finally launch their attack on Hemont Wood and Beuge Wood. The attack on Beuge Wood was a joint operation between the 37th and 79th Divisions. If these woods could be secured, it would be possible to continue the advance to the village of Cierges and from there open up the road to Romagne and the Kriemhild Line. At 9.00 am, the 37th took Ivoiry. The Germans launched a counterattack, but the village remained firmly in American hands. While the Americans advanced, the Germans repeatedly blasted the whole skirmish line with high explosive and gas shells. By noon the 37th and 79th had managed to secure Beuge Wood at the expense of heavy casualties. The 37th Division managed to take Hemont Wood (*Bois Hémont*), a kilometre to the west of Beuge Wood, without much opposition; but they could not hold onto it because of intense enemy artillery fire. The wood, now saturated with phosgene gas, was evacuated by nightfall.

Morning, 28 September, the right flank, Nantillois:
The 315th was leading the attack
The 314th was in support

The 315th Regiment
At 5.00 am, the German artillery opened fire on the American lines; there would be no let up, this would continue for the whole day. The fury of

the German artillery found no real answer from the American guns. The preliminary barrage was very weak, only coming from four batteries, the only ones that had been able to get to the front through the traffic jam. At 7.30 am, when the American artillery fire grew fainter, the troops moved forward. The First and Third Battalions were in the line, with the Second Battalion in support, following the centre of the attacking battalions. Company E and one platoon of the machine gun company attached to the Second Battalion were detailed as a liaison group on the right flank to keep contact with the 4th Division. The advance of both leading battalions was to be directed against Nantillois, the First Battalion enveloping the town from the west and south, and the Third Battalion attacking directly from the south. As soon as the troops moved across the top of the ridge between Montfaucon and Septsarges, the German artillery opened up. First Lieutenant Arthur H Joel wrote in his diary that,

'Outflanked and unsupported, the regiment was forced [by German shelling] to leave the hill [Trou de Cailloux on present-day maps] and take a new position farther back in order to reorganize and again advance. Shortly after passing the big windmill [in the Trou de Cailloux] to the right of Montfaucon, the fading of darkness announced the arrival of a new day with its fortunes and misfortunes of battle.'

Nantillois

The area of attack of the 315th Regiment; Nantillos is situated in the valley behind the barn.

Fortunately, there was still some artillery available to support the attacks on Beuge Wood and on the village itself. Despite the poor barrage, the 315th made good progress as they were able to advance without facing any sizeable opposition. The leading companies reached the crest of a ridge south of Nantillois, but from that point on experienced terrible raking fire from snipers and machine gunners in Beuge Wood. Along with that, the German heavy artillery laid down a terrific barrage over the entire slope leading down into Nantillois and on the ridge itself and poured a withering fire into the advancing waves from the flanks. Joel noted:

'There was an advance [in the direction of Nantillois] over rolling country with considerable shelling on the hill tops. Finally a position was taken on the reverse slope of the hill west of Nantilois. Enemy one-pounders and seventy-sevens, shooting almost point blank, shrieked directly overhead most of the night. To add to the comforts and pleasures of the situation there was a steady downpour of rain. The night was spent in the muddy shell holes, with only overcoats and raincoats as protection against the elements. The cold drizzle, the shells, the fatigue and hunger of this night and the next seemed to sap the last bit of strength of bodies already overtaxed. So fatigued were the overworked and undernourished bodies, that a man could sleep even in mud and rain. But in the morning one felt far worse than after a night of intoxication. Dead nerves, stiff muscles and rheumatism produce a state of mind dangerous to a soldier, the attitude of caring little what happens to him. The knowledge that two sergeants had disappeared didn't help matters or morale in the least.'

The men pressed forward in short rushes. Corporal Louis A Berkowitz, Company L, advanced recklessly across the open ground to give first aid to a wounded comrade and applied a field dressing, only to be killed by shell fire as he rejoined his squad. Sadly, his body was never found; his name is one of the many inscribed on the Tablets of the Missing in the Meuse-Argonne American Cemetery. Despite all opposition, the advance moved on until at 10.50 am the men of the Third Battalion swarmed into the ruins of Nantillois, capturing a German battery of six 77mm guns on the Nantillois-Brieulles road in the process.

By this time, most of the Germans defending Nantillois had already withdrawn to the north, in the direction of Cunel, where the well-prepared trenches and shelters of the Giselher Line were waiting for them. The news of the capture of Nantillois was taken by runner to Colonel Oury, who at 11.25 am sent the message to General Kuhn that Nantillois was taken and that they were in desperate need of ambulances, stretchers and doctors. Snipers in Nantillois caused the doughboys considerable problems even after the village had been captured. Regimental headquarters were established in the crypt of the ruins of the church.

The German trenches ran along the slope in the foreground; in the centre is the village of Nantillois and behind that are the wooded heights of the Kriemhild Line.

Ruins of Nantillois; the building on the left is the Mairie, the Town Hall.

Wounded men of the 316th in a truck on their way to the field hospital in Cuisy. Note the German prisoners. 28 September 1918.

Nantillois had been taken, but at a heavy cost. By now the front line companies had each lost on average a third of their men, killed or wounded. Support companies mopped up the town and cleared the ruins of snipers. This was accomplished under heavy shelling of high explosives and gas. The rest of the regiment moved through the village and pushed on the advance to Hill 274, which lies just one kilometre north of Nantillois, under a continuous shower of shells. At about 1.00 pm a halt was ordered and the battalions were reorganised. Five hundred metres beyond the crest of Hill 274 rose the grim outline of Ogons Wood, whilst to the north west of this natural bulwark lay Madeleine Farm. These woods and farm had been organized as one of the outlying strong points of the Kriemhild Line, one of the last of the great German defence lines.

Samuel Franklin Bartine Vasey from Lumberville, Pennsylvania, served as a private first class with Company D, 311th Machine Gun Battalion, 79th 'Cross of Lorraine' Division. He participated in the attack on Nantillois and luckily survived the ordeal. After the war, Samuel Vasey took up his old job as a well driller. He died at the age of 94.

Samuel Vasey's 'Welcome Home' pin.

Noon, the left flank, 28 September, Wood 268:
The 316th was leading the attack
The 313th was in support

'Beuge Wood was very dense with underbrush, being almost impenetrable, excepting by several narrow paths, through which the troops pushed. Many short trench lines and machine-gun nests were scattered around the wood, forming a flexible defence line. When one stronghold was given up, the defenders moved to the next. On the northern edge was a great German P.C. covered with heavy steel plates, but there was no time to explore. In spite of unabated artillery fire over the whole front, and in spite of another open approach to wood-crowned "268", the advance continued. At 1.42 pm Captain John McI Somers, commanding the Third Battalion, reported, " We are at 10.2-81.8, on assigned sector, with right on the Nantillois-Cunel road." One platoon under Lieutenant Chambers had even crossed the open land north of Wood 268 and was entrenched in Wood 250, near Madeleine Farm. On the right of Wood 250, just across the Nantillois-Cunel road, lies Ogons Wood. In the afternoon the regiment reorganized in Wood 268, the regimental P.C. being established on the south-eastern tip. The

French tank company which had followed the troops in the attack through Beuge Wood maneuvered west of Nantillois and then retired to Montfaucon. All day the German artillery violently shelled the entire area.

At 1.30 pm the heavy Brownings of the 312th Machine Gun Battalion were advanced sufficiently to open fire, covering the Third Battalion of the 316th advancing up the slope in the direction of Wood 250. Here it engaged in direct machine-gun fire; a German nest to the north was the objective. The retaliatory fire of the *Bavarian 12th Reserve Regiment* inflicted severe casualties. Wounded and dead dropped all around. Private 1st Class William N Brazel, under heavy fire, disassembled a Browning gun which had been jammed by a flying piece of shrapnel, extracted the shrapnel, reassembled the gun and recommenced firing. After the German machine gunners had fled, Private 1st Class Brazel assisted in carrying Privates 1st Class William J Compher and William A Eopolucci to the first aid station, where they died shortly afterwards. Later on, the 312th M.G. Company located a retreating body of German troops about 1,200 metres to the north, causing them to scatter and preventing them from manning a piece of artillery. Later they found the bodies of four Germans and two dead horses on that spot. They also inflicted heavy casualties firing on a company of marching Germans.'

The Regimental History of the 316th

In the middle of the afternoon the 316th was reorganized in Wood 268, about two hundred metres beyond Beuge Wood. With the Germans shelling them constantly, the orders were given to dig in for the night. At dark, Lieutenant Chambers' platoon was forced to abandon Wood 250; the place had become untenable. The men of the 312th Machine Gun Battalion were placed in position as cover in case of counterattack.

The 313th Regiment, in support, moved up through Beuge Wood and, with the 37th Division on the left flank, took up a defensive position on Beuge Wood Ridge. The P.C. was established in the open on a narrow gauge railroad embankment close to the woods and the officers and men lay down in the mud and rain to try to get some much needed rest. At about 11.00 pm the supply company reached Nantillois; rolling kitchens and water carts went up to distribute some much-needed sustenance to the troops in the form of hot coffee and food. Some of the men were too exhausted even to collect their share. The last time anyone had eaten was three days earlier, when they had consumed their reserve rations.

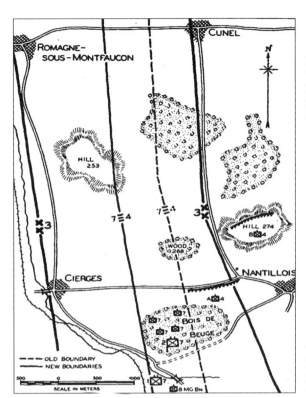

Map of the area. To the north of Wood 268 lies Wood 250; to the north of Hill 274 lies Ogons Wood.

At 11.00 pm, 28 September, rolling kitchens reach Nantillois.

146

Noon, 28 September, the right flank, Hill 274 and Ogons Wood:
The 315th was leading the attack
The 314th was in support

By 4.00 pm, the First and the Third Battalions of the 315th had reformed. Only one battery of supporting artillery remained at the disposal of the regiment and it directed its fire at Ogons Wood and Madeleine Farm until 4.30 pm. Supported by six French tanks, the 315th Regiment launched itself against the woods ahead. The advance had barely begun when a deluge of bullets from machine-gun emplacements hidden in Ogons Wood struck the advancing line. After this died down, German batteries, which were massed in the wood behind Madeleine Farm, opened fire. A few minutes later heavy calibre guns, located on the heights east of the Meuse, joined in and enfiladed the entire southern edge of the wood with a storm of high explosive shells. Two of the tanks were put out of action by direct hits before they had even started. In spite of the storm of shells bursting around them, the Americans went forward and penetrated the southern edge of Ogons Wood. No sooner had they come to the edge of the woods than the German machine guns again let rip with a murderous fire, creating a barrier of flying steel in front of the advancing lines. Sergeant George N Churchill (Medical Department) went from shell hole to shell hole and, in the open and with shells bursting all around him, gave first aid to the wounded and carried several wounded men to the

An over-optimistic note about the taking of Hill 274.

147

safety of shell holes. The combined fire of artillery and machine guns proved too powerful to sustain the attack, so the Americans withdrew to the southern side of the crest of Hill 274. By this time the Second Battalion had arrived on the hill and were awaiting orders.

At 6.00 pm, the tattered remains of the 315th, with the aid of a half-hearted artillery preparation, launched a second attack on Ogons Wood and Madeleine Farm. The diary of an anonymous non-commissioned soldier gives a vivid description of it:

'The Germans seemed to be preparing for a counter attack here. They were pouring a heavy machine-gun fire on us. Major Patterson ordered our company to form a skirmish line and go over after them. We formed our line, first and second platoons in front and the fourth in support. A shell landed just in front of where I was standing, killing Buckwald and wounding two officers. I was thrown about ten feet but fortunately was not injured. Lieutenant Bagans jumped out in front of the company and led us on the run for the woods. How many of us got there is more than I can tell. Bullets pelted around us like hail. We managed to get to the edge of the woods. We had to fight for every inch of ground. We saw some wooden shacks about two hundred yards in the woods, and these we bombed with grenades. We captured several machine-gun nests and took eleven prisoners. We worked our way into the woods and finally captured the shacks. These turned out to be officers' quarters and artillery chart rooms. We got some valuable papers and maps there. We discovered a large building [Madeleine Farm] about 100 yards further in the woods with a Red Cross flag flying over it. At first we thought it was a hospital but we found out later that it was a regular fort. They had a machine gun in every window. Lieutenant Bagans had about decided to investigate it. We would all have been killed. The woods were full of machine guns and snipers and several of our men got hit. We were making good progress when we were ordered out. Word had been received that the Germans were going to set the woods on fire, so we had to give it up. We got out just in time, for the Germans started a terrific bombardment and almost levelled the woods. We got back to the hill [Hill 274] under heavy shell fire and were ordered to dig in.'

Retreating to Hill 274 was the only option that had been left to the doughboys, the German artillery being too strong; the hill quickly became known as Suicide Hill. All night the Germans continued raining shells on

148

Fox holes on the southern slope of Hill 274, Suicide Hill.

View of the area between Hill 274 and Ogons Wood.

Hill 274, which again took their toll of dead and wounded. Sergeant Joseph T Labrum (314th Regiment) recalled:

'The shelling was the worst we had ever been under, Fritzie most of the night keeping us in a box barrage that for its intensity of fire could hardly be equalled. The right and left and our front and rear was a halo of steel from four o'clock in the afternoon until the next morning, but fortunately our position was almost impregnable to artillery fire.'

Thus ended the third day of the ordeal, aiming to force a breach in the Kriemhild Line. The 314th and 315th Regiments spent the night in

The ruins of Nantillois looking north; note the shell-pocked landscape.

Gunfire at night.

Nantillois and on the southern slope of Hill 274; the 316th and the 313th in the edge of Beuge Wood, with a skeleton deployment of men trying to maintain their hold in Wood 268. All night shells rained down on their positions.

The Germans.

The *5th Bavarian Reserve Division* War Diary:

'On both 28 and 29 September the Americans launched several mass attacks at us. *Regiment 147* and the *10th Bavarian Reserve Regiment* successfully offered stubborn resistance. The assistance that we have got from gun batteries situated on the Meuse Heights

150

must not be underestimated. On the other hand, in spite of forcing the enemy several times to a bloody retreat, in the end we were forced to give up Beuge Wood and Nantillois and retreated to Wood 250 and Ogons Wood. The area under the command of the *5th Bavarian Reserve Division* runs from Brieulles on the bank of the River Meuse to Wood 250, somewhere between Nantillois and Cunel. The situation remained the same until 4 October.'

The War Diary for *Group of Armies Gallwitz* noted on the evening of 28 September:

'On 28 September the enemy continued his attacks west of the Maas [Meuse]. They were directed against the sector from Cierges to Brieulles-Wald [Brieulles Wood]. While the attack at Beuge-Holz [Beuge Wood] and east thereof was repulsed, the enemy gained ground at Cierges and outflanked Beuge Wood. Under this pressure the *117th Infantry Division* withdrew to the south edge of Ogon-Wald [Ogons Wood]. The *Bav. 5th Res. Div.* and the left flank of the *7th Res. Div.* were withdrawn east as far as the southern edge of Brieulles Wood. At 9.30 am the *115th Inf. Div.* counterattacked with two regiments from Romagne southward. Towards noon the western half of the Cierges-Nantillois Road was reached. About midday further fighting developed in the wooded terrain west of the Cunel-Nantillois Road near Ogons Wood, and as far as Etanche-Mühle [Etanche Mill]. The enemy here threw strong forces against our lines, employing tanks. Initially, all attacks were repulsed. Later, the enemy succeeded in pushing forward to the northern edge of Ogons Wood. Our counterattack at that point was met by the enemy advancing in force, accompanied by tanks, and we were, therefore, unable to gain ground. In the late afternoon *Fifth Army*, west of the Meuse, was on the line Franzen-Hof [La Grange au Bois] – north portion of the east edge of Cierges – east slope of Hill 253 – south edge of Wald von Cunel [Cunel Wood] – south edge of Fays-Wald [Fays Wood] – north edge of Brieulles Wood.'

29 September, Ogons Wood, Wood 250 and relief by the 3rd Division:
Over the next two days the Americans made virtually no progress. Their positions remained the same, in spite of attack after attack being launched at the Germans defending the Giselher Line. It was not the numbers of Germans who were occupying these positions that was the problem; the major obstacle was the open terrain that had to be crossed. Every time

the Americans started an attack, they were relentlessly punished by the German artillery. To add to the American woes, by now the whole of the 79th Division was completely exhausted, almost dead on their feet. Time and again they leapt forward, only to end back at the point from where they had started. Lieutenant Colonel DuPuy:

'We received an order from our Division Headquarters to push on at all costs. The men were so exhausted that they did not seem to have strength even to cry out but went forward with jaws drooping and eyes listless.'

On the evening of 29 September, word had spread that the 79th was going to be relieved by the 3rd Division. First Lieutenant Joel (314th Regiment):

'Another seemingly endless night of rain and shrieking shells, spent in the unheated rooms of Hotel de Shell Hole failed to improve the condition of dazed nerves and almost senseless bodies. But the star of luck was at last due to glimmer with at least a faint sparkle. With daylight came rumors of relief. These were quickly confirmed by actual orders to prepare to be relieved by the Third Division. Hobos could hardly look more rough than the columns of soldiers trailing over the ruins of Montfaucon on the evening of 30 September. With seven day beards, clothing ripped and shredded by barbed wire and a thick coating of Argonne mud cemented to the hide with perspiration, the men hardly looked human. Everyone was famished and hollow-eyed, most of them suffering from bad colds and related ills. Swollen feet and stiffened muscles were the common lot of all. Guns and bayonets were covered with thick layers of rust. Even the ordinarily well-dressed officers were hardly presentable to a self-respecting hobo.'

But even after their retreat the ordeal was not yet over, as Lieutenant Colonel DuPuy (311th Machine Gun Regiment) wrote after the war:

'At 11.30 am on the morning of October first, the Third Division came in, fresh, to relieve a handful of men, their faces drawn, their eyes sunken with a dead look, and almost all affected more or less from shell shock, and so weak were some that they died of exhaustion on the trip to the rear. Others were so used up that they could not carry their ammunition belts and rifles, being just able to stagger along at a pace of not more than a mile and half an hour. When they finally came out of the fight, with more than one-third

The first rations reach Malancourt, 28 September 1918.

Tearing down a wall of a ruined building to rebuild the road in Nantillois, 29 September 1918.

of their horses and mules killed, dragging their mule-carts by hand, they looked more like a defeated force than a victorious one. They were so exhausted that I had to halt them about three kilometres behind the line and give them a few hours' rest. Here fate continued to follow us, for from 11.00 pm until 7.00 am the next morning we were shelled continuously by large calibre guns, increasing our casualties among men, horses and mules.'

153

The Germans.

The *5th Bavarian Reserve Division* War Diary:

'At the moment, the fighting has ceased. Cierges and Gesnes are still in our hands. For several days [after 30 September], there is not much activity on the front and we use that time to relieve and strengthen our regiments.'

30 September, the Meuse-Argonne Offensive grinds to a halt:

The whole American offensive had ground to a halt by this stage of the battle. Divisions like the 79th were completely spent and needed to be relieved. In fact, all of the original assaulting AEF divisions needed to be reorganized, relieved and resupplied. A very significant problem within First Army, added to the numerous others – supplies, organisation and the shortage of qualified officers, was the number of so-called 'stragglers'; soldiers that for whatever reason lost contact with their own unit, were intermixed with other divisions or were just loitering around an unknown somewhere. During the first days of the offensive, as many as twenty per cent of a unit's personnel were AWOL, absent without leave, contributing significantly to the chaos in the units. However, most soldiers eventually returned to their own units within a couple of days and continued to fight. Whilst some may well have been disinclined to be in the front line, it would be an error to ascribe this motive to all or even the majority of these 'shirkers'. Largely inexperienced soldiers, inadequately trained, with a shortage of NCOs and officers, lack of knowledge of the ground, confusion caused by the enemy, broken country – all these conditions provide ample reasons why a man might get detached from his unit.

The German opposition in the Giselher Line was so formidable that the sector at Nantillois was divided in two. The 3rd Division was tasked with taking Wood 250 (often on maps described as Hill 250) and the 80th Division with taking Ogons Wood. However, these positions remained firmly in German hands until 6 October, when they were finally taken by the 3rd and 80th Divisions at the cost of huge losses. The main German defences on the Kriemhild Line were only two to three kilometres away from Nantillois; but in some sectors it took more than two weeks of dogged fighting finally to reach that line.

Charles Richard Clubb from Baltimore, Maryland, served as a sergeant with Company E, 313th Infantry Regiment

On 30 September, Charles Clubb was killed in action, presumably near Ogons Wood, north-east of Nantillois. He died at the age of 24. The

154

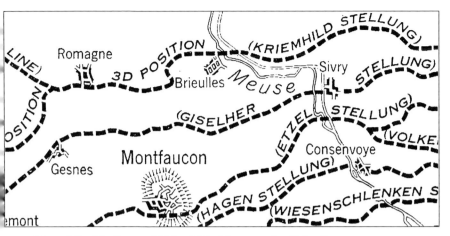

Map of the Giselher and Kriemhilde Lines, north of Montfaucon.

body of Charles Clubb was never recovered; his name is listed on the Tablets of the Missing at the Meuse-Argonne American Cemetery. These tablets hold the names of 954 men whose bodies have not been recovered or identified. Rosettes mark the names of four men that have been recovered and identified after their 1930 inscription on the tablets.

The German perspective of the battle: conclusion.

On 30 September, *Group of Armies Gallwitz*'s Operations Section reported:

Charles Clubb, missing in action, 30 September 1918.

'It has been definitely ascertained that the enemy has moved considerable forces, including the best American front line divisions, from opposite *Composite Army C* [roughly the St Mihiel sector] to the attack front on the Meuse. To exploit this situation, forces of *Composite Army C* will be shifted to the *Fifth Army*. As soon as possible after the arrival of these forces, *Fifth Army* will attack the American forces that have advanced west of the Meuse and

155

The death certificate of Charles Clubb that was sent to his wife.

will throw them back. The attack will be prepared immediately …
'

The *Group*'s summary for 30 September:

Following the heavy and indecisive fighting of 29 September, at
the termination of which Gesnes remained in our hands, the night
of September 29/30 passed without special combat activity in the
Fifth Army and *Composite Army C*, except for feeble harassing
fire by enemy artillery into the rear area. The day was generally
quiet. …'

Naturally enough, the victors and the vanquished had very different
experiences in the Meuse-Argonne Offensive. Whereas for the Americans
the offensive came to be known as 'America's deadliest battle' and served
an important role in the international coming of age of the USA, to the
Germans the Meuse-Argonne Offensive appears to have been not much
more than a footnote in history. The breaking of the Hindenburg Line on
the Somme and the surrender of their allies, Bulgaria, which both
occurred in late September 1918, were of much more significance to the
German High Command than developments in the Argonne (disturbing
as they were) as they completely undermined German morale. Because

156

of these events, Kaiser Wilhelm II was pressured by the military into accepting governmental reform. The Somme and Bulgaria were the important game changers and speeded up the negotiations that would ultimately lead to the Armistice.

The German defences proved that the combination of good observation and well-positioned gun batteries could hold up and destroy a much larger enemy force. During the first two days of the offensive the Germans had been outnumbered at least five to one but the Americans did not manage to achieve the much desired breakthrough at Montfaucon on the first day. How significant this setback was to their success and the duration of the offensive has also been the subject of considerable discussion. During 1 October the Germans actually improved their positions, 'regaining Ogons Wood and the small woods west thereof. Continuing to advance, we also reoccupied Hill 266, south of Ogons Wood. An enemy attack against this hill was repulsed.'

To the Germans the loss of Montfaucon was painful, but there were still many other significant heights in their possession; in any case, once the lines forward of Montfaucon had been lost, its value to them diminished considerably. Its place as the 'eyes' of the artillery could be

A rifle grenade: now in perfect symbiosis with a tree, Ogons Wood.

German prisoners being marched off to the rear, Malancourt, 28 September 1918.

adequately taken (as was shown again and again over the coming weeks) by observers on the Meuse Heights and on the high ground to the north of the Argonne Forest. On the other hand, Montfaucon acted as a symbol of the loss of the defensive lines before the main, 'Hindenburg', defence system.

The liberation of Montfaucon, fought on 26 and 27 September 1918, came at a high price: on 26 September, the 79th Division alone lost over a thousand casualties. The liberation of Nantillois was almost equally as costly: 950 casualties. The estimated German losses are about the same, although an unknown number of prisoners must be added.

Tours

Car Tour 1

Introductory Car Tour
Duration: three to four hours, allowing for stops.
Distance: sixty kilometres **OR** 115 kilometres if you start from Verdun.

Please note: the tour (and others) are designed for cars or smaller means of transport. Should you be considering a bigger vehicle, certainly anything larger than a small minibus, it would be advisable to make an initial tour of any route before you commit to it. Many of the roads in the area, whilst having excellent surfaces, are narrow and have numerous bends and blind spots, as well as running through extensive woodlands.

This tour starts at the American 316th Regiment Monument in Sivry-sur-Meuse (N49°19.725' E005°18.576') and ends at the American Monument in Montfaucon. Ideally, if you start in the morning, you can combine the car tour with one of the walks. From Verdun the easiest way to reach the starting point of the tour is to take the D964, which brings you through the villages of Belleville, Charny, Samogneux, Brabant and Consenvoye to Sivry. Do not forget to bring a pair of binoculars and a bottle of water.

The route is covered by the map 'Sites de la Guerre 1914-1918 en Meuse' and IGN map 3112 Ouest, Montfaucon. For the centenary of the Great War, IGN produced some special overprinted maps at 1:75 000 for a number of especially significant areas during the war, with useful (generally accurate) additions, as well as indicating some of the memorials and many of the war cemeteries. The one entitled *Bataille de Verdun* includes the whole of the area covered in this book (indeed much of the area of the Meuse-Argonne Offensive). These maps can usually be purchased at several locations, such as Fort Douaumont, Museum Memorial de Verdun in Fleury, Douamont Ossuary and the Leclerc Supermarket in Verdun, amongst other places. At the time of writing, there are cafe and/or toilet facilities in Montfaucon, Nantillois, Consenvoye, Varennes; the Meuse-Argonne American Cemetery Visitors Centre in Romagne-sous-Montfaucon has a rest room and a well presented exhibition on the battle. There are petrol stations in Consenvoye, Varennes and Dun-sur-Meuse. There are supermarkets in the latter two and a couple of bakeries in Varennes.

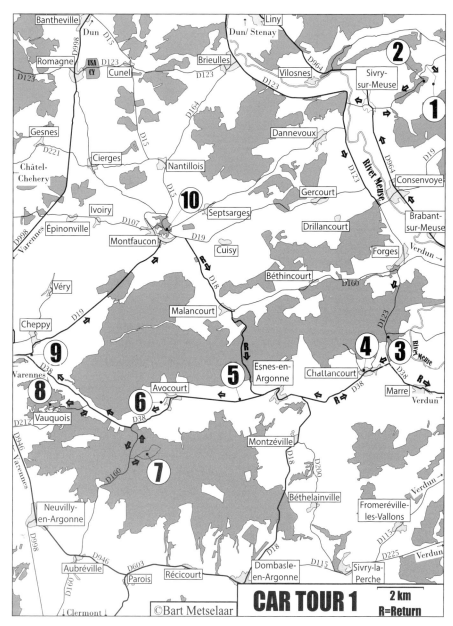

NOTE 1: In spring and autumn it can be extremely foggy in this area; as there are many panoramic views to be seen on this tour it requires clear weather if its full benefit is to be enjoyed.

160

NOTE 2: **Stop 7** can only be reached on foot and is quite a steep walk; but the extra effort is well worth your while.

GPS coordinates for Car Tour 1

(1) 316th Infantry Regiment Monument   (N49°19.725' E005°18.576')
(2) American dugout   (N49°19.779' E005°18.196')
(3) Cumières, destroyed village   (N49°13.903' E005°16.826')
(4) Chattancourt, Tranchée de Verdun   (N49°13.065' E005°15.974')
Open 15 April to 30 September, 2.00 pm-6.00 pm.
(5) Esnes-en-Argonne National Cemetery (N49°12.416' E005°11.489')
(6) Avocourt National Cemetery   (N49°12.404' E005°08.276')
(7) Hesse Wood, Hermont Observation
     Post   (N49°11.214' E005°07.683')
(8) Vauquois Hill   (N49°12.245' E005°04.048')
Open all year round. Guided tours: first Sunday of the month, 9.00 am-11.00 am.
(9) Missouri Monument   (N49°13.497' E005°03.363')
(10) Montfaucon American Monument   (N49°16.332' E005°08.514')

This tour is specifically designed to give a better understanding of the lie of the land and of the position of Montfaucon in relation to the surrounding country as well as leading visitors to vantage points from where they can assess the significance of the hill and its place in the German defences. Several sites of the 1918 front line are included in the tour, but there are also a few famous 1916 Battle of Verdun sites; in many places the front lines of 1916 and 1918 were roughly the same. The panoramic views from the allied side offer a spectacular view of Montfaucon, proving its dominance as an area observation position.

An appreciation of ground is an essential military skill; it is – or should be – as important to a military historian who aims to write a critical assessment of the Offensive or any part of it (which applies, of course, to all such engagements). Equipped with masses of documentation (preferably from both sides), copies of orders and assessments, personal accounts, unit and formation histories and good quality mapping – and yet. Unless such criticism is based on an excellent understanding of the ground in all its aspects – topography, infrastructure and so forth – it will be flawed. It also has to take into account the numerous imponderables – the state of readiness of the troops, their experience, the condition of the formations, communications, the ever present 'fog of war'. There can be no objection to harsh critiques of individuals (usually those in command) or of individual formations; but these deserve little respect unless the foundations of that criticism is based on the reality of the battlefield and of the state of those who were involved.

This tour aims to illustrate one of these issues, the topography – but even then it can only give a broad brush idea of what faced the men of the 79th Division and their German opponents.

Sivry-sur-Meuse, 316th Infantry Regiment, 79th Division Monument (1). (N49°19.725' E005°18.576')
Start this tour by leaving Verdun on the D964, the main road to Stenay, or in Sivry. At Sivry-sur-Meuse, a somewhat faded white sign, *Monument Américain*, indicates a right turn at a point where the main road makes a 90° bend to the left. Follow the road to the right for about four kilometres. The monument is situated at a height of 369 metres on a hill in the hamlet of *Sillon-Fontaine*. Almost at the top of the hill, there is a sign pointing

The 316th Regiment's Memorial at Sivry.

View from the 316th's Memorial towards Montfacucon.

to the right that reads: 'To La Grande Montagne and the monument of the 316th Infantry AEF'. You should already see the pine trees that line the lengthy approach path leading up to the monument. Coincidentally, this hill was also liberated by the 79th Division; but that action has nothing to do with Montfaucon. It was freed of Germans between 3-7 November, during the Third Phase of the Meuse-Argonne Offensive.

NB! *Note that the approach road from the D964, whilst perfectly adequate, is narrow, can be surprisingly busy and should be driven with considerable caution; the approach from this 'C' road towards the monument is over a rough, but serviceable, track.*

Once at the monument, there is a clear, indeed magnificent, view over the Meuse Valley; Montfaucon (both the memorial column and the very handy red and white television mast to its east) is clearly visible in the distance. Before the Americans wrested this hill from the Germans it was an important artillery observation position. In fact, it was part of a whole range of artillery positions that were built on the Meuse Heights, of which the *Grande Montagne* formed just a small part. From these heights, especially as the American line pressed northwards, the Americans would have been increasingly hit in enfilade. Intense and terribly accurate gun fire, directed by observation posts on Montfaucon and here, made it extremely hard for the men of the 79th Division (and of course many other divisions) to reach their objectives. Most of the gun batteries were in action during the better part of the American attack and were responsible for a significant proportion of the American casualties.

Most of the German gun batteries remained in action during the greater part of the American attack; the right bank of the River Meuse did not come under any significant attack during the first weeks of the offensive (it has to be said much to the surprise of the Germans) and the guns positioned there were mainly responsible for harrying the whole American offensive and for a significant proportion of casualties. It is notable that the hill – and therefore all the advantages that it offered – remained in German hands until the last week of the war.

The monument, erected in 1928, commemorates the casualties of the 316th Regiment of the 79th Division during the course of its operations in 1918, seventy-eight officers and 3,128 soldiers. With Captain Carl E Glock, a former member of the 316th Regiment, from Pittsburgh as the driving force behind the project, Marcel Delangle was hired to be the architect of this privately funded monument. At the time of its construction the monument was a source of controversy. According to an American law *no memorials should be erected to any unit of the American Army in France of lesser size than a division.* General Pershing became the American Government's 'Supreme Coordinator' for American Battle Monuments abroad; he urged the French Government to destroy the monument. Fortunately, the French Prime Minister, André Tardieu, refused this request, coming up with a fistful of admirable bureaucratic reasons, the ace card being that it was erected on private property. Indeed, he was only surpassed in wiliness by the Regimental Association. He offered to amend the memorial by adding a bilingual memorial plaque, to be inscribed, 'In memory of the high achievements of the American troops that fought in this region during the World War'. This was reluctantly accepted by Pershing, but in the end the plaque was never added to the memorial; over time the controversy died away, the memorial remained and for that the modern battlefield visitor must be truly thankful. It has remained a fine (and, pleasingly, recently restored) regimental memorial.

NB! Before you leave, take careful note of the line of conifers and the shape and location of the memorial: it is a very useful marker point, visible from many places on the west side of the Meuse.

Drive back in the direction of Sivry-sur-Meuse and stop at an **American dugout (2)**. (N49°19.779' E005°18.196') Of course, check if it is safe to stop on this narrow road, which sometimes can be surprisingly busy. The dugout is situated on the left side on the road and is constructed of recovered German curved sheet metal, often called elephant steel or iron. During and after the fighting in November, the Americans built numerous shelters into the side of Hill 378, 'Corn Willy Hill' as they called it; many

Dugout at the side of the road.

'dugout' holes remain along the side of the road and on the hill but whose sheet metal roofs are long gone, having been used by farmers in the area. They are silent witnesses, testimony to the fighting that took place that autumn of 1918.

Return to Sivry and rejoin the D964 in the direction of Dun-sur-Meuse. After some 200 metres, the Church of Sivry-sur-Meuse is situated on the right side of the road; just opposite the church turn left into the Rue du Moulin. At the end of this street there is a campsite (Le Brouzel); turn left here and cross the bridge over the Canal de l'Est and a second bridge over the River Meuse. Once at the T-junction, take a left turn. This is the D123 and takes you, via Forges, to our next stop. Once you leave Forges (obliterated during the war), you are entering the battlefield of 1916; as you drive through the forest, traces of shell craters and trenches are visible all around. At the southern end of the battlefield you will see the site of the destroyed village of **Cumières. (3)** (N49°13.903' E005°16.826') This village was completely destroyed during the Battle of Verdun. The heights of Le Mort Homme or Dead Man's Hill are located within the French commune of Cumières-le-Mort-Homme, about ten kilometres northwest of Verdun, and earned tragic notoriety for being the scene of bitter fighting. It is one of the famous 'nine destroyed villages of Verdun', although in fact there are several more villages that have never been rebuilt in this area. Cumières had the misfortune of being situated on the spur of Mort Homme. The hill has two summits which are named after their height in metres: the northern crest is Cote 265 and the southern one is Cote 295. Mort Homme overlooks the villages of Béthincourt to the

Trenches in the area of Cumières in 1918.

northwest, Crow Wood and Cumières to the east and Chattancourt and Esnes-en-Argonne to the south. It was a great vantage point – stripped of trees, the field of view from the hill in all directions was remarkable.

In late February 1916, following German attacks on the right bank of the River Meuse during the Battle of Verdun, the French established artillery batteries on the hills on the left bank with a commanding view of the German-occupied right bank. These batteries wreaked such havoc that the Germans, belatedly, also decided to attack southwards, along the left bank of the Meuse. The key

One of the plaques on the war memorial in Cumières.

objectives were Cote (Hill) 304 and Mort Homme. Over the next few months the Germans launched repeated attacks, destroying the French lines, rushing their positions and ejecting the French from their wrecked trenches. French artillery would then batter the Germans and counterattacks would drive them out again, the French infantry re-occupying the shell holes where once the trench systems had been.

Despite the terrible cost, the Germans were able to advance slowly, first capturing a neighbouring hill, Cote 304, which dominated the approach to Dead Man's Hill. On 16 March, the Germans finally managed to take the summit and on 24 May, they took the second summit, Cote 295. The taking of both hills did not mean that the fighting in this area ceased; the French desperately tried to remove the Germans from these key positions and continued to launch attacks on the Germans until well into December. They succeeded in partly pushing the Germans out of their trenches; but a second battle was needed in August and September 1917 to finish the job and to drive the German troops off the summits completely. By that time, the whole area, including Cumières, had virtually ceased to exist. The village had been so utterly destroyed and the soil so heavily poisoned by gas that after the war the rebuilding of the village was deemed impossible.

Continue to Chattancourt along the D123 until you arrive at the crossroads; turn right onto the D38 in the direction of Esnes. Once you have entered Chattancourt follow the main road and turn right where the road forks. At the fork, there is a small signpost that directs you to the **Tranchée de Verdun (4)** (N49°13.065' E005°15.974'), the entrance to which is fifty metres further along the road on your right. The 100 metres long trench system is a private initiative and has been rebuilt by local French World War One enthusiasts; there is a small visitors' centre. Should they wish, visitors can walk through the trenches and see the dugouts. However, you enter at your own risk; the ground can be slippery, particularly after rain. Groups are welcome.

One of the reconstructed dugouts in Chattancourt.

Open from 15 April to 30 September from 14.00-18.00. entrance fee: Adults 4 euro, children 2 euro. For more information: http://www. tranchee-verdun.com/index.php/fr/

Return to your car and continue along the D38 in the direction of Esnes. Pass through the village and once at the T-junction follow the sign **Esnes-en-Argonne National Cemetery (5)** (N49°12.416' E005°11.489'). Park on the right side of the road and take a look at the panoramic photograph to get a better understanding of the lie of the land. The Americans at the beginning of the offensive started their approach to the front line and No Man's Land from the D38, the road on which your car is parked.

Enter the cemetery. During the war, there were no trees left standing to the north and as a result there was a clear view of Montfaucon in the distance behind the cemetery. The 316th Regiment Monument in Sivry is hidden behind the trees on the far right; but it is possible to see the top of the tower of the Ossuary at Douamont off to the east south east.

The cemetery is the final resting place of 6,661 soldiers who were killed between 1914 and 1918; many of them were fatalities in this area in 1916 during the Battle of Verdun. By the time the fierce fighting in 1916 had ended, the whole area around you and, indeed, as far as you can see, had become a barren wasteland. During the advance of the 79th Division this was a front-line cemetery attached to a regimental aid post that operated from the cellars of Château d'Esnes. The cemetery was enlarged between 1920 and 1930 in order to accommodate the bodies of those soldiers who were exhumed from temporary cemeteries and isolated field graves. At the back of the cemetery 3,000 bodies are buried in two mass graves. During the advance of the 79th Division, whatever remained of the woods behind the cemetery was completely destroyed.

Go back to your car and continue along the D38 in the direction of Avocourt. The divisional boundary between the 37th and 79th Divisions was approximately 800 metres before entering Avocourt. During the

168

Hermont Hill   Butte de Vauquois

Left: Hermont Hill, a French observation area. The Butte de Vauquois is on the right.

course of the war this village was entirely destroyed by shelling but remained in French hands. On the morning of 26 September 1918, the 37th Division climbed over the French occupied piles of rubble that had been there since the fighting in 1916 to find their way to the German frontline.

Once you have entered the village, turn right and follow the somewhat weather-stained signs to **Avocourt National Cemetery (6)** (N49°12.404' E005°08.276') As you stand facing the cemetery, look at the panoramic photograph over the page. As for the cemetery near Esnes, there were no trees here by 1918 and Montfaucon was in plain view.

The cemetery was started in 1916, but was extended in 1921, 1925, 1930 and 1934. This was largely due to the fact that the bodies exhumed from temporary French cemeteries in Jubécourt and Récicourt were reinterred in Avocourt. Many of the bodies in the Avocourt sector found during the inter war years are buried here. In 1954, forty-nine bodies from a Second World War military plot in Esnes-en-Argonne Communal Cemetery were reinterred in this cemetery. These men were French colonial troops, nicknamed the *Marsouins* (porpoises), who had defended Cote 304 in May 1940. In total, 1896 soldiers are now buried here; in 1963 the cemetery was renovated to its present state.

169

Turn your car and drive back to the main street in Avocourt – this was one of the road junctions that became effectively completely jammed over the first day or two of the Offensive. Turn right at the T-junction on to the D160 and head back to the D38; continue in the direction of Varennes. After three kilometres you reach another T-junction; take the D160, one of the crucial life lines of the AEF, to Aubréville and follow this for about 1,200 metres.

The memorial at Avocourt French Cemetery.

To understand the battle (indeed, any major battle) it is vital to consider the whole business of logistics – that is the supply and maintenance of an army in the field. During any major activity at the front, road and rail track systems ranked in importance with every other aspect. Now consider the road along which you have been travelling: during the war it would have been narrower, without a tarmac surface, without drainage and designed for, generally, nothing much heavier than farm carts. Every army worried about their supply roads. The AEF, despite herculean efforts by its engineers, faced more problems than most – problems that persisted for weeks after the offensive began.

The next stop is at the second forest track on the left. Make sure when you park your vehicle that you are not blocking the track, which leads to (the French) **Hermont Observation Post (7)** (N49°11.214' E005°07.683'). NOTE: This walk is about one kilometre along this track. Note: it is quite steep in some places; so anybody who intends to do this walk needs to be physically fit.

You are now standing at the French Army's version of Montfaucon;

Montfaucon Hill and the Memorial

View from Hermont Hill towards Montfaucon; No Man's Land lies in between.

One of the eight French observation posts.

the concrete observation posts are built on the ridge on your right. One look across the battlefield in the direction of Montfaucon makes everything immediately clear. Although thirty metres lower than Montfaucon, Hermont Observation Post was built directly opposite the German observation posts at Montfaucon. The French constructed seven concrete observation posts here, all connected to tunnels, underground shelters and a telephone exchange. The men had exactly the same task as their German counterparts at Montfaucon: observing enemy movements and relaying information back to headquarters and gun batteries. With the aid of light signals the French could reach any signal post between the right bank of the Meuse and the Argonne Forest. On 26 September, this was roughly the start line of the American 90th Division. By that time the installations on Hermont Hill were being used by American observers from the Signal Corps. The forest was a hive of activity, the American occupation beginning roughly a week before the offensive started and continuing right up to the Armistice.

For the real enthusiasts, what follows are the coordinates of the **observation posts**: (N49°11.256' E005°07.987') The easiest way to reach the bunkers is to follow the muddy track uphill on your right. Once at the top, follow the fence that starts on your left; this will lead you directly to the bunkers. NOTE: Keep away from any unexploded ordnance!

Return to your car and drive back to the T-junction; turn left onto the D38 in the direction of Varennes. After about two kilometres, turn left onto the D212 in the direction of Vauquois. Pass the church and turn right at the junction; proceed to the parking area at the foot of the **Butte de Vauquois,** or **Vauquois Hill (8)** (N49°12.245' E005°04.048'). What follows is a short history of this impressive site.

One of the most poignant reminders of underground warfare anywhere on the Western Front can be seen at the Butte, a pronounced hill in the foothills of the Argonne Forest. The French abandoned it on 24 September 1914 and the Germans soon realised that it would make an ideal observation post. Aware of their mistake, the French launched attack after attack on the Butte until, finally, in March 1915 they managed to take its southern slope; the Germans still firmly held the northern slope. From this moment on both sides commenced construction of what became a maze of underground tunnels in order to blow the opposition off the hill. In the course of three and a half years the Germans and French detonated over 500 charges on this one hill alone; they dug seventeen kilometres of tunnels, extending over three levels, which incorporated fighting tunnels, hospitals, shelters, workshops, kitchens and battle stations. This situation continued throughout the war until, on 26 September 1918, Vauquois Hill, or what was left of it, was liberated by the American 35th Division.

Vauquois was taken surprisingly quickly by the Doughboys, even though the hill was defended by the elite *1st Guard Division*. On 26 September it took the 35th Division just forty-five minutes to surround the hill and flush out the enemy. The 35th succeeded in doing what the

View from the Butte de Vauquois to Montfaucon.

French had been trying in vain to do for over three years; though it should be noted that the garrison had been reduced to no more than about forty men. However, at many places on the hill the fighting was fierce as the Germans fought to the bitter end. It has been estimated that during the course of the Great War 15,000 men were killed on the Butte alone.

A German trench mortar at Vauquois.

The site is open to the public all year round and is free of charge. However, every first Sunday of the month there is a guided tour of the tunnels on Vauquois Hill, starting at 9.30 am and takes about ninety minutes. The walk through the tunnels of this underground world is a trip into the past. If you are thinking of doing this tour you need to wear sturdy boots, a warm coat and you also need to be in good physical condition. On site there is also a fascinating exhibition of the objects that were found in the tunnels during restoration work. *Guided Tours Fee: Currently, adults 5 euro, children 3 euro. Excellent value.*

However, there is a well presented **self-guided Vauquois walk,** which takes approximately an hour to complete.

173

Walk uphill via the footpath on the right. **NB!** This is a very steep climb. You are now on the French side of Vauquois Hill. Once you are at the top, you are confronted by the sight of huge craters, the remains of the savage mine warfare that once raged here. As you walk towards the *French memorial*, there is an information panel that features a photograph which shows you what the Butte de Vauquois looked like before the war. The hill was originally fourteen metres higher at the summit and on and immediately around which the village was situated.

Follow the path that runs between the craters. You are now crossing the front line and entering the German side. Turn left in the direction of the German trenches that are visible in the distance. Follow the path that runs alongside the craters and stop at the *information table.* You can see Montfaucon looming in the distance, dominating the surroundings and underlining its importance as an observation post; you have now completed a semi-circle tour south of Montfaucon. The views here at the Butte de Vauquois and at various other sites that have been visited make it clear that neither army could lightly afford to lose the prominent observation posts in their possession, as they provided spectacular views of each other's territory: if the integrity of the line was to be maintained in this sector, such observation posts were crucial.

Continue along the path until you come to the partly restored *German trenches*; you can walk through the trenches but you do so at your own risk. When entering structures be sure that you do not bang your head. Do not enter the tunnels! Alternatively, you can follow the path that runs alongside and above them. When you reach the end of the trench, you can choose either to follow the path down along the lip of the crater, or the path that runs through the forest; they both end at the car park.

Return to your car and leave the Butte de Vauqois. Go over the speed bumps, continue to the junction and turn left. Follow the D212 back to the D38 and turn left here in the direction of Varennes/Cheppy. When you reach the junction of the D38 and the D19, turn right onto the D19,

A panoramic view from the top of the American monument, Montfaucon.

The 316th Regiment's Memorial

View from Montfaucon to the 316th Regiment's Memorial at Sivry.

direction Cheppy-Montfaucon. After about fifty metres you will come to a car park with picnic benches on the left hand side of the road (N49°13.492' E005°03.252'). It is safer to park your car here and walk to the **Missouri Monument (9)** (N49°13.496' E005°03.364'); alternatively, if in a car, you can park in front of the monument.

This monument, a stone base with a bronze statue of a woman looking towards the sky grasping a victory wreath of laurel in her raised right hand while holding an olive branch in her other hand, was erected in 1922 by the State of Missouri (although the 35th Division was unofficially known as the Kansas-Missouri Division, originally mobilised with some

lfe de ancourt   Cuisy Wood   Hermont Hill   **Butte de Vauquois**

9,000 National Guard from Kansas and 14,000 from Missouri). At this place the division stormed a strong German section of the northern branch of the Hagen Line. It is a fitting location in that Captain Alexander Skinker, a Missourian, was awarded the Medal of Honor for his actions during the fighting near this spot in the autumn of 1918. On the afternoon of 26 September his company was held up by intense fire from machine guns. While personally leading a team equipped with the French Chauchat automatic rifle/light machine gun (both the divisional and regimental histories note that their composite units were yet to be issued with the far more effective Browning Automatic Rifle [BAR]) in an attack on a machine-gun post, Captain Skinker saw that the ammunition carrier had been killed, whereupon he grabbed the ammunition himself

Captain Alexander Skinker Medal of Honor.

and kept feeding the Chauchat until he also was killed. With utter disregard for personal safety, he had sacrificed his life to save the men of his company. On 26 December 1918 American newspapers reported that Captain Skinker's body had been found in a shallow grave at the side of the road. It was lying side by side with that of Private Maurice Walter, who had volunteered to go with his captain to eliminate the machine-gun post. Captain Skinker's body was repatriated to the USA in 1921.

Return to your car, pass through Cheppy and continue along the D19 in the direction of Montfaucon, which is reached after about five kilometres: stop at the crossroads. Go straight ahead and continue onto the D15a. At the end of the D15a, turn left; this road leads you to the **Montfaucon American Monument (10)** (N49°16.332' E005°08.514'). From the top of the monument (no elevator!) and with the help of the panoramic picture (see pp. 174–175) a great view of the battlefield can be appreciated. For a description of the monument and its surroundings, see p. 190.

From Montfaucon it is easy to return to Verdun as it is clearly signposted **OR** use this stop as the starting point of one of the walks. The nearest toilet facilities are in the bar that is situated in the centre of Montfaucon, the museum in Nantillois (two kilometres, open Thursday-Sunday, 12.30-18.00) or at the American Cemetery in Romagne (eight kilometres, open daily, 9.00-17.00).

Car Tour 2

From Esnes-en-Argonne to Montfaucon

Duration: three and a half hours: allow extra time if you wish to explore Cote/Hill 304 in more detail; there are battlefield walking trails there. Distance: seventeen kilometres.

The tour starts at the Monument aux Morts, Rue de Varennes (D38) in Esnes-en-Argonne (N49°12.480' E005°12.683') and ends at the American Monument in Montfaucon. Ideally, if you start in the morning, you can combine the car tour with one of the walks. The area of the tour is covered by IGN map 3112 Ouest, Montfaucon. At the time of writing, there is a café/bar in Montfaucon. There are no public toilets along the way, the nearest are in the grounds of the Meuse-Argonne American Cemetery, which is situated just a ten minute drive from Montfaucon.

To reach the starting point of the tour from Verdun, take the D964 in the direction of Bras-sur-Meuse. Once you have arrived there, take a left turn onto the D115, in the direction of Charny-sur-Meuse. After about one kilometre, turn right onto the D38 and continue via Marre and Chattancourt to Esnes.

NOTE: The former frontline area around Hill 304 can be extremely muddy and boggy all year round. However, the monument can easily be reached by large vehicles, including a bus. For more information about the 1916 battles in this area, see Christina Holstein's *Verdun, The Left Bank*.

GPS coordinates Car Tour 2

(1) Panorama Esnes, Hill 304,
    Mort Homme   (N49°17.897' E005°08.277')
(2) Esnes Old Cemetery   (N49°12.591' E005°12.607')
(3) Panorama, start line 79th Division (N49°12.593' E005°11.951')
(4) Hill (Cote) 304 Monument   (N49°13.504' E005°12.432')
(5) Hill 304, Monument Georges Fabre (N49°13.513' E005°12.424')
(6) Haucourt, Monument Louis Durand (N49°14.235' E005°11.356')
(7) Haucourt, Monument Maurice Petit (N49°14.209' E005°11.050')
(8) Malancourt, French observation post (N49°14.279' E005°10.997')

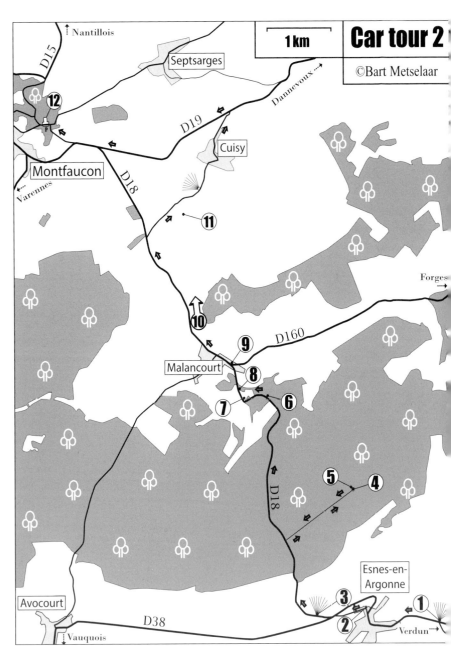

(9) Malancourt, German shelter   (N49°14.543' E005°10.658')
(10) Panorama, view of Demon Redoubt (N49°14.833' E005°10.331')
(11) Demon Redoubt observation post (N49°15.628' E005°10.011')
(12) Montfaucon American Monument (N49°16.332' E005°08.514')

178

Coming from Chattancourt, follow the D38 and stop at the top of the hill at the T-junction Esnes-Montzéville. You can either stop at the side of the D38 Road (direction Esnes) if you are driving a standard sized car to take in the view. However, if your vehicle is larger than that it is advisable to take the left turn to Montzéville, find a place to turn around and return to the T-junction. On the right side of the road there is more than enough space to park on a (usually quite firm) verge. This location is a perfect viewing point to look at **Esnes, Cote 304 and Mort Homme (1)** (N49°17.897' E005°08.277'), all important parts of the 1916 battlefields. The French guns positioned on Hill 304 and Mort Homme were a real thorn in the side for the Germans attacking the French defences in front of Verdun on the right bank.

Return to your car and continue along the D38 in the direction of Esnes. During the first weeks of the Meuse-Argonne Offensive, there were huge traffic jams in this village, with countless vehicles, horse-drawn and motorized, all trying to make their way to the frontline.

Destruction and chaos in Esnes, October 1918.

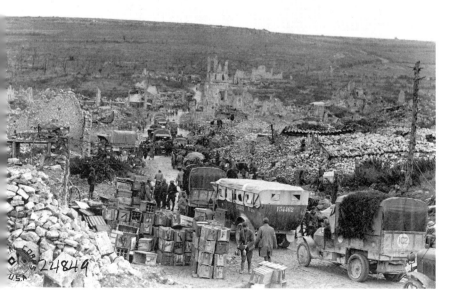

Drive into the village; just as the D38 (direction Varennes) heads out of the village, stop and park your car on the side of the road. Walk back along the road for a short distance and go up the cul-de-sac on your right. Once in the cul-de-sac, keep to the right and walk past the white farmhouse that is on the right, shortly before the road bends to the left. Climb the flight of steps beyond the farmhouse and enter the pre-war Communal Cemetery of **Esnes (2)** (N49°12.591' E005°12.607'). The cemetery was heavily damaged by shelling but the remains of many broken headstones are still standing, including a superb central monument made of cast iron.

American and French troops at the destroyed memorial in the Communal Cemetery in Esnes in October 1918. Note the shell on the edge of the monument on the right.

The cemetery today.

Return to the car and drive up the hill until you are at a T-junction; the monument on the corner is dedicated to the French 173rd Regiment that was drafted from Corsica and that lost a great number of men on Cote 304 during the fighting in 1916. Turn right here onto the D18 in the direction of Malancourt/Montfaucon. When you reach the highest point of the hill, stop at the side of the road. You are now at the approximate **start line of the 79th Division (3)** (N49°12.593' E005°11.951') When they started to move forward from this position, the Doughboys had to walk across two kilometres of utterly devastated No Man's Land before they made contact with the enemy.

Continue along the D18 in the direction of Malancourt. After about one kilometre turn right onto the D18a and follow the signpost to the **Cote 304 Monument (4)** (N49°13.504' E005°12.432'). The monument stands at the end of a 750 metres long, narrow approach road and was inaugurated in 1934. It is dedicated to the 10,000 French soldiers who were killed during the French counter-offensive of August-September 1917 and during the battles of 1916. Close to the monument stands the memorial to Lieutenant **Georges Fabre (5)** (N49°13.513' E005°12.424'). Aged forty years old, he was killed on 18 May 1916 during a French attack. He was awarded the *Croix de Guerre*. There are several more monuments on this site, often original burial sites of the individual concerned.

The Hill (Cote) 304 monument.

Cote 304 in 1918; note the helmet and skull.

Lieutenant Georges Fabre's memorial.

It is also possible to take a
marked walk around the
battlefield here: see the
wooden information panel.

A useful, well produced and multi lingual information panel about the
events on the site is on the south side of the circuit road around the main
memorial; behind the panel one can look in the general direction of
Verdun (though obviously better to do so when there is no foliage). These
panels are found at the major Great War sites in the area (and also, for
example, in the St Mihiel Salient) and are a most welcome addition to
those following events on the ground.

Return to the D18 and follow the road for about two kilometres until you see (which might be difficult in the summer) the **Captain Louis Durand Monument (6)** (N49°14.235' E005°11.356'), set back a short distance on the right side of the road. This monument commemorates the deaths of Captains Louis Durand, Léon Goury and an unknown number of men who were killed by shelling whilst seeking shelter in a cellar in Haucourt. Killed on 22 March 1916, the bodies were transferred to Avocourt Military Cemetery in 1921.

Captain Louis Durand's memorial.

Go back to your car and continue along the D18 for a few hundred metres. Just beyond the bridge, you enter Haucourt and after a 90 degree bend in the road, on your right-hand side stands the monument to **Captain Maurice Petit (7)** (N49°14.209' E005°11.050'). He commanded the First Company of the 69th Regiment and was killed in action on 5 April 1916 in the last-ditch defence of Haucourt. His body was later reported missing. This monument was erected in 1927.

A short distance along the same road there is a **French observation post (8)** (N49°14.279' E005°10.997'), also on your right. Built in 1915 by

Captain Maurice Petit's memorial.

the French to observe and control the valley leading to Montfaucon Hill, the Germans wrested it from the 69th Regiment on 30 March 1916.

The observation post in Haucourt.

The observation post in Haucourt before destruction.

In 1913, the population of the villages of Malancourt and Haucourt totalled 723 residents; in 1916, both villages, the gateway to Cote 304, were completely destroyed by German shellfire. Haucourt, just a mere 200 metres from Malancourt, fell five days later. The memorial plaque on the bunker commemorates the fact that the 69th Regiment lost thirty-seven officers and 1,390 other ranks in six days. The 69th had been ordered to fight to the last man and in the event the only survivors were one lieutenant and a small number of other ranks. By the end of 1917 Mort Homme and Cote 304 were back in French hands; but Malancourt/Haucourt remained under German control until 26 September 1918; what was left of both villages was taken by the troops of the 79th Division. Once in the hands of the Americans, the French

The plaque on the pillbox also mentions 'our brothers in arms of the 79th Division'.

observation post was destroyed; the Americans took this measure so that the Germans could not reuse it should the doughboys have to retreat. The marble plaque on top of the bunker commemorates both the events of 1916 and 1918. A few years ago the memorial was desecrated when the centre helmet of the three French helmets that form part of the memorial was stolen by disrespectful souvenir hunters. Unfortunately, this type of crass behaviour is becoming all too common.

Malancourt before the war.

Drive into Malancourt, go towards the church on the Rue de Haucourt and continue in the direction (Rue Principale, D18) of Montfaucon. Park your car on the side of the road at the Malancourt War Memorial (the figure that dominates it is well done). Across the street from the memorial is a **German shelter (9)** (N49°14.543' E005°10.658'), located to the bottom right of the grassed area opposite the memorial; it is hidden under a clump of trees. This is the approximate site of the pre-war Malancourt Brewery. The structure of the shelter is made from curved sheets of elephant steel bolted together to create a domed shelter. This was later covered with earth and was strong enough to provide the men inside with protection against shell splinters and shrapnel, though it was not shellproof, ie it could not withstand a direct hit.

Detail of the Malancourt 14-18 War Memorial.

A German shelter in Malancourt.

Follow the D18 in the direction of Montfaucon and stop after about 250 metres; notice in the distance a large barn to the right of the road. On the ridge beyond the barn you can just make out (except when crops get in the way!) the rectangular shape of a pillbox, forming part of **Demon Redoubt (10)** (N49°14.833' E005°10.331').

Demon Redoubt Bunker

The German observation bunker is just visible on the horizon.

The German observation bunker of the Demon Redoubt, part of the Hagen Line.

This German observation bunker was part of the Hagen Line, which blocked any further advance to Montfaucon. The pillbox and surrounding defences were one of the two 'traps' the Germans had set for the Americans; the other one was the Golfe de Malancourt defence system. The wooded ridge on your left, Belsace Wood, was well defended by several German machine-gun crews. On the afternoon of 26 September, when the men of the 314th and 315th Regiments left Malancourt to continue the advance to Montfaucon, these German defences wrought havoc amongst the doughboys; the huge losses suffered and the chaos they caused with the ranks made it impossible to advance any further that day.

Drive along the D18 in the direction of Montfaucon. Once you are at the top of the hill, turn right and follow the sign to Cuisy. After about a hundred metres you will see the **Demon Redoubt observation post (11)** (N49°15.628' E005°10.011') in the field on the right of the road. NOTE: Keep out of the fields when the crops have been planted to avoid causing any damage; these crops are the farmer's livelihood. Should the field be without crops, a closer inspection is well worth while: the bunker is in good condition and the significance of its location is made quite apparent.

On top of this ridge a complex system of German trenches ran east to west; the observation post is all that remains of the Hagen Line in this sector. On 26 September it directed machine-gun fire (some of which, at least, would have been indirect) at the advancing Americans in Malancourt. Early in the morning of 27 September, the whole valley before you was covered in thick mist (or fog – different sources mention both). At 4.00 am several Americans patrols set out to test the German's strength and cleared out several isolated machine-gun posts. Before the mist had cleared, the American artillery laid down a barrage on Demon Redoubt Ridge. After two hours of fighting, the attack successfully drove the Germans out of the Demon Redoubt defences and off the ridge but at a heavy cost; it had taken practically twenty-four hours to dislodge the Germans from the Hagen Line and there were hundreds of casualties on both sides; the ridge was littered with dead and wounded. Finally, Demon Redoubt was taken and the advance continued.

Return to your car and continue in the direction of Cuisy. About one hundred metres before you enter the village, look into the valley on your left. When the light is good the outline of a line of shell holes is visible at the left side of the field. Very soon after the liberation of Montfaucon

Shell craters in Cuisy, still identifiable after a hundred years.

Part of the American field hospital in Cuisy, October 1918. A huge red cross is visible to the left of the tents in the centre of the photograph, although partially obscured by trees.

a large field hospital was established here; dozens of tents were put up at the bottom of the valley that was protected against incoming fire by the steep ridge on the north side of the valley. Continue into the village and turn left at the church onto the D19a. At the T-junction, turn left to reach Montfaucon; follow the signs 'Monument Américain'.

Montfaucon American Monument (12) (N49°16.332' E005°08.514'). The monument and its surroundings are described in *Walk 1, Stop 1, pp. 190–193.*

From Montfaucon it is easy to find the return route to Verdun as it is clearly signposted **OR** use this stop as the starting point of one of the walks. The nearest toilets can be found in the bar that is situated in the centre of Montfaucon or at the American Cemetery in Romagne (eight kilometres, open daily, 9.00-17.00).

Walk 1

Montfaucon Old Town

Duration: two hours
Distance: three and a half kilometres.

A similar walk is in the first book in this series, *The AEF in the Great War Meuse-Argonne 1918: Breaking the Line*. In this case, the route is the same but the narrative has been revised and new accounts and photographs have been included.

The walk starts and ends at the Montfaucon American Monument, Rue d'Amérique, on the D15a in Montfaucon (N 49°16.332' E 05°08.514'). It is covered by IGN map 3112 O Montfaucon. Should you decide to do this walk it is advisable to bring a flashlight/torch and a pair of binoculars with you. Most of the walk is along tarmac roads and tracks, so the going is easy. A large car park is situated in front of the monument. Opening hours in the summer are from 9.00 am to 9.00 pm, in the winter from 9.00 am to 5.00 pm. Note: The tower is not equipped with a lift! It is a health-giving climb to the top – 234 steps. At the time of writing, there is a café in the centre of Montfaucon.

NB! For Walks 2 and 3, Montfaucon Old and New Town, note the list of surviving bunkers given in **Appendix 5**. Many of these bunkers are visited in the course of the tours. Many other bunkers lie in private property.

GPS coordinates Walk 1: Montfaucon, old town.

(1) Montfaucon American Monument	(N 49°16.332' E05°08.514')
(2) Montfaucon cemetery	(N49°16.373' E005°08.532')
(3) Montfaucon church ruins	(N49°16.377' E005°08.497')
(4) German shelter	(N49°16.365' E005°08.421')
(5) German power station	(N49°16.482' E005°08.298')
(6) Observation post of the Crown Prince	(N49°16.499' E005°08.259')
(7) German signalling post	(N 49°16.535' E005°08.187')
(8) Orientation Table	(N 49°16.510' E005°08.123')

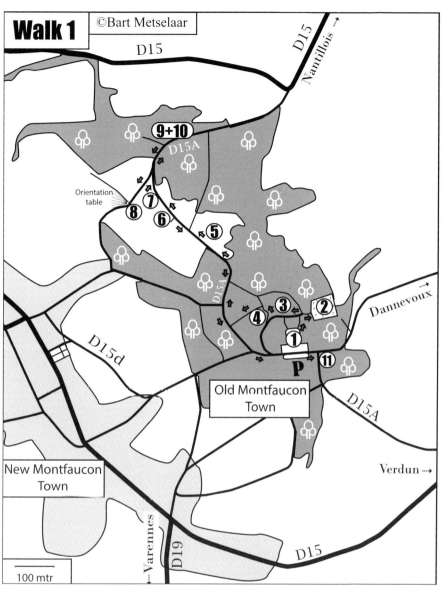

(9) Crucifix	(N49°16.607' E 005°08.239')
(10) The JF Cadell story	(N49°16.607' E 005°08.239')
(11) German bunkers	(N 49°16.332' E 05°08.514')

The impressive **Montfaucon American Monument (1)** (N 49°16.332' E 05°08.514') is a fifty-seven metres high classical column, surmounted by a figure representing Liberty. It was designed by the famous New

York-based architect, John Russell Pope. During the construction of the monument the discovery of tunnels on the site added to the problems the builders had to confront. While digging out the foundations, workmen found an underground passage running from the ruins behind the monument to the foot of the hill. A cemetery, which probably dates from the Middle Ages, was found some four feet under the ground to the left of the monument. Three old cellars, one on top of the other, were found to the right of the column. One of the cellars contained evidence that indicated that it had previously been in use as a dungeon.

Construction of the monument was completed in 1933 and it was officially dedicated by Albert Lebrun, President of the Third Republic, on 1 August 1937. General Pershing and Marshal Pétain were also present at the ceremony. President Roosevelt was not in attendance but he addressed the crowd by radio from his yacht on the Potomac River.

The Montfaucon American Monument. It was dedicated in 1933 to commemorate all of the American divisions that participated in the Meuse-Argonne Offensive.

Ruins of the church. Note the German observation tower, left centre.

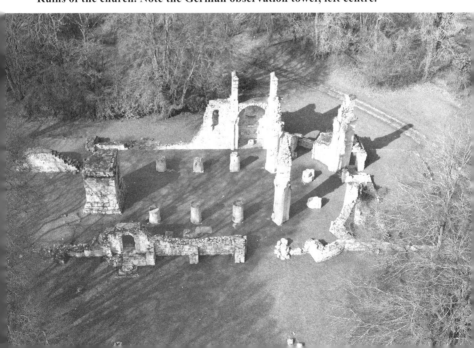

The church in 1914.

The monument faces towards what were the First Army's start lines on 26 September, 1918. From the observation platform at the top there is a 360 degrees view over the surrounding countryside. On a clear day a large part of the former Meuse-Argonne battlefield can be seen as well as the Ossuary of Douaumont, which is situated in what was once the Verdun sector, and the 316th Regiment's Memorial above Sivry. The platform is reached by a circular stairway leading up from the base of the shaft, a climb of 234 steps. Eleven of the thirteen landings have benches so that the weary climber can take a little rest.

Carved on the walls around the main terrace are the names of the divisions that formed First Army. They are, from left to right, Meuse Heights, Barricourt Heights, Romagne Heights and Argonne Forest. The names of the divisions which formed the First Army are also listed; inscribed under the name of each are the names of the places where that division was involved in the fighting.

The architect of this impressive monument was John Russell Pope. Pope was born on 24 April, 1874 in the Borough of Manhattan, New York City. He studied architecture at Columbia University, graduating in 1894. In 1895 he was the recipient of the McKim Travelling Fellowship and gained a fellowship to attend the American Academy in Rome. While studying abroad, he travelled through Italy and Greece, studying the buildings that would later influence his architectural style. Following his studies in Rome, he attended the *École des Beaux-Arts* in Paris. He returned to the United States in 1900, working for three years for Bruce Price before setting up his own architectural firm. In October 1921, John Russell Pope married Sadie G. Jones-Pope. The ceremony took place in New Hanover, North Carolina, where Sadie was born. Over the years, the couple had three daughters, Mary, Sarah and Jane.

On 27 August 1937, Pope, aged 63 years, died of cancer. He became noticeably ill at the beginning of August and was brought to the Harkness Pavilion Medical Center for treatment. Despite an operation, Pope's condition deteriorated due to the complications he developed and from which he finally succumbed. He is buried in Berkeley Memorial Cemetery, Middletown, Newport County, Rhode Island. Besides the tower at Montfaucon, he designed the Lincoln Memorial, Hodgenville, Kentucky; the Metropolitan Museum, New York City; the Jefferson Memorial, Washington, DC; the west wing of the National Gallery of Art, Washington, DC; the Museum of Natural History in New York and the National Archives and Records Administration Building, Washington, DC.

Once you emerge from the monument, turn left and go up the steps facing you. You are now at the rear of the monument and the ruins of the church are in front of you. Turn right and walk to the **present-day cemetery (2)** (N49°16.373' E005°08.532'). On the afternoon of 27 September, a few men from the 313th Regiment of the 79th Division set up a telephone exchange in one of the monumental crypts in the cemetery. The Americans were not the only ones to desecrate the crypts; the Germans converted one into a makeshift observation post.

A crypt in Montfaucon Cemetery turned into an observation post.

Today, all that remains from the period of the Great War are just a few headstones that somehow miraculously escaped destruction, but there are also two French soldiers buried in this cemetery. They both died at the beginning of the war. Originally they were buried in temporary graves close to where they were killed but after the war they were reburied in Montfaucon by their relatives. *Sergeant Major Georges Henri Auguste Zunhamer*, 369th Infantry Regiment, fought in the Limey sector, not far from St Mihiel. Zunhamer, only twenty years old, was killed on 21 September 1914 (N49°16.373' E005°08.554'). The second French soldier is *Jules Omé*, a native of Montfaucon, born on 14 June 1888. He was a corporal with the 18th BCP (Battalion Chasseurs au Pied) and was based in Stenay. On 30 August 1914, Omé, aged twenty-six, was killed in Châlons-sur-Marne (N49°16.376' E005°08.546'). Walk out of the cemetery to the road and you will see Septsarges in the valley below (4th Division's area) and, on a clear day, the 316th's Memorial above Sivry, a view that should underline the significance of the German artillery's observation over much of First Army's operations.

Once the Germans had evacuated Montfaucon they started shelling the hill on a regular basis. For the Americans, Montfaucon not only served as an observation post but also as an important road junction and supply dump. The Germans were fully aware of this fact and tried to frustrate every move the Americans made. It will be recalled that Colonel Sweezey set up his command post in the cemetery on 27 September (and, indeed, was forced to return to it when he was shelled out of one further forward, near the road to Nantillois).

Return to the **ruins of the church and abbey (3)** (N49°16.377' E005°08.497'). Stop at the information panel. Have a look at the old photograph of the church as it was before it was reduced to the ruins you see before you today. Montfaucon, 'hill of the falcon', dates back to the sixth century when Benedictine monks built a monastery on the hill. It is one of the most prominent hills in the area and rises 336 metres above sea level. For centuries invading armies took advantage of the commanding presence of Montfaucon. Even the Romans used it to build a signal beacon on its summit. The area around Montfaucon has been the scene of many battles; one of the most notable was the battle against the Norsemen, the Vikings, in 888. The Vikings, skilled sailors and navigators, had sailed all the way from Scandinavia to the north of France, via modern Belgium and Holland along the River Meuse, with one purpose in mind – to ransack and plunder this area. In July 888 the Vikings were finally defeated. According to existing records as many as 19,000 were killed in the battle. For centuries the area around Montfaucon has been known as the Val Dunois, the Valley of the Danes. The medieval buildings were largely destroyed by anti-clerical mobs during the French Revolution of 1789 (the monks had long departed before then and it had become a Collegiate church), though the church itself became the parish church. Montfaucon has been destroyed eight times during the course of its history, the last time during the First World War.

When the Germans began fortifying the hill in 1915 they naturally used materials that were already available in the village, which had grown over the years around the monastic enclosure. The observation tower, built amidst the ruins of the church at the start of 1916, was constructed of stone that had been recycled from the church and abbey. The roof of the new structure was reinforced with railway girders. The observation post was built inside the church as the surrounding walls hid it from prying French eyes. However, by the end of 1916 large parts of the church lay in ruins. Two years later only the observation slit was visible while the rest of the bunker was covered with debris from the shelled church. This, of course, provided excellent camouflage and further security against shells. In 1918 the ruins and debris provided a major headache for the doughboys of the 79th Division who liberated Montfaucon on the morning of 27 September; there were many German snipers still hiding there. It took much time, effort and numerous casualties before every German was finally cleared from the hill.

American and British officers standing on the rubble in front of the observation post in the church in 1919.

Leave the church and head towards the wooden information panel. Walk down the old stairs (two steps) of the church. Keep the wooden panel on your left. Cross the chalk path and keep going straight ahead. After forty

Remains of a German shelter.

Remains of walls from homes that would originally have been standing along Montfaucon's main road.

metres turn right and follow a small path that leads to a **German shelter (4)** (N49°16.365' E005°08.421'). The shelter is clearly visible from where you are standing. It is possible to enter it through the doorway in front of you, but an easier and safer way in is to go around the back of the structure. Once inside, it is clear to see that in the past this bunker had been the basement of a house that the Germans converted into a shelter.

The ceiling and the walls of the cellar date from before the war. Step outside and walk around the shelter; you can see that the roof is heavily reinforced with railway girders and concrete. The building materials needed to construct the roof and outer walls were not difficult to find as they used the debris of the destroyed houses, the Germans taking full advantage of the buildings that war had reduced to ruins. The garrison at Montfaucon was equipped with stoves and electric light so that during the relatively quiet times of 1917 to September 1918 the men who were stationed here lived in relative comfort compared to the frequently poor conditions in the trenches. About twenty observation posts and shelters still survive in the vicinity. The tunnels are not accessible to the public and are sealed off.

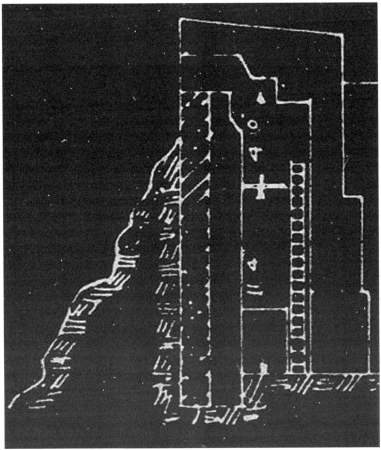

A schematic plan of the German observation post. (App 5, No 4)

Leave the shelter, return to the track and proceed downhill. There are several concrete structures to your left and right, all built by the Germans. When you are at the tarmac road, turn right. Note the ruins of walls and fences on both sides of the road. There were many houses along this street before the war; it used to be a busy village and even had a market. On your right a German observation post is visible amongst the trees. Keep on following the road that now bends to the left. After about a hundred metres you will see a modern yellow bungalow on your left, across from which, in a hollow in the field, are the remains of the façade of the **German generating station (5)** (N49°16.482' E005°08.298'), now marked by a big tree. The generating station provided electric lighting for the tunnels and shelters. The structure housed a gas (petrol) engine and next to it were several entrances to underground shelters.

The generating station as it was left by the Germans, 27 September 1918. See also Appendix 5, No. 3.

Part of the liquid gas engine that powered the generator, 1919.

Continue along the D15a, pass the yellow bungalow and turn to your left after fifty metres. You are now standing in front of what was once a magnificent entrance made from stone and wrought iron. Behind it was the site of the former Château Leriche. All that remains of the once grand building are some holes in the ground and a few concrete walls, remnants of the cellars and not visible from the road. During the war the Germans built a concrete observation tower inside the château. After the war it became known as the **Observation Post of the Crown Prince (6)** (N49°16.499' E005°08.259'). Crown Prince Wilhelm commanded *Fifth Army*, tasked with executing Operation Justice (or Judgement), better known as the Battle of Verdun. Army Command ordered the engineers to build an observation post inside the partially ruined Château Leriche, to be used to direct German artillery on targets on and around Mort Homme and Cote 304. Inside the tower, the Germans installed a powerful telescopic periscope range of fifty kilometres. The observation post relayed the coordinates of targets to long-range German guns. The building was demolished after the war, the periscope was shipped to the U.S. as a war trophy and is now housed in the U.S. Army Artillery Museum at Fort Sill, Oklahoma.

An American platoon passing the Crown Prince's observation post, 29 September 1918. They are all equipped with the P17 American Enfield rifle instead of the Springfield rifle, as was 80% of the American Army.

Site of the Crown Prince's observation post today. (App 5, No 2)

Remains of the cellars of the observation post.

American observers in the attic of the observation post.

Carry on along the D15a until a track appears on your left. Follow this track for about thirty metres; the little knoll on the left hand side houses the remains of a **German signalling station (7)** (N49°16.535' E005°08.187'). This station, built on the other side of the hill, was extremely important to the whole operation on Montfaucon. In case of a power cut and/or when telephone lines were down, from this place it was possible to relay the information gathered by the observation posts with battery operated signal lights. The signals were ultimately received by other signalling stations that were built on the hills in the Argonne Wood.

View from the signal post (App 5, No 1) over the Argonne.

Proceed along the track for another forty metres until you are at the **Orientation Table (8)** (N49°16.510' E005°08.123'), which was unveiled on 26 September 1968, to commemorate the fiftieth anniversary of the Meuse-Argonne Offensive. The Argonne Forest now appears directly in front of you. As a result of the ravages of war, all trees and houses in this area had been destroyed and so the Germans had an unobstructed view of the surrounding country for miles around. For over four years Montfaucon was a thorn in the side of the French. As soon as the Germans observed any movement in the French front line or beyond, artillery started firing. Therefore, it is no surprise that the hill was shelled time and time again by French artillery. However, the French had their 'own' Montfaucon, their own observation post: on Hermont Hill, in Hesse Wood, where the French built several concrete observation posts connected by a tunnel system on the side facing Montfaucon. Although Hermont Hill is thirty to thirty-five metres lower than Montfaucon, it nevertheless provided the French with a splendid view over many of the Germans positions.

Information table.

Return to the D15a, turn left and follow the road for about fifty metres until you are in front of a rather battered **crucifix or *calvaire* (9)** (N49°16.607' E 005°08.239'). It dates back to the nineteenth century and is still in its original state, having survived four years of war. If you take into consideration that all other buildings in the vicinity were completely destroyed, it is something of a small miracle that the cross is still standing. Most of the damage was caused by German shell fire on 27 September 1918, when the Americans liberated Montfaucon. A large German camp, complete with wooden barracks and more permanent structures made from concrete and cement, had been established in the valley behind the crucifix. The buildings were demolished after the war and the materials were used to build shelters at other locations. These served as temporary housing for people who were rebuilding their farms and homes. The reconstruction of the village started as late as 1921 and was completed in 1935. The remains of the camp are now on private property; there are cows on the field almost all year long. French farmers have a habit of adding a bull to their herd; be warned …

Remains of the *calvaire*.

While at the crucifix, take a closer look at the limestone pedestal; there are several carvings in the stone. This is all First World War graffiti, scratched out by American soldiers. At the back of the pedestal one name is clearly legible: **James Fulton Caddell (10)** (N49°16.607' E 005°08.239'). The limestone pedestal has several distinct markings made by American soldiers. Clearly visible is a large inscription in the centre '148. F.A. MONTANA', which refers to the 148th Field Artillery, 41st Division. This artillery unit took up positions near Nantillois during October 1918. Above and beneath this inscription are two illegible markings, presumably soldiers' names. In the lower left corner on the same side of the pedestal

Graffiti carved by James F. Caddell.

is a smaller inscription 'J.F. Caddell Lowell Mass 1918'. His fascinating story has been researched and written by Peter Wever.

James Caddell was born on 5 April 1888 in Lowell, Massachusetts. He moved with his parents to Clear Lake, Montana, where his father died in 1915 while filing a homestead claim. The 1917 draft registration lists

James Caddell as still living in Clear Lake, where he worked as a self-employed farmer and supported his mother. On 8 June 1918 the Chouteau County Exemption Board sent 30-year-old James Caddell to Camp Lee, Virginia, to serve as a stock raiser. There, Private Caddell was allocated Army Service Number 2723520 and was assigned to the 151st Depot Brigade. On 22 June he was transferred to Company E, 303rd Infantry, 76th Division; by 7 July he had sailed for Europe.

Once in France most of the 76th Division troops were used as replacements for other units. On 2 August Caddell was transferred to Company B, 116th Supply Train, 41st Division, which had also been designated as a replacement division. However, several of its units saw action. Companies B and D of the 116th Supply Train are specifically mentioned among the units comprising V Corps during the Offensive, implying his active participation in the operation. On 6 November, five days before the Armistice, James Caddell was transferred to Company A, III Corps Artillery Park, which was a I Corps unit during the Meuse-Argonne Offensive.

Caddell made his limestone inscription in 1918 some days or even weeks after the Americans had captured and secured Montfaucon and so presumably between early October and 31 December. The other illegible names on the pedestal were inscribed by soldiers who, like Caddell, were also from Montana and served in a 41st Division unit and might, therefore, have been his comrades.

On 30 June 1919, James Caddell sailed from St. Nazaire to Hoboken, New Jersey, while assigned to Casual Company No. 1182. Upon arrival home on 12 July, he was sent to Camp Merritt, New Jersey and was honourably discharged on demobilization on 18 July. Later in life he worked as an electrical engineer and moved subsequently to Indianapolis, Indiana, Nashua, New Hampshire, and finally to Sarasota, Florida. He died there on 16 December 1969, aged 81.

Walk back along the D15a and return to the car park. Near to the car park there are several **German bunkers (11)** (N 49°16.332' E 05°08.514')

View from Bunker 14 across the front line towards the French intelligence centre on Hermont Hill.

The Crown Prince's shelter (App 5 No 15), built in April 1918. It is quite unlikely that he ever stayed here; there were more comfortable and, more importantly, much safer quarters in what has become known as the Crown Prince's observation post.

and shell holes are clearly visible. Take your time to have a good look around this area but be careful where you walk as there is still a lot of debris lying about. Before the war the site of what is now the car park used to be one of the busiest streets in the village and there were numerous houses. Over 800 people lived and worked in and around Montfaucon. When the Germans invaded this part of France in September 1914 the inhabitants were evacuated. Not many of the original inhabitants returned after the war; there was not much to return to, they had lost everything they owned. Many started a new life elsewhere.

Walk 2

Montfaucon, the New Town

Duration: three hours
Distance: five kilometres

This tour starts and ends at the Delpech Monument (N49°16.190'
E005°08.936'), situated on the D15 at the base of Montfaucon Hill. It is
covered by IGN map 3112 O Montfaucon. This walk is designed to visit
the monuments that have not been included in Walk 1. Keep in mind that
the village was rebuilt at a different location; before the war there was
nothing here but fields. The tour takes the visitor along a short stretch of
track over which the 313th and 316th Regiments advanced on 27
September.

The memorial of Corporal Delpech and his comrades of the 67th Regiment.

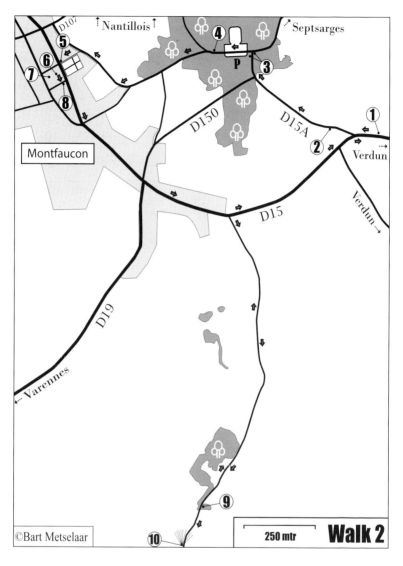

Good walking shoes are indispensable and in summer it is advisable to bring bottled water with you. Most of the walk is along tarmac roads and tracks and the going is easy. Like many French villages, Montfaucon has just a bakery (mornings only); there are no other shopping or refuelling possibilities. At the time of writing there is a cafe close to Stop 5, but you can also bring everything you need for a picnic that could be eaten at, for example, Stop 9.

GPS coordinates Walk 2: Montfaucon, New Town.

(1) Delpech Monument 1914	(N49°16.190' E005°08.936')
(2) German anti-tank barrier	(N49°16.187' E005°08.831')
(3) German bunkers	(N49°16.304' E005°08.562')
(4) Liberty Tree	(N 49°16.322' E 05°08.455')
(5) Meuse-Argonne Memorial	(N 49°16.306' E 05°07.996')
(6) German 10.5 cm howitzer (1916)	(N49°16.295' E005°07.979')
(7) American Sherman tank (1944)	(N49°16.290' E005°07.968')
(8) Hospice, 37th Division Memorial	(N 49°16.273' E 05°08.009')
(9) La Grande Fontaine	(N49°15.520' E005°08.433')
(10) Panoramic view	(N49°15.317' E005°08.369')

You can park your car at the **Delpech Monument (1)** (N49°16.190' E005°08.936'). Make sure your car does not block the road. This monument was erected by veterans of the 67th Regiment to honour Colonel Delpech and other men who fell in the fighting in and around Montfaucon on 2 September 1914; Colonel Delpech was killed by a German shell. On 3 September, after several severe bombardments, the Germans charged Montfaucon and pushed the French off the hill. Crown Prince Wilhelm of Prussia was amongst those present. In the wake of the retreating French Army, many of the local population fled south.

Continue along the D15 in the direction of the American Monument, clearly visible on the skyline. At the bend in the road, keep right. After about forty metres stop at the left hand side of the road where the hedge ends. This is the approximate site of one of several **German anti-tank barriers (2)** (N49°16.187' E005°08.813') that were blocking the roads leading to the centre of Montfaucon. Unfortunately, but inevitably, during the first days of the offensive all such obstacles were removed by the Americans. When the Americans were making their way into the town on the afternoon of 27 September they found that all the roads leading into Montfaucon were blocked with anti-tank barriers.

The barriers consisted of three one metre square reinforced concrete pillars placed across the width of the road. Buried one metre into the ground, the pillars were about three metres high. The structure was strong enough to withstand the heaviest tank. Added to this, machine guns were trained on the barriers to prevent the infantry from blasting the obstacles.

Walk uphill for another 800 metres until you see several **German bunkers (3)** (N49°16.304' E005°08.562'). The one on the left is built into the bank of the road and was used as a shelter; note the double row

The road from Malancourt leading into Montfaucon was once barred with anti-tank obstacles.

Americans taking a breather at one of the tank obstacles in Montfaucon, 28 September 1918.

208

German shelter (App 5 No 16); the roof has been heavily reinforced with railway girders and concrete.

of railway girders sticking out of both sides of the structure. Built originally as the cellar of a house, it was reinforced with concrete and served as an entrance to subterranean shelters. These shelters are no longer accessible; the remaining structure still is but beware of the rubble and rubbish on the floor.

Built on the bank on the right of the road, a large structure can be seen; this is one of the many remaining observation posts that still watch over the hill. The metal plates visible on the exterior of the building are iron railway sleepers. They were used to reinforce the structure that was

German observation post. (App 5 No 17)

originally built inside a house. Behind the observation tower is a chart room and sleeping quarters that were used to house the men who were on duty. For more details see Chapter 2. There are many more bunkers on this site; they are all accessible but at your own risk. Beware of bats, rubble and holes in the floor.

Once finished exploring the area, go to the T-junction and turn left. Pass the monument (for the monument, see Walk 1) and stop at the notable fir tree that is at the right hand side of the road. This is the **Liberty tree (4)** (N 49°16.322' E 05°08.455'). It was donated and planted by the American Committee on the French Revolution on 8 May 1991 to commemorate the bonds between France and the United States. The planting of 'Liberty Trees' was common to both nations at the time of their revolutions – it became an official symbol of the French revolution in 1792.

**The Liberty Tree
at Montfaucon.**

210

The short-lived French Constitution of 1791 was the first written constitution in France; one of the basic precepts of the revolution was the adoption of constitutionality and the establishment of popular sovereignty. The Declaration of the Rights of Man, adopted on 27 August 1789, eventually became the preamble to the constitution adopted on 3 September 1791. The Declaration contained sweeping generalizations about rights, liberty, and sovereignty. Together with the English Bill of Rights of 1689, it was the inspiration for the American Bill of Rights. Articles Three up to and including Twelve were ratified as additions to the American Constitution on 15 December, 1791, becoming Amendments One to Ten inclusive of the Constitution.

Walk along the D15C and follow the sign for Montfaucon. Go down the hill, follow the bend in the road and pass the church on your left hand side. Just a little bit further on there is a green fence and a playground; pass through the gate on the left and continue to the main road, the Rue Raymond Poincaré. The **Meuse-Argonne Memorial (5)** (N 49°16.306' E 05°07.996') is hidden behind shrubbery on your right and becomes clearly visible just as you reach the main road. The monument was erected by the French on 26 September 1989 to commemorate the 80th anniversary of the Meuse-Argonne Offensive and is literally dedicated to all the 'Sammies', the French nickname for the Americans, after Uncle Sam, that participated in the battle.

The 80th anniversary monument of the Meuse-Argonne Offensive.

Two interesting monuments are situated across the street in the village square, the Place du General Pershing. The **German 10.5 cm howitzer (6)** (N49°16.295' E005°07.979') is a real part of local history. It was found in a barn not far from where it stands today. It dates from 1916 and was placed on the square by the same enthusiastic group of people who restored the Sherman tank that stands next to it. An interesting detail – when they began to prepare the gun for installation in 2015, the hay and chicken 'shit' was still on it! Operated in batteries of four, these guns inflicted serious damage; they were capable of firing shrapnel, high explosives and gas shells and had an effective range of about six kilometres. The 10.5 cm Feldhaubitze 98/09, as the Germans called it, was produced between 1909 and 1918. It is unknown how many were produced, but there were over 1200 of them in service with the German army at the outbreak of the war. Unfortunately, nothing has been done to restore or preserve the gun and the elements are now greatly speeding up its deterioration.

Next to the German howitzer, standing proudly on the village square is an **American M4 Sherman tank 1944 (7)** (N49°16.290' E005°07.968'), which dates from 1944. Interesting though it may be, it has not got much to do with wartime events as it was brought here by local Second World War enthusiasts who restored the tank. There was no fighting in this area in 1944 as the Germans who passed through the Argonne were on their way back to the River Rhine and Germany. Sherman tanks were in service from 1942 to 1957; this one dates from 1944. It was relatively easy to build and carried a seventy-five millimetre gun. By the time that the Americans ended production, almost 50,000 had been built.

American Sherman tank dating from 1944 with a German 10.5cm howitzer in the background.

The hospice donated by the 37th Division.

Pass the French War Memorial and return to the main road, the D15, and walk towards the building at the corner. This is the **Hospice 37th Division Memorial Building (8)** (N 49°16.273' E 05°08.009'). It was paid for and erected by the State of Ohio to commemorate the achievements of the 37th 'Buckeye' Division, mainly recruited in that state. The dedication ceremony took place on 28 September 1929 and was attended by a delegation of former members of the 37th Division and hundreds of French people. The presentation address was delivered by Captain McSweeney, who had been an aide to General Farnsworth, GOC 37th Division during the war. Also present at the ceremony were General Pershing, Marshals Joffre and Pétain and the ex-President of France, Raymond Poincaré.

Continue along the D15 (for safety reasons, walk on the left side) for about 750 metres until you see the sign 'La Grande Fontaine' on the right side of the road. Cross the street and follow this track, which is also accessible by cars that have sufficient ground clearance, for about one kilometre until you arrive at the site of **La Grande Fontaine (9)** (N49°15.520' E005°08.433'). This structure was built in 1835 and was

OHIO EXPEDITIONARY FORCE GOES ABROAD

COLUMBUS, Sept. 11 (U.P.)—An Ohio expeditionary force left here today bound for Belgium, France and the battle fields of the World war.

About 300 veterans of the 37th division and members of their families were in the party. They will dedicate war memorials, financed by the state of Ohio.

A newspaper clipping from the *News Journal*, Mansfield, Ohio, dated 11 September 1929.

La Grande Fontaine.

used by the people of Montfaucon at times when the water table on the hill itself was low and the wells were dry. After years of decline after the Second World War, it was finally restored in 1989. During the war this was a very popular spot for the Germans; it was the last stop to fill up the canteens before they moved up to the front. The place is described in many German newspapers, but also by the Americans; it was one of the few places where the Services of Supply could get uncontaminated water to bring to the front-line troops. Behind the building are the remains of a

Most of the wells in the area were either destroyed or deliberately polluted by (usually animal) corpses by the Germans. This well was repaired and was one of the few available watering places during the first week of the offensive.

large German shelter, the roof blown off by the Americans in the autumn of 1918.

Walk along the track for about 300 metres uphill until you are about a hundred metres from the edge of Montfaucon Wood. Stop where the hedge on your left begins and turn around. You are looking in the direction of Montfaucon; the monument is clearly visible. Look at the **panoramic view (10)** (N49°15.317' E005°08.369'); it clearly shows the opposing American and German positions on the morning of 27

A 75mm shell on the side of the road, not an uncommon sight in this area.

September 1918. This is what the Americans saw when they started the attack on Montfaucon on the morning of 27 September 1918. The open ground that had to be crossed by the 311th Machine Gun Battalion and 313th and 316th Regiments in order to reach Montfaucon was constantly subjected to artillery and machine-gun fire. Since the failed attack of the previous night, the 311th MG Battalion had occupied several shell holes and abandoned German trenches that were constructed on the ridges in front and to the right of you. When the area between these ridges and Montfaucon was cleared of Germans, and the Etzel Line was taken, the Americans were finally able to enter Montfaucon.

The wood behind you is Montfaucon Wood; the Americans spent a wet and miserable night here on 26 September. There are still many traces of the war in the forest but we will not be exploring the forest as part of this walk. However, for the adventurous, should you decide to explore you do so at your own risk. Walk into the forest for about 600-700 metres and you will find many old German trenches, all part of the Hagen Line. *Beware of unexploded ordnance! Do not touch or pick up bombs, hand grenades or things you do not recognise. It is not advisable to enter any structure, tunnel or dugout.*

Return along the track to the D15; take a right turn and walk a kilometre and back to your vehicle.

Walk 3

From Montfaucon to Nantillois

Duration: five hours
Distance: eight and a half kilometres

This walk covers the area of the right wing of the attack launched by the 79th Division (314th and 315th Regiments) on Nantillois on 28 September 1918. It is also designed to give a better understanding of the German movements in the area around Montfaucon. The tour can also be done by car or mountain bike.

The tour starts and ends at the parking area in front of the American Monument at Montfaucon, on the D15a (N 49°16.332' E 05°08.514'). For information about the American Monument, see Walk 1, Stop 1. The walk is covered by IGN map 3112 Ouest Montfaucon. It is advisable to wear sturdy walking boots and to bring a pair of binoculars and a bottle of water. Most of the walk is easy going and follows tarmac roads and tracks. In Nantillois you will find the Nantillois Meuse-Argonne 1918 Museum. Nantillois is the halfway point in the walk and it is a good opportunity to stop, visit the museum, use the restroom or have something to drink.

GPS coordinates Walk 3:

(1) Fayel Wood   (N49°16.378' E005°08.642')
(2) Artisane Trench   (N49°16.511' E005°09.073')
(3) German ammunition depot   (N49°17.184' E005°09.378')
(4) Panoramic view   (N49°17.426' E005°08.956')
(5) Narrow gauge railway loading docks   (N49°17.528' E005°08.628')
(6) German railway station and workshops (N49°17.688' E005°08.556')
(7) Story of Ashby Williams   (N49°17.777' E005°08.486')
(8) 80th Division Monument   (N49°17.875' E005°08.399')
(9) German telephone exchange bunker   (N49°17.844' E005°08.326')
(10) German officers' bunker   (N49°17.849' E005°08.302')
(11) Church   (N49°17.886' E005°08.323')
(12) Meuse-Argonne 1918 Museum   (N49°17.916' E005°08.306')
       Open: 1 May- 30 October, Thursday to Sunday, 12.30-6.00 pm
(13) 315th Regiment Monument   (N49°17.920' E005°08.292')

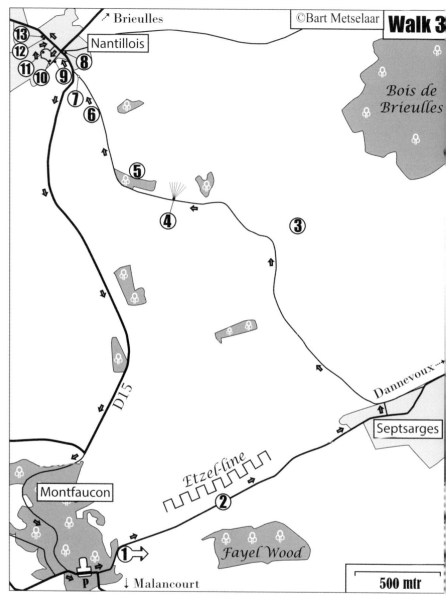

Walk 3

Brieulles

Nantillois

⑬
⑫
⑪
⑩ ⑨ ⑧
⑦ ⑥
⑤
④
③

Bois de
Brieulles

D15

Dannevoux

Septsarges

Etzel-line

②

Montfaucon

①

Fayel Wood

P

↓ Malancourt

500 mtr

After you have parked your car, face the monument. On your right are several sign-posts. Walk in the direction of Septsarges but beware of oncoming traffic. On your right there are several German concrete observation posts; once you come to the bend in the road on your left hand side you will find the remains of some of the homes that once stood

here and a draw-well, restored after the war and used by the workers who built the monument. Walk along the road for another 130 metres until you just pass the cemetery. Look across the fields and check the panoramic photograph to get an idea of the American and German positions. **Fayel Wood (1)** (N49°16.378' E005°08.642') was an important German artillery position in the autumn of 1918. Remember that during the war it extended up the slope towards where you are standing. After it was liberated by the 314th Regiment, the buildings and shelters that had been left by the Germans were put to good use by the Americans; several regiments used them as headquarters, telephone exchanges and storage rooms. The deep tunnels also provided excellent shelter against frequent German shelling.

Continue walking along the road for about 800 metres until you arrive at the top of a rise. Face left; you are now on the site of the German **Artisane Trench (2)** (N49°16.511' E005°09.073'). Look at the panoramic photograph. The trench system was part of the Etzel Line and an important link in the defence between Montfaucon on your left and Septsarges on your right at the end of the road in the distance. However

BEUGE WOOD   NANTILLOIS

important, the line was evacuated by the Germans before the Americans arrived in overwhelming force; after the evacuation of Montfaucon on 27 September and the breakthrough of the 4th Division at Septsarges on 26 September it became useless to try and hold the line. During the night of 27 September the trench was used by troops of the 315th Regiment to take shelter from German shelling (not altogether wise, as the German artillery would have known to the millimetre the location of these trenches – yet there was little realistic alternative to making use of them). From here you can get a good understanding of the route followed by the 314th and 315th Regiments on 28 September when they were on their way to attack the Germans in Nantillois. If you take a close look at the slope of Montfaucon, signs of the damage inflicted by the shells can still be seen in the fields.

Continue along the road, enter Septsarges and take the first road to the left, the one with the circular 3.5t weight restriction sign post. The next four stops were part of a German supply system that also provided the garrison in Montfaucon with rations and ammunition. The first stop is at the **German ammunitions depot (3)** (N49°17.184' E005°09.378'). On modern maps the hill top is indicated as '288'. During the war, the hill below ground was a maze of tunnels that were filled with stockpiles of artillery ammunition. A system of narrow gauge railways distributed the shells from the depot to where they were needed.

Continue for one kilometre and look at the **Panoramic view (4)** (N49°17.426' E005°08.956'); it explains why Nantillois was so important to the Germans – a centre for roads, railways and communications. Walk along the road for another 700 metres until you come to a hedgerow on the right side of the road. You are now at the site of the **narrow gauge**

BRIEULLES WOOD

316th Monument

E TRENCH

KRIEMHILD LINE

Beuge Wood   Station   Nantillois   Wood 250   Ogons Wood

railway loading docks (5) (N49°17.528' E005°08.628'). The docks are mostly gone but, if you look amongst the trees, you can clearly see the foundations of the storehouses that were built here. If you want, you can walk up to them. Please respect the farmer's work – do not walk over the fields if they have been ploughed and there is a crop growing; and if there should be animals then it would be best to be satisfied with a distant view.

The foundations of one of the workshops.

A short distance further along the road, on the left, stands a large barn. This, and the area around it, is the site of the former **German railway station and workshops (6)** (N49°17.688' E005°08.556'). The copse of trees on the right is the site of an artificial pond, dug by the Germans to provide water for the steam engines. In 1915 the normal gauge railway at Brieulles was diverted along the D164 to Nantillois to open up and supply the area that lies between the Argonne Forest and the River Meuse. Huge quantities of material were needed to build the front-line positions of 1915. Indeed, the line became hugely important during the Battle of Verdun in 1916. From the railway station supplies were transported all over the front line. The normal gauge locomotives that arrived from Brieulles continued their journey from Nantillois via Cierges and Romagne to Dun-sur-Meuse, where the train would be reloaded again. The supply system that was based here was the main reason that the village of Nantillois was so mercilessly shelled, beginning at the start of 1916. It was while attempting to destroy the German supply system that the French artillery largely destroyed the village; they were then followed by the Americans on 26 and 27 September; and the *coup de grace* was delivered by the Germans from 28 September to 1 November. The destroyed village was rebuilt from 1921 (starting with the mayor's home) and was not completed until well into the 1930s.

A section of the narrow gauge railway at Nantillois, 1915.

A partly destroyed workshop after a French air attack, 1916.

Continue uphill and stop at the point where trees surround the dip in the road. Two weeks after the start of the American offensive, Nantillois had become a very unhealthy place. To illustrate this, I have included an extract from a book written in 1919 by **Ashby Williams (7)** (N49°17.777' E005°08.486'), Commanding Officer of E Company, 320th Regiment, 80th Division, which vividly describes the situation in Nantillois on 7 October. The 'cut in the road' he mentions in the text is the road where you are standing.

The road along which Ashby Williams entered Nantillois.

A view Ashby Williams must have seen: the carcasses of horses on the side of the Montfacucon-Nantillois Road, currently the D15.

'No orders having been received on the night of October 6-7, I determined on the morrow to go forward to Nantillois and reconnoitre the route to the front and the terrain, and to visit Colonel Love of the 319th Infantry, under whose command I was to act until such time as my regiment should move up in that sector. In the morning, therefore, I started out with my Company Commanders and my orderly towards Nantillois. We followed for the most part the little trench railway that wound around the barren ridges until we reached the Nantillois-Septsarges Road at a point about five hundred yards from Nantillois. There were many evidences that a great struggle had taken place over this ground in the battle a few days before. Equipment and broken wagons and dead horses were everywhere. There were no dead men scattered over the fields, as they had been picked up and laid in a long row on the bank beside the road leading into Nantillois. There were perhaps a hundred of them. It was indeed a pathetic sight. They were Germans and Americans, lying side by side, calm and peaceful and unhating in death, waiting for that final act of the crude hands of the living to shove them into the waiting grave, back into the bosom of the mother from which they sprang, to be known and seen no more upon the face of the earth. As we entered Nantillois we passed through a cut in the road that formed a sharp impression on either side. Here horses and wagons and men were lined up as close as they could get for protection against the Boche shells that were searching the place constantly, as it was the main entrance to the town. Just beyond the cut, after we entered the town proper, the road was cluttered up with dead horses that had been killed by the Boche shells, evidently as soon as they cleared the cut and came into the open. They had been thrust into the gutter alongside the road to make the passage clear. Indeed, there was something almost as pathetic about these dead horses as about the dead men we saw. Not only were they pathetic, but they were horrible to look at. When horses are killed their food ceases to digest and begins to ferment and they swell up out of all proportion. Indeed, we were in no mood to gaze upon these torn, bleeding, swollen creatures and we therefore hurried on into the regimental headquarters, which was situated in what once had been a basement of a church but was now merely a vault, all the upper part of the structure having been blown away by shell fire. It was a very safe place on the inside, however, [as it was] a heavily reinforced cement affair upon the top of which heavy shells hit without appreciable damage. I remember when we went

224

through the front room of the vault I had to literally walk over the top of the men who were lying on the floor, so crowded were they, and the atmosphere was so tense that it could have been cut with a knife. The officers in Colonel Love's room were suffering under the strain of some excitement too, due to the fact, no doubt, that the Colonel's adjutant had been killed outside the door that day and another of his officers had been shell shocked at the same time. I remember, as we got into the Colonel's room, something happened which, under different circumstances might have been laughable, but betrayed the state of mind of the men in that room. The vault was closed up tight with heavy iron blinds, and candles were burning all around the room. My doctor had rolled a cigarette and he struck a match to light it. Colonel Love turned on him and said: "For God's sake, man, put out that light, do you want us all killed in here?'"

Walk along the hollow road until you are at the main road, the D15 and enter Nantillois. On the right you will find the *Place du Four*, the village square. To your immediate right stands the **Nantillois, 80th Division Monument (8)** (N49°17.875' E005°08.399'). The 79th Division was relieved on 30 September by the 80th Division. However, it was not until 8 October that the 80th finally achieved a breakthrough after days of heavy fighting in the vicinity of Ogons Wood. This feat is commemorated by the Memorial Fountain (no longer in working order) that stands on the village square, along with two French memorials. The monument to the 80th Division was erected by the State of Pennsylvania in 1927. Most of

The 80th Division's Monument in Nantillois in 1933; note the absence of buildings behind the monument.

225

the soldiers of the 80th Division were draftees from the 'Keystone' State. Estimates are that about 1,800 Americans were killed or wounded in the fierce fighting in and around Ogons Wood and the breaking of the Giselher Line there.

In the village square you will also find the bust of Francois Boulanger, a former Senator from the Meuse and Minister of Foreign Affairs, who was born in Nantillois, as well as the Nantillois War Memorial and an information panel with a presentation of photos of Nantillois as it looked during World War One.

Facing the French War Memorial, from the village square turn right into Main Street (*Grande Rue*); after about twenty metres turn left into the Rue du Moulin. Walk sixty metres and on your left hand side you will find a **German telephone exchange bunker (9)** (N49°17.844' E005°08.326'), a three-room shelter built in 1916 in the bank of the road to provide maximum protection against incoming fire. From here, target coordinates were passed on to the appropriate batteries, which would then try to destroy the enemy before it could reach Montfaucon. Nantillois also relayed much of the information from the Montfaucon observation posts and was therefore an important link in the German defences in 1918. The officers stationed here were responsible for the defence of *Abschnitt Nantillois, Section Nantillois*, an intermediate line between the Etzel Line and the Giselher Line, that ran from Beuge Wood to Brieulles Wood.

The German telephone exchange bunker in Nantillois.

The German officers' shelter in Nantillois.

Opposite the bunker there is a track that leads directly to the church. Walk along this track; the slab of concrete immediately to your right is the roof of the **German officers' bunker (10)** (N49°17.849' E005°08.302'). The modern house in front of the barn was the site of officers' quarters. In case of enemy shelling or a bombing raid by aircraft, German engineers constructed this officers' shelter in 1916; in April 1916 there were twenty-one aerial bombing raids alone. Of course, for the ordinary German soldier there were seldom such luxuries as shelters. So here we have the whole German command structure of *Abschnitt Nantillois*: officers' quarters, telephone exchange and officers' shelter.

Walk in the direction of the church and follow the road that goes round it; turn left before you cross the creek and walk towards Main Street, the D15. At the corner of the house on your left, turn around and look at the **church (11)** (N49°17.886' E005°08.323'); compare it with the photograph in the book. During the war, the church was completely destroyed by shell fire; first it was shelled by the French, then in September 1918 by the Americans and when the village was taken what remained was destroyed by the German artillery. Originally, the bell tower was at the other side of the church. Amazingly, the tree on the left survived the war, whilst the stone cross that had stood on the church roof

The church in 1919.

The stone cross survived the war and now stands on the rebuilt church.

also survived the war and was placed back in its original position when the church was rebuilt in 1921.

Continue to *Grande Rue* and turn left. The **Nantillois Meuse-Argonne 1918 Museum (12)** (N49°17.916' E005°08.306') is on the left after a short distance.

This intimate and privately owned museum houses a fine collection of American uniforms, equipment and weapons, as well as showcases displaying a range of battlefield relics. German involvement in the war is well represented; however, the main emphasis in this museum is on the part played by the American soldiers, the 79th and 80th Divisions in particular, during the Meuse-Argonne Offensive. Every year there are also temporary exhibitions. *Entrance fee: 3 Euros. The museum owner, who speaks English, also offers guided tours of the battlefield.*

Nantillois, 315th Infantry Regiment, 79th Division Monument (13)
(N49°17.920' E005°08.292')
Right beside the Meuse-Argonne 1918 Museum is Nantillois Community Hall, built in 1930 and dedicated to the 315th Infantry Regiment of the 79th Division. Over 900 of its members were killed and wounded during the liberation of Montfaucon and Nantillois. It has been estimated that German losses were about the same. The village was taken at noon on 28 September, at a very heavy cost; the front-line companies had each lost a third of their men, killed or wounded. The supporting companies mopped up the last German resistance in the village, as there were numerous isolated riflemen hidden amongst the ruins.

The remainder of the 315th Regiment moved through the village to keep pressure on the retreating Germans. Together with the rest of the division, they launched attack after attack on Ogons Wood, a kilometre north of the village, but none of these were powerful enough to break through the Giselher Line situated there. Over the next two days the 79th Division maintained their attacks but the Germans proved too strong. On 30 September the division was finally relieved by the 3rd and 80th Divisions.

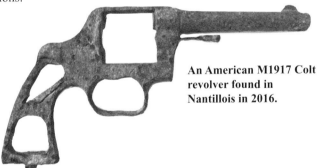

An American M1917 Colt revolver found in Nantillois in 2016.

Many American troops passed through Nantillois once it was liberated as it was part of an important supply route to the front. Like Montfaucon, it was centrally positioned on the battlefield and an important road junction, just as it had been for the Germans in previous years.

This is the end of the tour; the walk back to your car will take approximately forty-five minutes. Return to the village square and follow the main road, the D15 (keep to the left side of the road) in the direction of Montfaucon. After walking about one and a half kilometres you come to a T-junction (the main road bends sharply to the right), continue straight ahead and up the hill. This road leads you directly to the car park. Do not follow the sign to Montfaucon, as this takes you to the present village.

The severely shelled main street in Nantillois, photographed in the winter of 1917.

Troops returning from the front line using the Montfaucon-Nantillois Road, currently the D15.

Appendix 1

Order of Battle of the 79th Division in September 1918

GOC:	Major General Joseph E Kuhn
Chief of Staff:	Colonel Tenney Ross
157 Brigade:	Brigade General WJ Nicholson
313th Regiment:	Colonel Claude B Sweezey
314th Regiment:	Colonel WH Oury
311th Machine Gun Regiment:	Major CM DuPuy (96 guns)
158 Brigade:	Brigade General RH Noble to 26 September; Colonel AC Knowles, 27 September; Colonel WH Oury, 27 September to 12 October.
315th Regiment:	Colonel AC Knowles
316th Regiment:	Colonel OJ Charles, from 30 September Lieutenant Colonel RL Meador
312th Machine Gun Regiment:	Major Stuart S Janney (96 guns)
154th Field Artillery Brigade:	Brigade General A Hero Jr.
310th Machine Gun Regiment:	Colonel HL Landers (24 77mm guns)
311th Field Artillery Regiment:	Lieutenant Colonel CG Mortimer (24 77mm guns)
312th Field Artillery Regiment:	Colonel HP Wilbur (24 155mm guns)
304th Trench Mortar Battery:	Captain WG Huckel (12 15cm mortars)
Divisional Troops:	
310th Machine Gun Regiment:	Major JL Evans (68 guns)
304th Engineer Regiment:	Lieutenant Colonel JF Barber
304th Field Signal Battalion:	Major ZH Michtum
Headquarters Troop:	Captain EW Madeira
304 Trains HQ:	Colonel WC Rogers

Appendix 2

Average American Divisional Strength in Numbers, September 1918.

The maximum authorized strength (sometimes known as 'the establishment') was 991 officers and 27,114 men. The effective strength in the field was 16,000 rifles, roughly divided over the four regiments.

Division: 16,000 men, comprising two Brigades, four Regiments
Brigade: 9,000 men, comprising two Regiments
Regiment: 4,400 men, comprising four Battalions
Battalion: 1,100 men, comprising four Companies
Company: 275 men, comprising four squads
Squad: 70 men

Companies A, B, C and D – 1st Battalion
Companies E, F, G and H – 2nd Battalion
Companies I, J, K and L – 3rd Battalion

Strengths of the American forces on 26 September 1918.

The Americans started the offensive on 26 September with 193,329 men in the line (but this excludes Corps and Army troops); the Germans had some 65,000 men in the sector.

77th Division: 25677 men
28th Division: 23312 men
35th Division: 19849 men
91st Division: 20794 men
37th Division: 18222 men
79th Division: 14322 men
4th Division: 21511 men
80th Division: 25112 men
33rd Division: 24530 men

Guns: 2,775; half of these were manned by French crews.

Aircraft: 821; approximately a quarter of these were flown by French pilots.

Estimated casualties of the 79th Division 26-30 September.

Killed: 942 killed
Wounded: 3,000 wounded
Total casualties: 4,000

Official figures for the total AEF casualties in the Meuse-Argonne Offensive.

Killed: 26,277 killed
Wounded: 95,786
Total Casualties: 122,063

This does leave the question of how prisoners – and there most definitely were prisoners – were accounted for. The 'missing' category that is usually found in the statistics of other combatants is also not evident, so that the figures themselves, whilst very definite, are not particularly detailed.

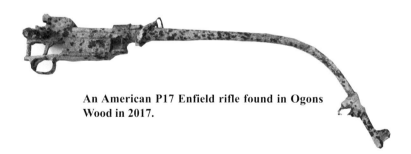

An American P17 Enfield rifle found in Ogons Wood in 2017.

Appendix 3

German Organization

The German troops defending the Meuse-Argonne sector was *Fifth Army*, commanded by General von Marwitz, part of *Group of Armies Gallwitz*.

The main German division that was engaged with the 79th Division during the first two days of the Meuse-Argonne Offensive was the *117th Division*. A German division was divided into three regiments and the *117th* consisted of the *11th*, *157th* and *450th* Regiments. The German regiment equated approximately to a British brigade by this time and comprised three battalions.

During the night of 26 to 27 September, the *37th Division* and the *5th Bavarian Reserve Division* appeared on the scene to reinforce the Montfaucon sector. On the 26th alone, the *117th* suffered about 1,500 casualties in dead, wounded, gassed, missing and prisoners.

The 117th Infantry Division:
11th Regiment
157th Regiment
450th Regiment

The 117th Division was created in April 1915 and was composed of several regiments from different divisions as a consequence of a major reorganisation of the structure of divisions in the army, which was gradually implemented across it over a period of months. Immediately after its establishment, they fought battles in Champagne, Artois and Flanders. In 1916, it was involved in the Battle of the Somme and in 1917 it was deployed in battles in Russia, Romania and Italy. In May 1918 the exhausted division rested for two weeks near Madeleine Farm, four kilometres north of Montfaucon, after which it was deployed on the Somme again. On 8 August, the so-called 'black day' of the German Army, the division lost about 2,700 prisoners. What was left was withdrawn to the Argonne Forest, where it received thousands of replacements.

On 12 September the *117th* relieved the *37th* in the line near Avocourt. Parts of the German line were overrun by the Americans on 26 September, but elements of the division kept up the fight until 29 September, when they were withdrawn after having been pressed back to the area around Cierges, north-west of Beuge Wood and Nantillois. Its total losses in three days were estimated at 3,200, including 1,861 prisoners; the division was in fact almost destroyed. In spite of this, it received replacements, and stayed in action from 2 to 11 November. By German standards, in 1918 this division was rated as second-class.

The 37th Infantry Division:
147th Regiment
150th Regiment
151th Regiment

The 37th Division, mobilized in 1914, originated from East Prussia and was engaged in several major battles. At the end of 1916, after one of its detached regiments had suffered terrible losses during the Brusilov Offensive on the Eastern Front, it was sent to the Western Front, to the Alsace area of France, to regroup and rest. The first five months of 1917 were spent in a quiet sector near Switzerland, but in May the division was transported to the Sedan area to take a weeks' rest. They went in line in the Chemin des Dames, where they suffered heavy losses. They were involved in heavy fighting at several places on the Western Front during the German spring offensives in 1918, ending with the last of these major attacks on the Marne, staying there until the end of July. In August they were transferred to the Argonne front, where the *37th Division* relieved the *231st Division* to the north of the village of Avocourt.

Relieved by the *117th Division* on 12 September, it reinforced that same formation on 26 September, the opening day of the American Meuse-Argonne Offensive. At the Golfe de Malancourt, near Montfaucon, they launched a powerful counter-attack that temporarily stopped the American drive. It was heavily engaged until withdrawn on 1 October. The men of the *37th Division* moved several kilometres west, to the hamlet of Exermont, in anticipation of the second American drive, which began on 4 October. It was engaged in a number of minor actions that proved quite costly; its losses in prisoners alone was 962 men. Despite numerous large drafts of replacements, it suffered such high losses that by the time the Armistice came into effect regiments had been reduced to a mere 350 men, compared to 2,500 at the start of 1918. The *37th Division* was considered to be a first-class shock division by the Germans in 1918.

The 5ᵗʰ Bavarian Reserve Division:
7ᵗʰ Reserve Regiment
10ᵗʰ Reserve Regiment
12ᵗʰ Reserve Regiment

In 1914, the *5ᵗʰ Bavarian Reserve Division* was part of *Sixth Army*, Crown Prince Rupprecht of Bavaria, and was deployed in the Franco-German border area of the Moselle. At the end of the year they were engaged north of Arras. In 1915, the division suffered heavy losses at Souchez; it was reorganised and remained largely in the Arras sector. In 1916, the Bavarians were sent to the Somme; from August to September the *5ᵗʰ Bavarian Reserve Division* was engaged near Maurepas, where it had heavy losses: for example, the *10ᵗʰ Reserve Regiment* was reduced to 150 men. During the following months the regiment was deployed along almost every part of the front line in France; at the start of 1918 it found itself near Zonnebeke, in the Ypres Salient.

However, very soon the division was transferred back to France. On 23 September 1918 it arrived in the Argonne area and detrained at Dun-sur-Meuse. From there the division was marched to the front, where on 27 September, the second day of the American Offensive, it was engaged with the U.S. 80ᵗʰ Division at Dannevoux.

The 5ᵗʰ Bavarian Reserve Division was engaged throughout the Battle of the Meuse-Argonne. On 28 September, between Montfaucon and Nantillois, it was forced back, sustaining heavy losses; early in October it received 500 replacements, but losses had been far greater than that. On 28 September alone it had lost several thousand men, dead, wounded or taken prisoner. The initial company combat strength averaged sixty men; on 4 November this had been reduced to twenty. Despite the considerable casualties that the division had suffered over the years, in 1918 the Germans rated it as a second-class division. By the time of the Armistice its effectiveness had drastically decreased to the point that any energy they might have had was almost used up – yet it was still functioning, despite being a shadow if its former self.

'Histories of 251 Divisions of the German Army which participated in the War (1914-1918)', see *Selective Bibliography*.

Appendix 4

Major Parkin's Affidavit

'Chaplain Wright of my regiment, the 316th of the 79th Division, which captured Montfaucon, that is the 79th Division did, remained in the regular army after the war. He told me, after the war, that he had served with the colonel, also after the war, who had commanded the left regiment of the 4th Division during the Argonne battle. This regiment was in touch with the right regiment of the 79th Division (ours) all during our bloody frontal attack on the high and stoutly defended town of Montfaucon. It was the 313th Infantry which captured this town, the 316th, my regiment, was in close support.

This colonel told Chaplain Wright that his regiment got beyond Montfaucon on the first day of the battle, and realized that we were having a very hard time in front of Montfaucon, and were losing heavily. He said he could easily have sent a battalion to attack the town in the rear, and have helped us take it, if the Germans had not vacated it upon their approach, as they most certainly would have done. But the colonel dared not do this without authority as he would be going out of the sector of his division, the 4th. The matter was referred back to brigade headquarters and to division headquarters, and finally to corps headquarters, where General Bullard said that he would not help General Cameron, our corps commander, win any battle laurels, so on account of this nasty jealousy between high officers, the help was not sent to us, and the 4th Division went ahead with its much easier advance, and left us to be slaughtered by hundreds in a frontal attack against the machine guns in Montfaucon.

Bullard received all the high military decorations of America, France, England, and Belgium. What he deserved was a long term in military prison for deliberately murdering hundreds of American soldiers.'

H. D. Parkin (signed)
Ex Major, 316th Infantry, 79th Division
Balboa, Calif. 9/14/36
Parkin was awarded the DSC and the Silver Star for Valor in 1924.

Reproduced, with permission, Collection William T. Walker Jr., Musselman Library, Gettysburg College, Gettysburg, Pennsylvania, USA.

Appendix 5

List of German Observations Post and Shelters

According to the 304th Engineers, 79th Division, survey of 1918, originally there were seventeen observation posts built on Montfaucon; today, there are only twelve left. Several have been demolished since the war, either to recuperate the iron or for safety regulations. Additionally, one shelter has dissappeared; standing on private property, it is covered with dirt and is now part of a flowerbed.

NOTE: Bunkers 2, 3, 11 and 12 are built on private property and should be treated as such. Permission was granted by the proprietors to the author to take pictures. Entry of the bunkers are entirely at your own risk.

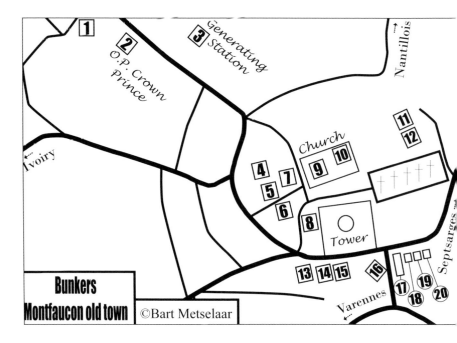

1. Signalling post (N 49°16.535' E 05°08.178')

2. Observation post, Crown Prince's (N49°16.499' E005°08.259'). See pp. 239–248.

**3. Generating station
(N 49°16.486' E 05°08.324')**

**4. Observation post
(N 49°16.387' E
05°08.369')**

5. Observation post (N 49°16.366' E 05°08.401')

6. Observation post (N 49°16.374' E 05°08.421')

241

7. Shelter (N 49°16.367' E 05°08.493')

8. Observation post (N 49°16.360' E 05°08.460')

9. Observation
post (N 49°16.381'
E 05°08.473')

10. Shelter
(N 49°16.394'
E 05°08.490')

11. Shelter (N 49°16.422' E 05°08.536')

12. Signalling post (N 49°16.419' E 05°08.533')

**13. Observation post
(N 49°16.309'
E 05°08.442')**

**14. Observation post
(N 49°16.305'
E 05°08.470')**

15. Crown Prince's shelter (N 49°16.308' E 05°08.482')

16. Shelter (N 49°16.306' E 05°08.554')

**17. Observation post
(N 49°16.319' E 05°08.564')**

**18. Observation
post (N 49°16.312'
E 05°08.588')**

19. Observation post (N 49°16.326' E 05°08.593')

20. Observation post (N 49°16.320' E 05°08.600')

Advice to Travellers and Useful Addresses

The Meuse-Argonne region is not very densely populated and is an area dotted with small villages. Most people make their living from agriculture. To do the weekly shop people have to go to one of the larger towns e.g. Verdun or Stenay. On the former battlefield, an area of 30 by 40 square kilometres, there are only a few places where you can fill up the tank, buy your battlefield tour rations and have a cup of coffee. However, the area can be easily reached from Verdun. From there, it is only a drive of a little over half an hour to the heart of the battlefield.

Language:
In this area, most French people do not speak English (or any other foreign language for that matter), although it is, albeit rather slowly, starting to change. However, most of the time the local people are very helpful if you give them a chance. A few French words can work miracles.

Petrol stations:
       Varennes, Dun-sur-Meuse or Consenvoye.
Supermarkets:
       Varennes, Dun-sur-Meuse or Doulcon.
Cafes and/or lunch facilities:
       Consenvoye, Dun-sur-Meuse, Vauquois, Nantillois, Romagne-sous-Montfaucon and Varennes

For serious collectors of military antiques, there is an excellent shop in Dun-sur-Meuse, Passé au Présent, 6 Rue de l'Ile, passeau present@live.fr. Opening hours: Thursday to Sunday from 10.30-12.30 and 14.30-18.30. English spoken. (N49°23.096' E005°10.936')

Where to stay:
There are dozens of B&Bs in the Meuse-Argonne. The list below contains the names of B&Bs that are centrally located on the former battlefield and whose owners speak English. For other B&Bs, search on Google using 'Chambres d'hotes' or 'Gites de France'. Many B&Bs have a restaurant licence and offer good quality three course dinners at reasonable prices. This saves you a lot of time on arrival or if you want to make the most of the day.

14-18 Nantillois – Nantillois – www.14-18nantillois.com
Le Coq d'Or – Montfaucon-d'Argonne – www.bblecoqdor.com
Le Mont Cigale – Vauquois – www.lemontcigale.fr
L'auberge d' Argonne – Apremont – www.hotel-argonn-auberge.com
Villa Nantrisé – Romagne-sous-Montfaucon – www.nantrise.com

Group accommodation (10 or more people)
Hotel Le Rale des Genets – Dun-sur-Meuse – www.hotel-le-rale-des-genets.com
Hotel Le Tulipier – Vienne-le-Château – www.letulipier.com
Hotel Du Grand Monarque – Varennes-en-Argonne – www.hgmgambini.wixsite.com/hoteldugrandmonarque

Ordnance:
The bomb disposal unit in the Meuse-Argonne consists of ten brave people who, day in day out, put their lives on the line to clear the former battlefields of the deadly heritage of the First World War. Every year these men collect some 100 tons of shells of all types – gas, shrapnel or high explosive, as well as hand grenades. Travellers are strongly advised not to pick up anything from the ground and to use their common sense. Munitions are designed to kill and sometimes they still do.

Maps:
A useful, general map of the Meuse-Argonne region is the Michelin 'Sites de la Guerre 1914-1918 en Meuse' map, which you can buy locally, or ordered at www.michelin-boutique.com. If you want to study the area in more detail, the maps in the IGN Série Bleue map 3112 Ouest, Montfaucon is highly recommended. Again, these can be purchased in Verdun at the bigger supermarkets or ordered on various internet sites. For the centenary a special 1:75 000 map was published by IGN: *Grande Guerre – Bataille de Verdun 1916*. Although the overprinting of the line and unit deployments relate to the Battle of Verdun 1916, it is very useful, covers the area of this book and also indicates places of interest, such as cemeteries and major museums.

Roads and speed limits:
The roads in this area are, for the most part, well maintained. Maximum speed in villages, towns and cities is 50 km/h, on national roads (N and D roads, i.e. N209, D15) 80 km/h (from July 2018) and on motorways 130 km/h (110 km/h in rain) unless indicated otherwise. Remember to drive on the right-hand side of the road! For up to date information on

the ever-changing French road regulations, check with the websites of motoring organisations such as the AA or RAC.

The weather:
In summer, the weather in this area can become quite hot. As regards the rest of the year, the weather is usually quite good but from time to time you may need a pair of Wellingtons, a rain coat and an umbrella. Tip for a pleasant trip into the forest: apply a good brand of insect repellent. Wear sturdy boots.

Water:
It is quite safe to drink water from the tap in this area. The French constantly monitor the quality of drinking water.

Hospitals:
There is a very good hospital in Verdun. Most doctors and specialists speak English or at least have the basics.

Hopital Saint-Nicolas
2 Rue d'Anthouard, 55100 Verdun
03 29 83 84 85

Acknowledgements

The amount of assistance I got for this project has been heart-warming. So many people generously offered their time and knowledge to help me out when I got stuck. Sometimes help came from an unexpected place; for example, Dr. Matthieu, my General Practitioner, whose practice is in Montfaucon and whom I have known for years, revealed to me that he is an enthusiastic collector of period maps and photographs. There is a small group of people who have been a great and continuous source of help through the years; Peter, Orla and Bart, I could not have done it without your loyal support. Thank you so much! However, any errors in this book are solely my responsibility.

In no particular order, I would like to thank Orla Kuiper-Ryan, for proof reading and correcting the manuscript; Bart Metselaar, who once again drew excellent maps for the touring section, Nigel Cave, the series editor, for his help, advice, support and patience. (By the way, I really enjoyed exploring the battlefields with you!) The people at Pen & Sword Books; Jack Sheldon for generously sharing his information on German units and formations; Tom Gudmestad for his general advice and hunting out sources and photographs from his vast collection; Mr. James Bertelson, Assistant Superintendent of the Meuse-Argonne American Cemetery, Romagne-sous-Montfaucon; the American Battlefield and Monuments Commission; James Shatler; William T. Walker; the National Archives and Record Administration, Washington, DC, who supplied me with great quantities of much yet unpublished (and outstandingly good) photographic material; and the Descendants and Friends of the 314th Infantry Regiment. Doubtless there are others: you know who you are and I am very grateful.

Special thanks go to Peter Wever, who researched and wrote the story of James Fulton Caddell.

This is my second book for Pen and Sword and I continue to appreciate very much the often unsung work of those who 'make' the finished article. So, to Matt Jones, Sylvia Menzies, Jon Wilkinson and Dom Allen, please accept a heart-felt thank you!

Nantillois, May 2018

252

Selective Bibliography

79th Division Summary of Operations in the World War, US Government Printing Office, Washington DC, 1944.

A Machine Gunner's Notes, France 1918, Lieutenant Colonel Charles M. DuPuy, Reed & Witting Company, Pittsburgh, 1920

American Armies and Battlefields in Europe, American Battle Monuments Commission, Government Printing Office, Washington D.C., 1938

Betrayal at Little Gibraltar, William Walker, Scribner, New York, NY, 2016

Die Bayern im Grossen Kriege, Reichsarchiv, Verlag Bayrischen Kriegsarchivs, München 1923

Fort Sheridan to Montfaucon, F.T. Edwards, Elizabeth Satterthwait, DeLand, Florida, 1954

Histories of 251 Divisions of the German Army which participated in the War (1914-1918), War Department, Government Printing Office, Washington, DC, 1920

History of Company G, 314th Infantry, Joseph T Labrum, Philadelphia, Pa. 1925

History of the 304th Engineers, 79th Division U.S.A. in the World War 1917-1919, J. F. Barber, Steinman & Foltz, Lancaster, Pa, 1920

History of the 313th Infantry 'Baltimore's Own', Henry C. Thorn Jr., Wynkoop Hallenbeck Crawford Company, New York, 1920

Les États-Unis dans la Grande Guerre, Léon Abily, Marines Éditions, Rennes, France, 2010

Machine Guns of World War One, Paperback edition, Robert Bruce, Windrow and Greene, The Crowood Press, Wiltshire, 2008

Regimental History of the 316th Infantry, Carl E. Glock, Pittsburgh, Pa, 1920

The 315th Infantry U.S.A. 1917-1919, The Historical Board of the 315th Infantry, Philadelphia, Pennsylvania, 1920

The 4th Division in the War, Bach and Hall, Country Life Press, Garden City, New York, 1920

The History of the Seventy-Ninth Division, A.E.F., J.F. Barber, Steinman & Steinman, Lancaster, Pa, 1921

The Story of the 91st Division, 91st Division Publication Committee, H.S. Crocker Co, San Francisco, CA, 1919

The Thirty-Seventh Division in the World War 1917-1918, Volume II,
  Cole and Howells, The Thirty-Seventh Division Veterans
  Association, Columbus, OH, 1929

The U.S. 79th Division in Nantillois 1918, Maarten Otte, ExpoSure,
  Rosmalen, The Netherlands, 2014

To Conquer Hell, Edward G. Lengel, Henry Holt and Company, New
  York, NY, 2008

Under the Lorraine Cross, Arthur H. Joel, Columbia University, New
  York, NY, 1921

*US Army in the World War 1917-1919, Volume 9: Operations – Meuse-
  Argonne*, Historical Division, Department of the Army, Washington
  DC, 1948.

With Their Bare Hands, Gene Fax, Osprey Publishing, New York, NY,
  2017

Your Brother Will, William Schellberg, JerryHarlowe, Patapsco Falls
  Press, Ellicott City, Maryland, 1992

Index

Gesnes, 154, 156, 160
Giselher Line, 132, 137, 142, 151, 154, 226, 229
Glock, Capt E.E., 110–11, 139, 164, 253
Golfe de Malancourt, xiv, xviii, 72, 74–5, 81, 87, 89, 92, 94, 99, 186, 235
Goury, Capt L., 183
Grande Fontaine, 207, 213–14
Grande Montagne, 163
Greenwood, Sgt H.L., 91

Hagen Line, 74–5, 87, 94–5, 103, 115, 118, 124, 176, 186–7, 216
Haig, FM Sir Douglas, 6, 50, 136
Haucourt, xiv, 56, 66, 74, 84–5, 87, 90–1, 94, 100, 125, 130, 177, 183–5
Hermont Hill, 161, 169–72, 201, 203
Hill 274, 144, 147–50
Hill 304, 64, 166, 177, 179
Hill 378, 164
Hindenburg, FM Paul von, ii, xiii, xviii, 6–7, 9–10, 16–17, 20–1, 23–5, 30, 69, 127, 156, 158
Hindenburg Line, xiii, xviii, 6, 9–10, 16–17, 20–1, 23–5, 30, 69, 127, 156
Hundred Days' Offensive, 4, 6

Ingersoll, Capt H., 88–9
Ivory, 108, 118, 133, 140

Jackson, Capt H.N., 89, 123
Joel, Second Lt A.H., 66, 68, 78, 82, 86, 95–6, 117, 130, 141–2, 152, 254

Knobelsdorff, Lt Gen K.S. von, 39

Kriemhild Line, 14, 19, 23, 27, 56, 132, 137, 140, 143–4, 149, 154
Kuhn, Maj Gen J.E., 56, 92, 104–105, 129–30, 142, 231

Labrum, Sgt J.T., 95, 115, 124, 149, 253
Langley, Maj J.R., 88–9
Liggett, Gen H., 58
Lloyd George, PM David, 5
Ludendorff, Gen der Infanterie Erich, 6–7, 106, 132

Madeleine Farm, 144, 147–8
Malancourt, x, xiv, xviii, 26, 54, 56, 63, 66, 68, 72, 74–5, 78, 80–7, 89–96, 98–9, 104, 115–16, 123, 131, 153, 158, 160–1, 177–8, 181, 184–7, 208, 218, 235
Marks, Lt S.J., 114
Marne, 4–5, 31, 37, 194, 235
Martenet, Pte E., 37
Marwitz, Gen der Kavallerie Georg von der, 6, 13–14, 234
Maxim, Hiram S., 17–19, 125
McCain, Maj Gen H.P., 39–40
McCawley, Sgt J., 97–8
McKenney, Lt Col H.J., 128
Medal of Honor, 39, 176
Meuse-Argonne 1918 Museum, 217, 228–9
Meuse Heights, 31, 48, 114, 118, 127, 137, 150, 158, 163, 192
Missouri Monument, 161, 175
Moore, Capt (Chaplain) J.C., 111
Mort Homme, 31, 42, 66, 165–6, 177, 179, 184, 199
Muller, L., 45

Nantillois, v, x, xiii, xviii, 22, 25, 46, 50, 52–3, 56, 64–6, 105,

Woods
- 250, 144–6, 151, 154
- 268, 144–5, 150
- Belsace, 186
- Beuge, xv, 22, 24–5, 56, 64, 114, 122–3, 125–8, 130, 132–3, 135–40, 142, 144–5, 150–1, 226, 235
- Brieulles, 24, 52, 133, 151, 226
- Cheppy, 26
- Cuisy, xiv, 72, 81, 92, 94, 99, 101–103, 110–11, 118
- Esnes, 64
- Fayel, 52–3, 123–4, 128–130, 217–19
- Fosse, 95, 98
- Hesse, 66–8, 161, 201
- Malancourt, 26, 72, 78, 80–1, 87, 92
- Montfaucon, xiv, 26, 54, 101, 215–16
- Ogons, 144, 146–9, 151, 154, 157, 225–6, 229
- Tuilerie *see* Fayel

Zunhamer, Sgt Maj G.H.A., 194